D1237802

Cynthia Pepper

Pigtails, Presley & Pepper
"A Hollywood Memoir"

Cynthia Pepper

with Victor J Hanson

AuthorHouse™ LLC
1663 Liberty Drive
Bloomington, IN 47403
www.authorhouse.com
Phone: 1-800-839-8640

Published by AuthorHouse 06/12/2014

ISBN: 978-1-4969-2000-3 (sc)
ISBN: 978-1-4969-2001-0 (hc)
ISBN: 978-1-4969-1999-1 (e)

Library of Congress Control Number: 2014910752

Forward

I have had the privilege and pleasure to know Cynthia Pepper for over 50 years. Yipes! Can that be right? Let me do the math. I have known Cindy (as I call her) since I was 9 years old. We became friends and co-workers while filming what turned out to be television's second-longest running situation comedy, a series called *"MY THREE SONS"*. The show originally ran for an amazing 12 years and 380 episodes! Since then, *"MY THREE SONS"* has played endlessly over the past 40 years in syndication and a variety of Cable TV Networks. Cindy played the character, *"Jean Pearson"* - the girlfriend of *"Mike"* (the oldest of the three sons) on the first year of the show. That was 1960. I played the precocious youngest brother, *"Chip Douglas"*. We also had a middle brother on the show, *"Robbie"*, played by actor and heartthrob, Don Grady. Cindy appeared in quite a few episodes the first year and made quite an impression on everyone - cast and crew alike. To put it mildly, her presence lit up the day. Even at 9 years old I remember being awestruck at how beautiful Cindy was. I remember feeling pangs of jealously when *"Mike"* (played by actor, Tim Considine) got to kiss Cindy. Call it an adolescent crush, I guess. Not only was Cindy beautiful... she was also extremely talented and professional. Other's thought so too and Cindy quickly moved on after the first year of *"MY THREE SONS"* to star in her own television series, *"MARGIE"*!

I lost contact with Cindy for a long while she was busy carving out a professional career for herself. When I was a teenager I ran into Cindy again... this time in a movie theater. Sitting in the audience of a darkened theater with bunch of my teenage buddies - there was Cindy up on the screen kissing Elvis Presley in *"KISSIN' COUSINS"*. It's good to be the King I thought.

I didn't see Cindy again until about 1990. I was now 40 years old. I had grown up, got married and had a family - and so did Cindy. We rekindled our long-lost friendship at a Celebrity Autograph Show and have been fast friends ever since. Cindy always talked about doing a book someday... and, well, lucky for you, that day has finally arrived.

Cindy's new book is an incredible read. Showbiz people all take a different path that leads to the same place - however, each actor has their own special "showbiz" journey... and Cindy is no different. Born to show business parents, Cindy, literally, grew up in the business. Like all of us, she's had her share of highs and the lows and ups and downs - but isn't that what makes life interesting? This is the story of an incredibly talented and beautiful woman whom the gods have smiled upon. An exemplary mother, wife, TV and movie star in her own right, Cindy is a show business survivor. She is also one of the most gracious, caring, compassionate and kind human beings I have ever had the pleasure to know. Cindy is also one of a select few Hollywood Starlets to actually kiss Elvis Presley. Come on... how cool is that!

Cynthia Pepper is a first class act, a beautiful woman and a treasured friend... and this is her story. Enjoy!

... **Stan Livingston** - *Actor / Director / Producer / Artist - played Chip Douglas on "My Three Sons"*

Kind Words From Other Friends

*

I have had the distinct pleasure of knowing Cynthia for more than fifteen years. During that time she has become a close and dear friend. My only regret is that I did not have the opportunity to meet her sooner as Elvis Presley talked about her on several occasions when he talked about his co-stars. She was one of his favorites. I found his description of Cynthia to be extremely accurate. In getting to know her I have had the pleasure of knowing a true lady just as Elvis described her. She is a person with a soul, a desire to do the right thing and someone with more compassion for others than can be imagined. To know her is to take a journey back in time, to when everything was good and beautiful, and she makes it so today.

... **Dick Grob** - *Personal Body Guard, and Chief of Security for Elvis Presley's tours - Author.*

*

Cynthia and I have been friends for a long time. She is a wonderful person and a great talent, not only for acting, but for relating to her fans. We have done many shows together and everyone just loves her.

I value our friendship and I am honored to call Cynthia my friend.

... **DJ Fontana** - *Elvis Presley's first drummer - Member of the Rock & Roll Hall of Fame - Appeared in the movies "Loving You", "Jailhouse Rock", and "G.I. Blues"*

*

When my dear friend Cynthia Pepper asked me if I would write a little something about her for her book, I was delighted.

Cindy and I go way back, and as the years go by, we have grown closer each day. In fact, I consider her more than a friend... she is like a sister to me, and I smile when she refers to me as her "little Sis". She is truly one of the sweetest, cutest, dearest friends I've ever known.

We talk just about every day, much to the chagrin of her darling English husband who for the life of him, can't figure out how we can have so much to talk about! ("...must be a "girl" thing") He loves to tease us by saying things like "You two are having lunch in an hour… get off the bloody phone!"

Cindy and I have shared many ups and downs, and many tears of joy, as well as tears of sadness as we have gone through so many losses in our lives. Our shared love of animals has created a special bond between us and is one of the reasons we have grown so close... That, and also that we make each other laugh… endlessly. Everyone who remembers her from her series *Margie* as well as starring with Elvis in *Kissin' Cousins* among other shows already knows what a wonderful actress she is, but even more importantly, she is a wonderful person. People, who meet her for the first time, immediately adore her. She lights up a room with her beautiful smile, and as pretty as she is on the outside, she is equally as pretty on the inside.

She is a friend whom I adore, respect, admire, trust and confide in, and one whom I can always count on... I consider myself blessed to call her my friend. I know you will all enjoy her book, as she has a wonderful story to tell.

I'm proud of you sweet Cindy and I'm grateful to know that ours is a friendship that will last a lifetime...

With love and affection "Sis"

…**Beverly Washburn** - *Actress / Author - "Shane", "Old Yeller", "Star Trek", "The Lorreta Young Show", "Superman".*

*

In 1964 Joanna Moore, Cynthia and I went to Rome and spent a month, making a pilot for a series based on the motion picture, *Three Coins in the Fountain*. When the shooting was over we had a three-week period of time that was free before we had to be back in Hollywood to loop sound. And because Cynthia and I had never been to Europe before, we decided to make a whirlwind trip which included visits to Florence, Venice, Vienna, Paris and London. Armed with the book *Europe on Five Dollars a Day* (I shudder to even think what that amount might be today) we set off for the adventure. And what an adventure it turned out to be! I won't spoil it by telling you all of the particulars but, instead, will let Cynthia do that because this *is* her book. Suffice it to say she was a wonderful and "game" traveling companion and we had an extraordinary trip, about which we still laugh today.

She and I also worked on the Elvis Pressley movie, *Kissin' Cousins* and I was a guest on her series, *Margie*. I can't think of anyone easier to work with, and always look forward to seeing her and catching up on both our activities when we're in the same town.

... **Yvonne Craig** - *Actress / Dancer / Author - Batgirl from TV's "Batman". "Star Trek", "Three Coins In The Fountain".*

*

I have known Cynthia for about fifteen years. The first time I met her I didn't have a clue as to who she was. When we first met and she told me her name, I never dreamed she had been one of Elvis co-stars. Having never been an Elvis fan - before I knew him, I had no idea who this lady was - but I liked her immediately.

Over the years, we have bonded and she had bonded so beautifully with my daughter Katey too - Katey always said that of all of the co-stars she had met, Cynthia was her favorite. Now, she has been one of my most favorite people/close friends in the world. When she comes to Memphis she stays with me and though I truly love her dearly, I am gonna really get her if she ever unplugs my coffee pot again. Cynthia has become my friend, my child, my caregiver - she has served me my meals and hot tea when I have been tired after one of the many Elvis Presley Memorial Dinners that I host. I would not take anything in the world for her friendship. Cynthia - I love you dearly girl!

... **Marian Cocke** - *Author / Elvis' Nurse, caregiver, close friend and confidant for the last two years of his life.*

Contents

Introduction

1. *Miss Congeniality* 1

2. *Who Is Cynthia Pepper?* 7

3. *Daddy, The Movies, Patty, Marriage, Hollywood* 20

4. *The Big Apple & My Broadway Debut* 27

5. *Everything's Bigger In Texas* 35

6. *Fresno To Hollywood* 53

7. *Look Out Hollywood, Here I Come / Room For One More / The Hollywood Ranch Market* 58

8. *Scary Incidents At The Elaine Apts. / Jr. High* 69

9. *Hollywood High* 91

10. *A Working Actress in Hollywood / Getting My Feet Wet / The River of Work / Mother & Daddy* 106

11. *I'm Getting Married In The Morning* 117

12. *My Three Sons* 124

Contents

13. Margie 138

14. The Show Must Go On? 152

15. Aloha 159

16. Margie Gets Direction / New York with Patty / TV Guide 164

17. How Do You Do '62 175

18. The Death of Margie - Or - Gee, I Didn't See That Coming 185

19. Sally & Sam / Take Her, She's Mine / Wagon Train 195

20. Kissin' Cousins - My Elvis Story 206

21. The Times They Are A Changin' / Bittersweet 237

22. My Boy, My Boy / Three Coins In The Fountain 252

23. When In Rome… / Europe on Five Dollars a Day? 261

24. Home Again, Home Again, Jiggety-Jig-Jig 272

25. Still Growing Up / Under the Yum Yum Tree 281

26. The River Is Down To My Ankles 288

27. Ivan, Goodbye Again 298

28. Saying Goodbye Is Never Easy 308

Acknowledgements

Introduction

Why Write A Book Now?

As children, we are taught to learn and practice the art of sharing. We are told that sharing is the right thing to do and a good way to go through life. However, I find that as we grow older and go through our life's experiences, it can get tougher and tougher to share. When asked to share our lives we don't mind sharing our triumphs and happy moments but it's harder to share our weaknesses and the bad times. Opening up your life means having to say you're sorry or at least admit that some things could have gone better.

Reminiscing about my friends, family, co-workers and the journey my life has taken has been fun at times. There have been moments of laughter and tears of great joy. There have also been moments of pain and sadness. Every person on the planet has a story to tell, and this one is mine.

We live in a world that is obsessed with sensationalized tabloid news (which is not really news at all), and so-called reality TV. (Which is TV, but it's not reality.) Most celebrity memoirs are expected to be a "tell all" book. I grew up in a different era with a few different values so I've written a "tell some" book. The stories are no less interesting but why hurt someone if you don't have to.

My friends know I love to laugh, and I hope that my humor comes through in this book. Feel free to laugh out loud if you get the urge. I won't tell.

Many people along the way have encouraged me to write my story, and I thank you all for the support and interest. (You know who you are. If you don't know who you are I encourage you to look into a mirror right now or seek immediate medical attention.) I've written this book for you.

One of the many pleasant discoveries I made while writing this book was of all the surprising connections I have to Elvis Presley. I only worked in one movie with him, but the connections that I had with Elvis before and even after working with him astounded me. We did a lot of research on the people that I've worked with and uncovered a lot of interesting links.

There are so many connections to Elvis in this book that we came up with sections at the end of certain chapters that we've called: "The Elvis Connection". These special sections provide some trivia and surprising facts that show how my life had been linked to Elvis at times when I didn't even know they existed. We thought of calling these sections "The Six Degrees of Elvis", but we didn't want Kevin Bacon yelling at us.

With all the Elvis connections we've made in this book we may have overlooked one or two along the way. I look forward to you telling me what we may have missed.

This is not an "Elvis Book". We only worked together once and became good friends during that experience. I've shared my experiences with him in this book along with the rest of my Hollywood life.

I truly hope you enjoy the book.

"Hollywood is a place where they'll pay you a thousand dollars for a kiss and fifty cents for your soul."

- Marilyn Monroe

Chapter 1

Miss Congeniality

I want to tell you a story, my life story. It's a Hollywood story in the truest sense. It's a story of love and innocence, of comedy and tragedy, of fame without fortune and how I killed Elvis Aaron Presley... Well almost. Before the story's done, I may even tell you the secret to life.

It's 6:15 a.m. on a balmy May morning 2004 in Las Vegas Nevada and look at me, I've got a job AND it's an acting job. I had been working at a local florist shop for a while, and it was enjoyable but not what I wanted to do with my life. I seemed to do pretty well when left on my own with a mindless task like cleaning the roses or carnations that arrived. No one at the shop knew that I was an actress or had knowledge of any of my past success on TV and in the movies. That and bringing home a regular paycheck was the best things about working there.

There was a time in the early 1960's when I couldn't walk down Main Street USA and not be recognized. I don't say that to brag but it was once a fact of life for me. From the year 1960 and into the early 1970's, I had worked on the big screen, the little screen and quite a number of live stage shows. I even had my own TV show for a while on ABC. These days things were different.

The two things you'll find out about me is that number one, I love talking to fans and B, I'm a survivor. Everyone's got a story to tell no matter what the differences may be between people and as my Daddy use to say, "That's what makes Horse Races."

Landing a job as an actor, which I had trained for from the age of 3 years old was very difficult to do so I picked up whatever jobs I could to help pay the rent. Along with my job in a florist shop, I'd been doing some work at the Elvis-A-Rama Museum on Industrial Rd. The Elvis Museum had been a wonderful opportunity for me to try and still make a living in the entertainment industry. Some days had a decent number of people coming in to visit, but other times people were few and far between. I had some long empty days there just staring at Elvis' old suits, jewelry, cars, and other expensive memorabilia with no one around. Those days were hard to get through, but you do what you have to do.

When tourists were there, I did enjoy the fact that I could be myself while talking to the great Elvis fans that visited. I was selling pictures and autographs to the various tourists that came from all over the world. Selling my memories to pay the bills is something that I'd gotten use to over time. I hadn't been working much as an actress for the past 30 plus years and finances had been tough, but I had my stories to tell to those that wanted to listen. In a way, you can say that Elvis came to my rescue.

I considered myself very lucky for having co-starred with Elvis in *Kissin' Cousins*, in 1964. That one acting job gave me access to and was now allowing me to stay in the Elvis world. Since his death in 1977 the demand for Elvis, his movies, music and people that had known him had grown in leaps and bounds every year. I would be asked to attend Elvis conventions and shows where I would usually get an appearance fee for telling my story. I would also make money selling memorabilia to the fans. After expenses, it brought in very little income but I was getting by. Elvis conventions are fan based just like the Sci-fi Conventions are. Actors in popular sci-fi franchises, such as *Star Trek* have an income and a forum for their pictures, memories and anything else they may have to sell. Most of those actors also get decent residual checks for their performances of past work. I don't get much in the way of residuals. *Kissin' Cousins* and television shows that I had worked on were made so long ago and don't sell much in today's rerun markets. Also, residual percentages were not as high as they are today. I was in a tough financial state that most of my friends, family and fans knew nothing about nor did I want them to.

But this May morning in 2004 was different. Today I was to be a working professional in the craft that I had honed for so long. Today I would make decent days' pay for a decent days' work doing what I love to do and with what I had always done best, acting.

After I say goodbye and kiss Steve the man that I share my dreams, hopes and love with I hug my beautiful babies goodbye. (Pepper, Jack, Lucky, Fluke, Sparky, and Rosebud… The best cats and dogs a person could ever ask for). I then jump into my 1996 dark green pearl metallic Toyota Camry better known to our family as the Green Goddess. I purchased it new in 1996 but now it was in some disrepair, and I couldn't afford to get all the work done that it needed. I just hoped it would turn over for me one more time. I don't know a lot about cars, but the general rule for me was that if the CD player and radio work then I'm happy. If it runs then I'm ecstatic. The 8 year old Green Goddess, (that's like 96 in human years) waited for my command. I said a little prayer, gently inserted the key into the ignition and gave it a twist. The engine of my on again off again vehicle was, thank God on again, and I was on my way.

I didn't get a lot of sleep the night before because I was thinking about my lines and was overall nervous. I didn't have many lines, but it was a big production being shot at the Venetian Hotel and my scene was with the star and producer of the film herself, Sandra Bullock. If you mess up your lines, it holds everyone up, and as they say "Time is Money."

In the year 2000, the movie *Miss Congeniality* was released and became a huge box office success. As Hollywood loves to make money, it was inevitable that only four years later Miss Congeniality 2: Armed and Fabulous was now in production. The fact that it was being shot in Las Vegas was the fabulous news for me as it was where I lived.

As I made my way to the Venetian Hotel on Las Vegas Blvd, my mind was racing with a thousand thoughts that were pushing my lines to the back of my mind. I was very happy to have a job in the vocation that I love, and that was paying me something just above scale, but I had also speculated on the great residual checks that would come in after the film was released. I got excited when I had heard that a couple of actors with very few lines in a movie shot, in

Vegas we're getting residual checks of up to $6,000.00 each. Oh brother, now that would pay off a few bills. I thought to myself: "I'm going to be rich."

It was a great day. My mind was running wild with positive thoughts. What could go wrong? Then I started to fixate a little too much on just what could go wrong. What if I mess up my dialogue? One of my lines was "Is it true you're seeing Prince William?"

As I was running it through my mind, it kept coming out as "Is it true you're seeing Prince Charles?"

Oh No! That would be a disaster. What if I missed my mark? What if they don't like the outfits that I picked out from home? Is my hair ok? What if Sandra Bullock turns out to be some kind of a superstar diva? A diva-Zilla? Is that even a word? What if they got someone else to play my part and didn't tell me? I wonder if the catering table will still have food on it by the time I get there. Why did they implode the beautiful Sands Hotel the same year the Green Goddess rolled off the assembly line in 1996 just to make the massive Venetian Hotel & Casino? I mean the Sands was good enough for Sinatra and The Rat Pack why change it at all? Should I valet or self-park? What are my lines again? How much wood could a woodchuck chuck, if a woodchuck could chuck wood? It's amazing what a little worry can do to mess up a performer's concentration.

As I pull into the Venetian, I remember that I only have a few dollars in my purse. I make a swift and wise financial decision to save some money, so I self-park. After parking and thanking the Green Goddess profusely for getting me there safely, I grabbed all my stuff and headed to the makeup and hair tent in the parking lot. It was so nice to be professionally done up and wasn't anything new to me. I had been doing movies and TV for a long time, just not recently. Years earlier on my own TV show *Margie* I had a fantastic makeup and hair person who took care of me. I eventually learned to relax in the make-up chair back then, but not so much today.

As I sat there in the make-up chair, I kept wondering if anyone would recognize me on the set. I realized that thinking those kinds of thoughts might make me sound like a completely self-absorbed person, but I'm not at all. When someone recognizes you it can be a boost to the ego, but then you might have to explain yourself when the questions start. Questions like: "Why are you here? Why do you have such a small part in the movie? What have you been doing for the past few decades? Is this a hobby for you now? Well, it's not like you need the work, right? After all you were a regular on *My Three Sons*, you worked on the Jimmy Stewart TV show; you were in movies with people like Sandra Dee, Bob Denver, Cary Grant, Audrey Meadows, Robert Morley, and even Elvis Presley. You must be living on easy street. You've lead a charmed effortless life. It must be all sugar and spice for you. So what's your next big project?"

How do I explain that my next big project is to head home and re-arrange my cutlery drawer! If I answer honestly people just look at me in confusion because it's not what they want to hear. If I take on the attitude that what's perceived is more important than what's real, it's sometimes easier to get by. In that case, maybe I should answer with: "Oh, my chauffeur will be by a little later on to drive me back to my palatial estate in Beverly Hills where I will be wined and dined by both Spielberg and Scorsese for their next big projects."

But then again, it's always nice to be recognized. That's showbiz.

At about 8:45 in the morning, the assistant to the assistant to the assistant director arrived to take me to the set. Now that I have calmed down a little I can now concentrate on my two lines. How did they go again? As we passed through the Venetian passageway and the alley of stores, we came to the set. We then made our way past numerous cameras, camera dollies, lights, grips, technicians, and what seemed like hundreds of other crew members until I was finally led into the Venetian bookstore. I was then introduced to the director John Pasquin. I was pleased to find that Mr. Pasquin was a very nice man and seemed well in control of what he was doing. I was then lead over to the couch where the star and possible diva-Zilla was sitting. As we said hello and shook hands I could see that she was in full costume and makeup ready for the scene and just like her pictures in the magazines, she was gorgeous. Cameras didn't do justice to her beauty. I kept wondering if a Hollywood star this pretty could also be a nice person. I had been disappointed in the past with some other actors. You might be surprised by who is nice and who is not in Hollywood. Being the eternal optimist my fingers were crossed. It turned out that I didn't have to wait long to find out. Mr. Pasquin said: "OK why don't we run the scene once just to see how it goes. Cynthia you have the first line so when you're ready..." I smiled at him and looked at Sandra Bullock. I opened my mouth... And nothing came out!

I had blanked. I didn't have a clue what my first line was. My face must've gone several shades of red. I was stunned and somewhat disappointed in myself. I wanted to scream out NO! WAIT! I'm a professional. I've been on *Perry Mason, The Flying Nun, Wagon Train, The Addams Family,* I Kissed Elvis Presley Damn It! I was snapped back into reality when I heard Sandra say: "Are you all right?"

She had a nice warm, concerned smile on her face. I said: "Yes I'm fine. I'm so sorry, I just blanked on my lines."

She responded with: "Don't worry about it. It happens to all of us. Let's just try it again and have some fun with it."

She made me feel so at ease that my lines popped back into my head instantly, and I was ready for action. Sandra was the complete opposite of a diva-Zilla. She was a nice-Zilla.

Sandra took a quick phone call from her new boyfriend Jesse James. We were then given some quick direction from Mr. Pasquin. We shot the scene three are four times until they got what they wanted. She wouldn't win her Academy Award for another five years, but I could see that with the right vehicle Sandra could go all the way to an Oscar.

On my way back to the Green Goddess and later on my drive home I could think of only three things. Number one, what a great set to have worked on, number two, I can't wait to get rich off those impending residual checks, and number three I hope the cutlery drawer isn't too messed up.

By the way, the first residual check I got for my work on this film was for $300.00. The next one was for $13.00 then $7.00 then $2.00... And that too is show biz.

Chapter 2

Who Is Cynthia Pepper?

Sorry, I'm getting ahead of things, and I have yet to introduce myself which is just not proper for an actress or a lady. I am Cynthia Anne Culpepper, Margie Clayton, Jean Pearson, Corporal Midge Reilly, Adele, girl next door, Maggie Walker, Liz Martin, Sally Marten, the vamp in booth number three, Susan Jones, Paula Cummings, Donna, Marsha, and the little girl peaking at Cary Grant. I am also the freaked out new neighbor Amanda Peterson, tourist woman, Robin, innocent little girl on the left, the best girlfriend of Sandra Dee, the wife, the girl next door, the girl that Jimmy Stewart yelled at, and a tourist woman hounding Sandra Bullock for an autograph, Cynthia Pepper, but my closest friends just call me Cindy. Before you think I'm a complete nut, those were just a few of the characters that I've brought to life on stage, in movies and on TV throughout my Hollywood acting career.

So where do we start? Well, you'll need a little background so let's start with my showbiz family. In order to do that, I have first to tell you about the Golden Age of Vaudeville. Long before MP3 players, DVD's, CDs, VHS, beta, cassette tapes, eight track tapes, Texas Hold'em, Karaoke Bars, Television, Movies, and Radio there was something fantastic in the world of live entertainment called Vaudeville. It was variety theatre at its beginning and its best. It was the most popular entertainment in the United States and Canada for about five decades. Vaudeville was also referred to as "The Heart of American Show Business".

Vaudeville began in the early 1880's and died off in the early 1930's. On any given night, the bill would include comedians, singers, dancers, jugglers, magicians, acrobats, athletes, lecturing celebrities, musicians, one-act plays, and even animal acts. You can see where Ed Sullivan got the idea for his long running TV show.

In 1881, a New York theater manager by the name of Tony Pastor decided to put together a show that was appropriate for the whole family. He called his shows "clean" Vaudeville. Any act that wished to perform in his theaters would have to meet the code of clean, acceptable entertainment. Alcohol was not for sale in his theaters. Pastor offered door prizes of coal or hams to get people to buy tickets for the shows. (Doesn't David Letterman still give out hams at his New York Theater? I guess some traditions are just too hard to give up.) Building upon the strength of this new theatre genre two men B. F. Keith and E. F. Albee built an empire of theaters and brought Vaudeville to the rest of the United States and Canada. Keith-Albee created a chain of Vaudeville houses across North America that was second to none. This alliance brought about block bookings that made the entire business much easier to manage. These bookings could range from two weeks to possibly a year or two on the circuit. A good act could start in Boston then go across North America doing one week in each town or city and a year later be back in Boston doing the same act. As long as the audience changed, the act didn't have to change. (Las Vegas shows still use that method to this day.) It was a tough life on the road, and you had to have a certain personality to handle it. Some towns and cities were tougher to play than others, which created the popular quote: "Yes it's good, but will it play in Peoria?" In other words, if an act could be successful in Peoria it could be successful anywhere. (They say that about New York now.)

A Vaudeville performance could have anywhere from five to eight acts per show. Here's an example of a typical Vaudeville show bill and why it was put together this way:

First act: (the dumb act) this could be acrobats, jugglers, or an animal act. This act was put on first because not everyone arrived at the theater on time, and there was very little attention required from the audience for these acts. People could arrive without interrupting the show.

Here's Daddy's name up in lights at Lowes State Theater in Manhattan, 1930. The amazing team of Barto & Mann was on the same bill. George Mann took this photo.
(George Mann Collection – by permission of Brad Smith)

Second act: (hoofers) this could be a solo dancer or dance team. A hot dance act would grab the people's attention so the stage crew could clean up after the animal act.

Third act: (thespians, known as Barrymore's) this would be a short sketch or part of a play. This helps to give the show some class.

Fourth act: (maestro) this could be an instrumental song by a refined featured musician. It would give the show even more class.

Fifth act: (novelty or freak act) a magician, mind reader, strongman, or quick change artist to wake people up.

Sixth act: (the big canary) a solo singing act that was the tenor or soprano singing the hits of the day.

Seventh act: (monologist) a popular solo or duo comedy act of the day with just the right amount of clean comedy.

Eighth act: (the closer) a bad singer or a bad instrumentalist. It could be any annoying act designed to get the audience to leave. A bad act gave the audience time, and motivation to leave the theatre and to make way for the next paying audience to fill the seats for the next show.

The amazing thing about Vaudeville performers is that they would do this lineup anywhere from three to five times a day. There were no microphones or sound systems to amplify their voices or instruments. The performers would get burnt out quickly and take to diversions such as gambling, alcohol or even drugs. It was not an easy life for them or their families. The most common saying back then among performers was, and still is: "You're only as good as your last show."

My Daddy - Edward Jackson Culpepper - Jack Pepper.

(Cynthia Pepper Collection)

My Father was a Vaudevillian performer through and through. Jack Pepper was a well-known and bonafide star of the stage in those days. He was in his early twenty's at that time and had the world by the tail. Performers in the entertainment business looked up to him and would ask for his advice and help with their own acts. On numerous occasions new and struggling performers trying to make their way in the business would benefit from the generosity of Pepper (as he was known to his friends). Daddy would provide a hot meal, a financial handout, or allow them to sleep on his couch for the night, if not for the month, when they had nowhere else to turn.

One such hopeful at the time was a young fellow originally from England, Bob Hope. Bob was a struggling vaudevillian surviving on low paying shows and his special brand of tomato "soup". (It was ketchup mixed with hot water that he'd get from a local Laundromat.) Daddy befriended him, and Mr. Hope never forgot his kindness or the many decent meals, provided by Daddy that they shared together in those early days. They became fast friends. Mr. Hope would return the help later in life. I still have a copy of a letter that Bob Hope sent Daddy in 1944. This was after Mr. Hope was a big radio star. It was a typed letter on Mr. Hope's private stationary and shows how devoted he was to helping my father.

April of 1944.

Mr. Jack Pepper

Frederick Bros. Artists Corp.

RKO. Building   Radio City

New York 20, New York

Dear Jack:

Received your letter with the script and I'm sending it over to Buddy De Sylva to see if he likes it. I hope he does, so Morrisey can open another show and you can be the star.

Stand by… I may want you to go to the Southwest with me in June. Write me… put down that bottle and write me quickly.

Happy sends her love. My best wishes.

Your straight man, Bob Hope

"Thanks For The Memory"

At the bottom of the letter he added a note written in his own handwriting which read:

P. S. Received the golf balls. You must really be using my jokes. Be careful baldy.

My Father was known in show business as a triple threat. He was an actor, a dancer and a singer. He was also an accomplished instrumentalist he played the ukulele. I guess that makes him a quadruple threat. Hang on, he was also a monologist or as we would say today, a comedian. So I guess that would make him a quintuple threat? (Is that even a word?) Did I mention he was also a songwriter? Hang on; once again I'm getting ahead of myself. Let us step back even further.

In 1902, a soon to be world class golfer named Bobby Jones was born. So was future photographer Ansel Adams, gangster Dutch Schultz, band leader Guy Lombardo, author John Steinbeck, one third of the Three Stooges Larry Fine, actress Norma Shearer, and aviator Charles Lindbergh. Best of all on June 14, 1902 in Palestine, Texas, my grandparents, George D. Culpepper and Josephine A. Chenowith gave birth to a bouncing baby ham... I mean boy. They named him Edward Jackson Culpepper, my Daddy. Knowing him as I did he probably bounced out of the womb, landed perfectly on his feet, danced a little soft shoe, and told a couple of jokes while singing and playing the ukulele, all before his first feeding. Show business was in his blood, and he was a charmer.

As a young man, Daddy began his entertainment career on stage with his sisters Helen and Winnie Mae and his younger brother Truett. I can only imagine what their act was like. Music, comedy, dance, and whatever else it took to win the audience's hearts. By all accounts that act didn't last too long.

My father first came to national prominence in the 1920's as part of the song and dance team, *Salt & Pepper*, with his partner Frank Salt. They were very popular on the Vaudeville stages throughout North America.

I'm sure the team was making pretty good money at this point. The money a Vaudevillian could make varied on the popularity of the act. An act just starting out might make $25.00 a week. On the other hand if they drew in a crowd they could make as much as $1,500.00 a week or more. That was a lot of money in the 1920's especially when you consider that a pound of bacon cost about 52¢, a pound of coffee was just 47¢, and a whole 10¢ got you a fresh loaf of bread. The average price of a house was $7,900.00, a new car could be had for $270.00 and gas for that new car sat around 22¢ a gallon. (I know these costs are all relative, but I think a few of you reading these prices just wished that you had a time machine.)

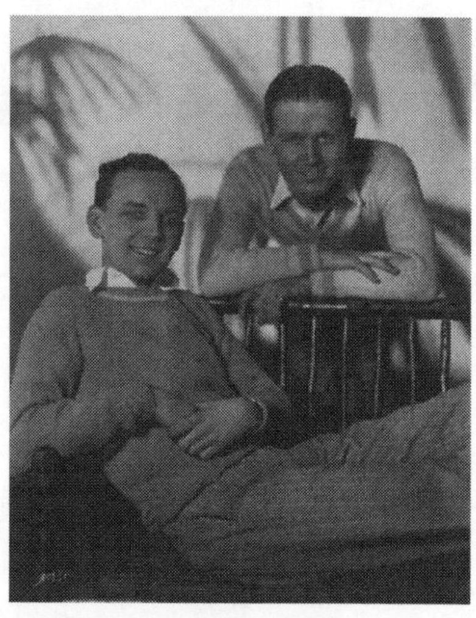

Vaudeville's Song, Dance, and Laughs a Minute team, Jack Pepper and Frank Salt better known as Salt & Pepper. Daddy is the one lounging on the bench.

(Cynthia Pepper Collection)

Salt & Pepper's popularity eventually brought them to Broadway where they performed in a few Broadway revues such as *Gay Paree* in 1925 and *The Merry World* in 1926. *Gay Paree* ran for about twenty weeks on Broadway and then toured Europe. *Salt & Pepper* were in the big time now. The cast of *Gay Paree* was fantastic, and included a young song and dance man named Jack Haley. I'm sure you know him as the Tin Man in *The Wizard of Oz*. Along the way *Salt & Pepper* performed on radio broadcasts, and recorded a number of recordings for *Cameo Records*. Daddy was always a charmer with the ladies and was drawn towards dancers. For a while he was engaged to a young Ruby Keeler while performing at a Chicago speakeasy that was frequented by gangsters and run by Texas Guinan who also had another establishment in New York City. When world famous Al Jolson came a calling for Ruby, Daddy and other suitors got out of the way pretty fast. Jolson was the Elvis of his day and everyone knew and respected him in the business, even though it had been reported that he could be a little difficult to work with unlike Elvis in later years.

The partnership with Frank Salt was altered somewhat in 1929 when Daddy married a young seventeen year old Champion Charleston dancer by the name of Ginger Rogers. You are now asking yourself, "Is that the same Ginger Rogers of stage, and screen fame?" The same Ginger Rogers that went on to later dazzle the world in now classic movies such as *Flying Down To Rio, The Gay Divorcee*, and *Top Hat* with some guy named Fred? The same Ginger Rogers that won the 1940 Academy Award for Best Actress in the movie *Kitty Foyle*? Yes that's the girl.

It was an interesting pairing at the time so much so that I had heard that later in 1943 there was a movie made which was kind of based on their interesting relationship called *The Hard Way* starring Ida Lupino and Dennis Morgan. Since I wasn't there when they first met, give me a break, I hadn't been born yet, I think that it's best to have Ms. Rogers tell you how these two lovebirds met. Here's what she had to say in her 1991 published autobiography, *Ginger: My Story*.

"During my Dallas engagement I was sitting in my dressing room at the Palace Theater when someone knocked on the door. "Who is it?" I asked.

"It's Jack Pepper, Ginger. I've come to say hello."

Jack Pepper! It was Aunt Jean's beau, Jack Culpepper, the man I had secretly fallen in love with while watching him smooch with my aunt as they sat on our front porch swing. I could hardly believe that he would come backstage to see me as a grown up. The haunting love theme of the past tugged at my heart the moment I heard his unmistakable voice. I couldn't get myself together fast enough to open the door and greet the man I had long identified as the most attractive man I had ever met. "Did you see the show?" was my fill in remark. "How'd you like it?"

"I thought it was swell." he said.

I waited for him to say, "My you have grown up, haven't you?" I was hoping that he would recognize that I had finally become a young woman. But his interest seemed to be in the performance I gave.

Ms. Rogers goes on to say how much she was in love with being in love. This was a time in the world when a lady didn't sleep around. If you wanted to find out about sex you didn't ask your mother. Most mothers didn't offer up any useful information either. The only thing left for a young girl to do was to get married and see what happened on the honeymoon. So on March 29, 1929 in the office of a New Orleans justice of the peace a seventeen year old Ginger Rogers became the wife of a 26 year old Edward Jackson Culpepper. (Yes I hear what your thinking reader and I'm sure the age difference was about to be a factor too). As we all find out in time, marriage is about a lot more than just sex. They both found out very quickly that this union was bound for disaster. He was working long days in the theater and as a dutiful wife she was there to make sure his suits were pressed and clean. She was relegated to the wings of the theater to watch the shows while never performing herself. That would frustrate almost any performer. Sitting on the sidelines is not what we do best. After taking all she could take, she finally packed her bags, moved back with her mother and resumed her career. In her book, Ms. Rogers goes on to say that my father had many good qualities but the one flaw that she could not tolerate was his constant drinking. You have to remember, this was a different time in American society. It was a time when men were men and alcohol bottles needed emptying. You weren't a real man if you couldn't drink. I think my Daddy was just trying to keep up with the crowd. Plus these were the days of prohibition. It's a well-known fact that if people are told they can't have something they just want it all the more. Thanks to the gangsters of that era they could get as much as they wanted. Thanks Al Capone. *(More on him later.)*

Before I continue, some people over the years have said that Ms Rogers and my Daddy were a Vaudeville team known as Ginger & Pepper. I would like to put that speculation to rest. I have yet to find any evidence to corroborate that they ever shared the stage together. Through the years of his life Daddy never once mentioned that the act existed. As a matter of fact, Ms. Rogers never mentions any such act in her book. Both of them possessed many great talents, and they would have been a great duo. Instead, it's just another Vaudeville myth. Besides, a two person act in Vaudeville always went by the last names of the performers. Examples of some famous duos include *Burns and Allen, Abbott and Costello, Smith and Dale, Laurel and Hardy,* and much later *Martin and Lewis.* If there had been such an act it would have been called Rogers and Pepper. I think the myth of an act called Ginger & Pepper started because the two names sounded good together. It's that whole play on the spice and seasonings thing.

Makes you wonder if an act called Nutmeg and Paprika could've made the big time?

Even though Daddy was very depressed about his failed marriage he continued on with Salt & Pepper. Ah, that old adage 'the show must go on' must have been what kept him alive. That and the hair of the dog, or the whole pelt even. Ginger and Daddy separated in 1930, but they didn't divorce until July 11, 1931.

I did have the pleasure of meeting Ginger Rogers once; however I have to admit that I embarrassed myself quite badly. I was called into wardrobe for a fitting during the filming of the pilot for my TV show *Margie* in 1961 at 20th Century Studios. I was walking through wardrobe when low and behold Ginger Rogers was standing just a few feet away from me. She was getting ready to film her pilot with co-star Cesare Danova. Ms Rogers' pilot was called *Vacation Playhouse: A Love Affair Just for Three*. I wanted to say hello but with her history with Daddy I was afraid that she may not even give me the time of day. I debated with myself for a minute or two and then decided, nothing ventured, nothing gained. Besides I was a big fan of her whole dancing and acting career and just wanted to tell her so. As I moved towards her I could see that she was even more beautiful in person than on the big screen and for a moment I was starting to feel slightly star struck. What would I say? What would she think of me? Is she holding a grudge against Daddy? Is she going to take it out on me? I wanted to make a good impression on her. Finally I walked up to her. I mentally placed my foot near my mouth and said: "Hello Miss Rogers. My name is Cynthia Pepper. I believe you know my father, Jack Pepper."

WHAT THE HELL WAS THAT? (My foot was now firmly placed in my mouth.) I couldn't believe what I had just said. He was her first husband and lover. Odds are she hadn't forgotten this fact. I felt like such a dope. I was ready to turn and bolt out of the room. However to her credit she smiled at me gave me a big hug and said: "Oh yes. How is the dear boy anyway?"

What a great lady. She was so sweet and sincere. We chatted about Daddy for a bit and had a wonderful conversation about the business for quite a long while. When we finally had to get back to work we hugged again and she said: "When you see Jack, give him my best."

That was the one and only time I met Miss Rogers. The whole meeting seemed surreal. It was such a heady experience for a young girl. I'm doing a pilot next door to movie star Ginger Rogers? How did all this happen? It got even more unreal when later my pilot was sold for a series and hers was not. The studio picked me over Ginger Rogers? That's was just dreamlike.

Eventually, my father decided to break away from Frank Salt to pursue a solo act as Jack Pepper. Once you are identified with a strong duo act it is very difficult to become a solo performer. Getting work can be tough initially as booking agents see you as being only half as good as you used to be. However, Daddy proved them wrong right away. He sang and played ukulele in a style similar to that of Cliff Edwards. He worked up new songs, comedy routines and even added emcee to his skill set. "Have Tux, Will Travel."

Jack Pepper (Daddy) when he was about 22 years old in his glory days of Vaudeville. He sure could he play that Uke.

(Cynthia Pepper Collection)

Daddy once told me about a Chicago club that he was working in during the mid-1930's. During that time, almost all of the entertainment industry was owned or somehow associated with organized crime. You couldn't work in entertainment and not rub shoulders with the guys in charge. My father never had anything to do with organized crime even though he was in the entertainment industry.

Through a lot of hard work Daddy had become very well known in the Chicago area and having his name on the marquee helped to bring the customers in. He was booked up town at The Green Mill club for a couple of weeks and was having a very good run. One night a bunch of tough looking guys, (a tougher than the usual cast of characters), dressed in handmade Italian suits came walking into the club. They quickly looked around and then announced that no one would be allowed to enter or leave the club for the next few hours. As my Father was wondering if the place was being robbed, a few more well-dressed guys and dolls came walking through the door. Daddy recognized one of the guys in this entourage. He was a thick lipped guy with a scar on one side of his face and a cigar on the other. It was the Chicago Mob Boss himself, Al Capone. Daddy had met him back stage once before. When Capone wants to meet you, there are no questions asked, you meet him.

He always referred to my father as Pepper. When Daddy heard Al shout: "Hey Pepper! Sing *Melancholy Baby!*"

Daddy grabbed his ukulele jumped on stage and started singing. When Big Al bellowed: "Hey Pepper! Make me laugh!"

Daddy said he let the jokes fly.

"Hey Pepper! Gimme some soft shoe!" Daddy hoofed up a storm while playing the ukulele, singing AND telling jokes. Sure, entertaining is about pleasing your audience, but entertaining Al Capone was more about staying alive. It was soon announced that Capone would be picking up the drink tab for all the patrons at the club. That was only fair since Al's crack security team was holding everyone hostage for the night. Daddy said it was a banner night for all.

This was one of "Salt and Peppers" big songs from Vaudeville.

(Cynthia Pepper Collection)

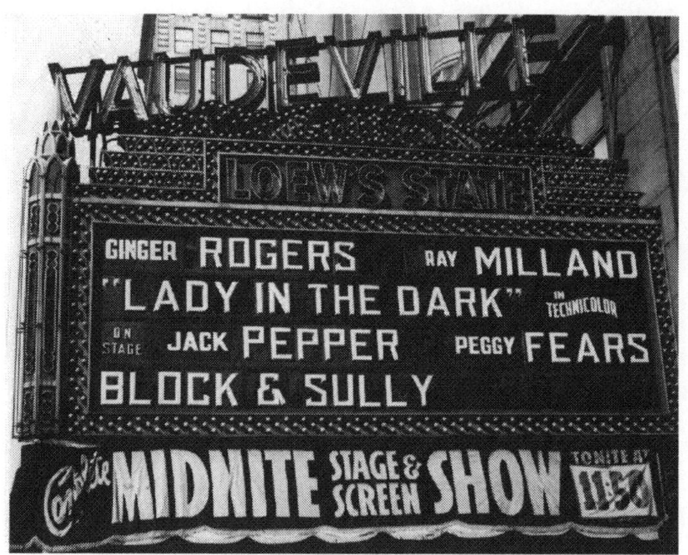

As Vaudeville was giving way to movies, the theaters started to combine movies with a live show. This marquee from 1944 states that Ginger's movie "Lady in the Dark" is playing, and Daddy was part of the live show. I wonder how happy he was with that.

(Rick Goeren Collection)

Chapter 3

Daddy, The Movies, Patty, Marriage, Hollywood

The advancement of movies started to threaten the live performances of Vaudeville. At the time, my Father said: "No one will pay good money to look at a flat moving image on the screen…" But he was wrong. Many people would pay a lot of money to look at that flat screen. Later, when movies added sound to their productions, my Daddy made his thoughts clear again. He felt that no one would pay good money to see a two dimensional moving, and now talking, image on a flat screen, as opposed to a live performance: he was wrong again. It wasn't long after the introduction of sound to the movies that he finally saw the future and reluctantly embraced it.

The year 1929 marked the first time Daddy appeared in what was then called "The Talkies." Silent movies were falling out of vogue and sound was a brand new concept for a film, and one that he was well suited to. He had a lot of music and jokes in his Vaudeville act and sound was what he needed to get to the next level of success.

My father's first movie short was called the *Metro Movietone Review of 1929* and ran about thirteen minutes in length. Here's what he said and did in that film:

Jack Pepper: (in a one shot - sitting down) "I'm going to try and sing a little song on this pork chop here... (holding up his ukulele) It's a little song I wrote myself. It's called Blue Skies by Irving Berlin."

(He starts to play the uke as he scats vocally. He abruptly stops playing then raises the uke to his lips, gives it a kiss and says...)

"Ahh, three more payments and your mine honey, I love you."

He then proceeds to play and sing fantastic versions of *Aint That Too Bad, Girl Of My Dreams* and *I've Got A Momma Down in New Orleans, Another Momma Up In Maine*. I'm so lucky to have this footage that shows what a talented performer my Daddy was, even in his early years.

From 1930 to 1937 my daddy's career was doing pretty well. He was constantly traveling from town to town, theater to theater and picking up anything else he could get. I'm sure he had a lot of girlfriends along the way as he was quite the nomadic charmer. He was married during this time to a lady I know very little about. She was known as Mutt. This was a nickname and not a slur towards her in any way. That marriage didn't last very long and once again he became a free, rambling, southern bachelor enjoying his lot in life. Then one day he met a beautiful dancer, twelve years younger than himself, that turned his head around so much that he actually considered marriage for a third time. Her name was Fairy Lila Stanton, but everyone called her Dawn. She was born September 8, 1913 in West Virginia. She was a beautiful southern belle and talented dancer with the *Ziegfeld Follies* in New York. As Daddy would say, "She was a looker." She had danced for Billy Rose in a number of his stage extravaganzas. She even had a contract with 20th Century Fox. She was a very talented dancer and worked a lot.

Her family, consisting of her parents, two brothers and one sister, had moved to Fresno California to find work in the 1920's. Mother spent many days picking fruit to bring money into the household, all while attending school. She would eventually graduate from high School in Fresno.

My mother's mother, my Grandmother, was a pistol. She told it how she saw it and didn't suffer fools lightly. Her name was Myrtle. She would lay down the rules and that was that. One day she left my Grandfather for a younger man. My Grandfather was truly heartbroken and never got over it. She and her new husband eventually moved to Seattle, Washington in the 1930's and opened a restaurant there. While all of that was going on Mother, now a young lady, had moved to New York to seek her fame and fortune as a dancer on Broadway.

Mother showing off her Dancer's gams and looking every bit of what the 1930's looked like.

(Cynthia Pepper Collection)

Mother couldn't afford an apartment on her own so she had to have a roommate to help pay the bills. Who was her roommate? She was a young dancing hopeful named Eleanor Powell. Ms. Powell would eventually be known as "The World's Greatest Tap Dancer". She went on to star in some great Hollywood films such as *Born To Dance, Lady Be Good, and Ship Ahoy*. I think she even showed Fred Astaire a thing or two when they performed together in *The Broadway Melody of 1940*. Ms. Powell would have been an interesting roommate.

Once Mother met Daddy she knew things would never be boring with a guy like him. Mother had a wonderful sense of humor. She was a great audience for him and Daddy loved nothing more in this world than a great audience. In the beginning, she would laugh at all his jokes. He was doing well financially at this time and was perceived as such by his peers and by all his theater contacts. He was immediately smitten with her and knowing how charming Daddy was; she would've been smitten with him too. As they say in Texas: "he was a hoot". Mother was still a little unsure of this comedic and musical Romeo. I'm not too sure how long they courted, but I do know that, on October 8, 1935 Mother and Daddy were married in the "Windy City" of Chicago. (She later claimed that even on the eve of their wedding she found him messing around with another woman. She said it was his ex-wife Mutt. "Oh, what a tangled web we weave...")

On the exact same day but in a different city in the USA, a young orchestra leader named Ozzie Nelson married a beautiful singer named Harriett Hilliard. This union created not only a marriage, but also a famous radio program and eventually the longest-running live-action sitcom in U.S. television history called *The Adventures of Ozzie and Harriet.* It became synonymous with the 1950s ideal of American family life. As time would go on, unlike the Nelson's TV show, the adventures of Jack and Dawn Pepper would prove to be far less idyllic than what was shown on TV.

Now it's time for a quick lesson in arithmetic. Math was never my strong suit, however, I think I have this one correct. Mother and Daddy were married October, 8, 1935. On March 17, 1936 Mother gave birth to my beautiful sister Patricia Faye Culpepper (Pepper). Now let's see, if you subtract the two dates from each other, carry the nine, divide by two and subtract 15% for the agent's fee, you will see that my parents had another good reason to get married. You have to remember that in the mid nineteen thirties having a baby out of wedlock was a pretty scandalous situation. Nowadays, they'd just make a funny movie about a story like that with a happy Hollywood ending. In the long run, my folks did make it a happy ending by getting married before my sister was born.

For the next couple of years, my parents were busy working, traveling, living out of a suitcase and bringing up my sister, Patty. This could not have been an easy time for the Peppers. Parenthood must have really scared my Daddy. I'm sure that he wanted to run away from the situation. However, my mother was the kind of woman that pulled up her bootstraps, and his too, and forged towards whatever the future held. My mother must have felt like she was bringing up two kids at that point in time.

Eventually, their search for work took them to live in Hollywood, California, the movie capital of the world, where they decided to try and make a go of it. In 1938, Daddy won a movie part and co-starred in an *Our Gang* episode. The *Our Gang* films, also known as *The Little Rascals,* were great comedy shorts and were produced by Hal Roach. They featured a gang of ragtag neighborhood kids that were always getting into some kind of trouble. The stars of these films were, of course the kids. There was Spanky, Alfalfa, Darla, Buckwheat and who can ever forget Pete, the lovable neighborhood dog with a big painted circle around his eye.

Daddy was in the *Our Gang* episode called *Bear Facts*. This episode was directed by Gordon Douglas. Mr. Douglas went on to direct many other successful projects such as Bob Hope's *Call Me Bwana,* Frank Sinatra's *The Detective,* Sidney Poitier's *They Call Me MISTER Tibbs*! And Elvis Presley's *Follow That Dream*. In *Bear Facts* Daddy played the part of Darla's father. Unfortunately, this role didn't turn out to be a springboard into the Hollywood movies that Daddy had hoped it would be.

1940 turned out to be a busy year for my father in Hollywood. He had a number of bit parts in different projects including *Rhythm On The River* starring Bing Crosby, Mary Martin and Basil Rathbone. He also obtained work on the movie *Road to Singapore* with Bob Hope, Dorothy Lamour, and Bing Crosby. Daddy did a radio show and sang a duet with a young lady that he had known since the Vaudeville days, Judy Garland. She was known as Frances (Baby) Gumm with The Gumm Sisters back in Vaudeville. Most theater history books say that a good friend of Daddy's in Chicago, George Jessel, suggested, in the mid 1930's, that the Gumm Sisters should change their name to Garland. For years there was a rumor going around our house, (started by Daddy), that he was the one that suggested the name change, not Jessel. Daddy was working in Chicago at that time, but I know that there's no way to prove his claim. I thought I'd throw Daddy's claim into the ring and let someone else look for the truth. Remember folks there's always three sides to every story: side A, side B and the truth. This has always been Daddy's truth.

I don't know how successful my folks were in the moneymaking department, but I do know that they were very good in the baby making department. On September 4, 1940 Mother gave birth to a bouncing baby girl: me. Cynthia Anne Culpepper (Pepper). The double take that Daddy did that day must have been priceless. By all accounts, it was a relatively easy birth for my Mother. I didn't want to cause any problems and was eager to, please, even at birth. To this day I'm not sure where Daddy was when I was born. He may have been in the waiting room with the other expectant fathers, or at the racetrack, or a local saloon with an old pal. But odds are that he was out seeking his fame and fortune at one of the movie studios at the time.

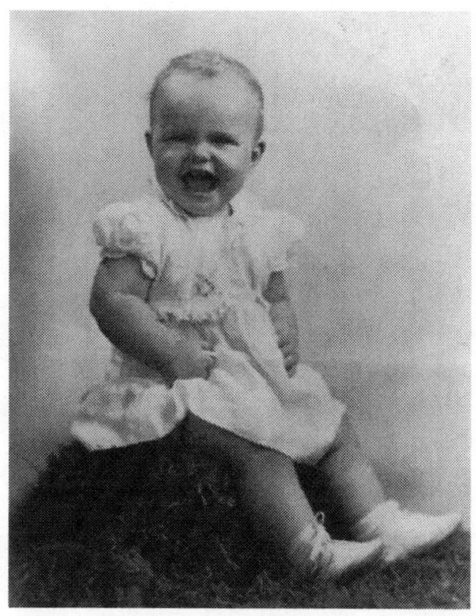

I'm not sure if I was laughing or singing in this shot. I sure do look happy.

(Cynthia Pepper Collection)

Daddy was not finding the success he desired. Throughout his Hollywood career, he would get many bit parts and several supporting roles, but he never won the elusive leading man role of his dreams. I know that the measurement of success is a subjective thing. Some measure it by money, some by awards, and other's by what you own or whom you've married. I don't know how he measured it, but I don't think he ever really felt like he had a lot of solid success. However, if he measured success by friendship, connections and fun then he was the most successful guy in Hollywood.

He worked with and was pals with some of Hollywood's elite. There was Bob Hope, Bing Crosby, Mary Martin, Clark Gable, Judy Garland, William Frawley, Basil Rathbone, Dorthy Lamour, Johnny Weissmuller, and the list goes on and on. Daddy was having too much fun to be worried about the business side of performing. Bing Crosby said that Daddy's favorite expression was: "Have fun now; get the bread later."

Here I am at my first New York catalog modeling job. I was either selling children's clothing, or backyard fencing.

(Cynthia Pepper Collection)

Chapter 4

The Big Apple & My Broadway Debut

Since Daddy was being ignored for the leading roles in Hollywood, my parents decided that maybe New York City was the place to be. New York City had many Broadway theaters, local clubs and a very strong support system for the arts in general. It seemed like there was a lot of opportunity for Daddy to perform live. After all, performing on stage was Daddy's forte. He hadn't been truly comfortable in front of the camera. So with a four year old and a newborn, Mother and Daddy moved us to New York.

I don't know how many people spent the beginning of their formative years growing up in a hotel, but I definitely did. We moved into the Windsor Hotel. It had two bedrooms, one for my folks and one for Patty. There was a bed for my folks and a crib for Patty. My bed was one of the clothes drawers in the dresser that was near the bed in Mother and Daddy's room. That doesn't exactly sound like a place where Ozzie and Harriet Nelson would have lived with their family, now does it?

Growing up in a hotel was like growing up in any other place for a kid. However, Instead of having a front yard, beautiful parks with trees, swings and other kids to play with I had a beautiful lobby, elevators, chairs and hotel staff to play with. I remember that there was, usually, someone playing the big, white piano in the lobby. They would play the hit songs of the day. Like *Don't Fence Me In* written by Cole Porter and Perry Como's big hit *Temptation*. I recall Patty and me hearing the beautiful music from the piano as we were being whisked through the Windsor lobby by Mother.

I stopped and told her: "I want to stay and listen to the piano music."

Me and Patty - the Pepper sisters.

(Cynthia Pepper Collection)

She said that we were going somewhere else to hear even more, better quality music with a big band full of musicians. We went out into the street and as she poured us into a taxi she informed us that we were going to see Daddy work. I was about to have my first visit to something called a radio studio.

In the 1940's a radio studio is where it all happened. Music, news, comedy, drama, product commercials were all created in this audio laboratory. Some studios had the audience behind glass so that they could control the sound of the crowd's reactions. The studio we were in was a big room that had raked seating for the audience and the stage below. The stage was deeper than it was wide. The orchestra was located towards the back of the stage and to the right. The stage had a number of microphone stands at center stage and more that were left and right of center. There were big electric signs above the stage that were very easy for the audience to read. They read "Stand By", "On The Air", and "Applause". There were a lot of men scurrying from stage left to right setting things up and checking wires and a lot of other things that I just didn't understand.

When we first arrived we were told where to sit and get comfortable as the show was about to begin.

I spotted Daddy on stage and yelled to him. Mother was not impressed with that at all, but he gave us a big wave and smile from across the room as the crowd giggled at my outburst. Daddy had a lot of papers in his hands. As I looked at the other people around him, I noticed they all had a lot of papers in their hands too. The big "Stand By" light sign came alive and the whole studio went silent. The silence was deafening but only lasted about ten seconds. Then the "On The Air" sign lit up. I could hear a man announcing the beginning of the show to us and the rest of North America. When the "Applause" sign came alive the show started and I was in a whole other world for the next thirty minutes. Even though he wasn't the star of the show I remember Daddy had everybody laughing. Then he'd sing and play his ukulele, after which they applauded wildly for him. I was so proud that he was my Daddy. His friend Bing Crosby was also in the show. He sang a song called *Don't Fence Me In*, but it was Daddy that I enjoyed the most.

After the show, we went for ice cream. I loved him beyond words and he could do no wrong in my eyes. I was Daddy's girl. He gave the best full hugs that anyone could ever want to receive. When he was around he would pick me up if I fell down, tell me he loves me and make all the monsters go away. Other times he behaved like a kid himself and would get down on the floor to play with me. This one-on-one playtime was something that no other adult in my life did with me until I became an actor and found lots of likeminded adults to play with on stage. In retrospect, all this love I received from Daddy could not have been that easy on my sister. He didn't ignore her, but I just seemed to get a little more of the love and I think Patty was aware of that.

By all accounts, Daddy was finding a lot of work in New York; so much work that a year or two later they decided to enroll Patty in the New York Professional School. She was learning to act, dance and sing while she was learning her ABC's. We found out that she was a pretty good singer.

Just before I turned five years old, Mother and Daddy were looking for other ways to make a buck and pay the bills. They had me modeling children's clothing for some magazines, and catalogues. One day they heard that The Playhouse Theatre on Broadway was looking to cast a cute young blonde haired girl for a role in a new play; they took me straight down for an audition. I don't know what I did that day to impress them, (I guess my baby girl cute factor was set on high), but I got the part. The play was called *It's A Gift*. It was a new, original comedy written by Curt Goetz and Dorian Otvos and starred a very young Julie Harris. This production marked Julie Harris's first Broadway play, and mine too. Julie Harris hit the planks of the Playhouse Stage at 19 years old. I was only 4 years old, beating her to the Broadway stage by a cool 15 years. She went on in her career to win five *Tony Awards*, three *Emmys*, and a *Grammy* and was nominated for an *Academy Award*. Ok, I'm done comparing myself to her.

Meanwhile back in 1945... The play was about a professor who learns that the sister he disowned for having an illegitimate child has died. She will leave money to him and his family of 12 children if the eldest female of his family has her own illegitimate child. WOW, now that's a pretty heady stuff for the day now wasn't it? Not only was Curt Goetz the playwright but he also played the professor in the production. I was playing the part of Julie's younger sister and at times I felt that I was nothing more than a human prop for the adult actors to work with. One incident sticks in my mind as clear as a bell to this day. It was something that changed my life. During a scene I was in, one of the actresses picked me up in her arms and held me as she delivered her lines. I'd always hit my mark and get scooped up every time. One night when I was picked up I could feel my little dress creep up my body, exposing my frilly knickers underneath. My backside was facing towards the audience and I knew my undergarments were now exposed. I reached back and in full view of the audience I began pulling my dress down to cover the knickers. Well, the audience roared with laughter. I heard the laughter and I liked it. The harder I tried to pull that dress back down the louder the laughter became. Somehow, even at that young age, I knew I was causing the crowd in the theatre to lose control and I loved it. I was hooked on the laughter and amazed that a simple action could create such a strong reaction. I caused a room full of people to laugh and it made me feel special. I knew it was a good thing because I was asked by the director, via Mother if I could do that again the next night and every night after that. Ha, just try and stop me! I was something special and I knew it.

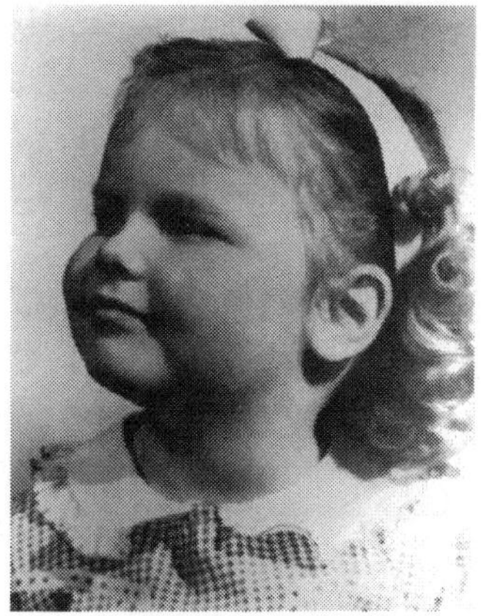

Modeling in New York. Check out those cheeks.

(Cynthia Pepper Collection)

I do remember one other thing about my first foray onto the Broadway stage; Mother gave me a lesson in humility. Mother was ironing some clothes while getting Patty and me ready for our day. Mother always seemed to be ironing a lot back then. To this day the sweet, fresh and somewhat tinny smell of the iron's steam will send me back to that hotel room and my childhood. (I'm here to say that aromatherapy is real and it works.) This particular morning Mother was flattening and creasing our clothes to perfection as I had to get ready for a matinee at the theatre, and Patty was getting ready to go to school. Feeling very special about myself and with a boastful tone to my voice I proclaimed to my sister: "Ha. You have to go to school and I don't because I get to go to the theatre!" Without hesitation Mother put down the iron, picked up her hairbrush, came straight over to me and gave me a couple of smacks on the behind. She scolded me: "Don't talk to your sister like that! You are no better than anyone else in this world young lady and you remember that!" I was stunned and confused as to why Mother was so upset with me. I was even more upset at myself for disappointing her on any level. Those words and the sting on my behind made me think twice about getting too smug or pretentious in life. It's a lesson that has affected me throughout my entire life. At the matinee that day, as embarrassed as I was I pulled that dress down extra fast so no one could see any stinging hairbrush marks below. I still got a laugh.

My role in the theatre production didn't extend for the full run of the play as the AEA (Actors Equity Association) claimed I was too young to be performing. I wasn't allowed to work in the play until I got older. Easy come, easy go. I was back to being a civilian again. (I was taught by Daddy that a civilian is anyone that's not in show business). One day you're in show business hitting your mark and getting the big laughs, and the next day you're out. "Quick, Get my Agent on the line!" Even at that age I knew I wasn't really going to be out of show biz for too long. I had been bitten by the performance bug and I liked it! I did some more clothes catalogue modeling, and tried to have a childhood on the side.

One day Daddy got a special letter from the United States of America. It was from his Uncle Sam. I had never met this Uncle Sam, but Daddy and Mother didn't seem to be too pleased to hear from him. The letter said that Uncle Sam wanted him and he had to go. Yep, Daddy was drafted into World War II. I didn't understand what war was but if they wanted him I thought it was for another show. As it turned out it was another show all right, just on a much bigger stage, the world stage. As a kid, I didn't understand why my Daddy was leaving or even where he was going, though I knew he'd be back home again soon. He had to come back as he would miss my hugs too much and I would miss his. In the end, he would be gone a lot longer than I had thought possible which left Mother alone to raise us as best she could. I knew I would have to get by with Mothers hugs until Daddy got home. My Mother was a great person and a great parent but Daddy was the perfect playmate. Mother was the loving disciplinarian and teacher, but Daddy was, well, just Daddy. My sister and I were brought up knowing about God and religion even though we didn't see the inside of a church too often. Mother would have us pray for Daddy before going to bed, to make sure that he would be safe. I always sent him a big hug and a prayer.

Once the Army found out about the fantastic gem of a performer they had just conscripted, (and with a gentle yet influential push from his now famous pal Bob Hope), Daddy was directed into the U.S.O. to entertain the troops. Unknown to me at the time, Daddy was touring the world with Bob Hope, Frances Langford and jazz guitar great Tony Romano. They toured England, Sicily, North Africa and the South Pacific. In Bob Hope's memoir, *Don't Shoot! It's Only Me!* he recalled how Frances Langford got the biggest laugh he had ever heard. While performing at a U.S.O. show in the South Pacific, Langford stood up on stage to sing before a huge crowd of servicemen. When she sang the first line of her signature song, *I'm in the Mood for Love*, a soldier in the audience stood up and shouted, "You've come to the right place, honey!" It brought the house down. I always wondered if it was Daddy that snuck out into the crowd and yelled that line as it sounded like something he would have come up with.

(L to R) an officer, Daddy, an officer that looks a lot like Clark Cable, Frances Langford, Bob Hope,& Tony Romano.

(Cynthia Pepper Collection)

While he was abroad, he would send money home to Mother to keep us alive and he would also send Patty and I coins from the different countries that he was performing in. They came in all different shapes and sizes and, best of all, they were very shiny. One day Patty and I decided that it would be a great thing to drop these coins out of the bedroom window onto the sidewalk and street below. We had no concept of the value of money, but we did think the thrill of dropping them out of the window would be more than worth it, and it was. Patty and I took turns pitching these beautiful pieces of foreign currency out of our third-story window. One by one we would let them fall just to hear the fascinating sounds they would make bouncing off an awning or a ledge or a car passing by. It made the pigeons fly and people were yelling at us. Once again I was doing something that got a reaction. Look at me, I was quickly learning Newton's law and I had not even spent a single day in school. "To every action there is always an equal and opposite reaction." We were having fun and laughing and the people below were angry and not laughing at all. When Mother realized what we were doing, she introduced us to another physics lesson. It involved mass, acceleration, and momentum or as I like to call it a good hard smack on the backside with a hairbrush. Mother always tried to send us down the right path and as I look back I realize now that it must have been very tough being a single parent when Daddy was in the Army. I think the term single parent should be changed to double parent as Mother had to be Mom & Dad to Patty and me even when Daddy was around.

(Standing L to R) Col Stanley T. Wray, Frances Langford, Col Charles E. Marion, & Daddy. (Seated L to R) Tony Romano, & Bob Hope.
(Mark Forlow Collection)

Chapter 5

Everything's Bigger In Texas

When Daddy returned home from his stint in the army, we lived in New York for another year. I was very glad to have his special hugs and love back in my life. He still wasn't around much as he was trying hard to make a go of things. There just didn't seem to be anything for him in New York anymore. The work in New York wasn't flowing in as Daddy had first thought it would. This must have been a huge blow to his ego in a number of ways. He had once played all the big theatres including the holy grail of Vaudeville, The Palace Theatre with a very successful and in demand act back in the day. Now most of his connections in Vaudeville were dead and gone. He didn't have a solid foothold in the new movie business and he was getting left behind. The fact that Ginger Rogers was now a big star on stage and screen must have stung a little too. Only ten short years before Daddy had been doing very well on the entertainment circuit in the "Big Apple" and beyond. As the future song would later proclaim: "if you can make it there, you can make anywhere..." And the bottom line was that Daddy wasn't making it there anymore.

Daddy spent more time at the track, and his gambling losses were increasing. His drinking was escalating and the tension between him and Mother was growing too. The Peppers used to take a bite out of the Big Apple but now it looked like the Big Apple was taking a huge bite out of the Peppers. Then one day Daddy was offered an opportunity in a place where he had his roots, Dallas, Texas. Daddy said it wasn't exactly the entertainment capital of the world, but he had been offered a good job. It was an opportunity to make a better living for him and his family, and maybe get another chance at stardom. Daddy was born just south east of Dallas in Palestine, Texas and certainly knew that area very well. Mother was also happy for a new start and a chance to get a job and contribute to the family financially, even if it was in civilian life. Mother had skills beyond her beauty, dancing and motherly attributes. The move to Dallas was also a good way to get Daddy away from the bars and gambling establishments of the big city.

Patty, on the other hand, was upset to leave her school and friends. She was nine going on ten years old and at that age it was very traumatic to leave all the relationships and best friends behind forever. I think that weighed on her mind for many years after we left New York. I was ready to follow Mother and Daddy wherever they went. They were my life at that point and I wanted what they wanted. When I was told that we'd be taking a train ride, I was over the top with anticipation.

Finally, the time had come. We were leaving New York for good. All the packing had been done, (not that there was a lot to pack), Patty had a good cry or two about the confusion and unfairness of leaving her friends, and I was getting dressed in my best little dress for our big adventure. The cab ride to the train station was short and sweet. As our taxi arrived at 42nd Street and Park Avenue I looked out the window and saw this monstrously huge building we were about to enter. It was Grand Central Station. There were so many people walking about and it echoed like a church. Could this be the Church of Sainted Travelling Folks? Were all these people going to Dallas too? If so, this Dallas, Texas must be one heck of a great place to live. That's when it happened. I heard the voice of God. It boomed through the concourse louder than any other voice. It was a strong and forceful voice with the confidence that only God could have. He said: "All those traveling to Dallas via Chicago on the Atchison, Topeka and the Santa Fe, please make your way to track number twelve as your train will be leaving in 15 minutes, thank you." I thought to myself: "God truly does know everything."

Our train ride to Texas was a very eye-opening experience indeed. All I had known to that point was skyscrapers, loud traffic, and the hustle and bustle of cars and people travelling about the city. Now I imagined myself as the Princess of New York heading to my new realm of Dallas. It was a long trip, but I didn't mind at all. When we first left the station, the city of New York was an amazing sight to see from our window. It all looked like it should. Then we left Midtown Manhattan and the concrete jungle that I had called home behind. As the train continued on, I was fascinated to see the high-rise and brownstone buildings give way to large smoking, chugging factories and houses. They were not apartments, but real houses with green lawns at both the front and back of the house, where real people lived and played. Some of the houses were two or three stories high. It was beyond thrilling to think that we would have our own house, that Daddy would be with us, and I would have my very own room.

When we arrived in Dallas, Texas in 1946, the population was around 300,000. The Peppers were about to bump that up to 300,004. As it turned out, Dallas was not quite the utopia that I thought it would be and our new house was far from being a castle. The house was very different from what I had in mind at that young age. Our new home was located in a place called La Reunion, Texas which was just outside of Dallas. Our house was attached to a row of other houses that looked just like our house. I found out later that these were called townhouses. At times, it wasn't all that different from living in an apartment. The house was small, on one level, and it was very easy to hear the neighbors yelling next door. The walls were very thin and the house had a clay shingled roof. There was a small porch at the front of the house completely made out of wood, except for the two or three concrete steps leading up to it. The front lawn consisted of a few strands of wild grass, a couple of wild cacti and a lot of dirt. It was really more of a sandbox than a lawn. The cats in the neighborhood loved it.

I would while away the hours playing with cars, jacks and neighborhood cats in the dirt with my friend Amanda McFarland. Amanda's mom Virginia was a wonderful and generous lady and all the neighborhood kids loved her. Amanda had three brothers Tommy, Rod (Roderick) and George also known to his family as Buddy. He was better known to the rest of the world as Spanky McFarland from the *Little Rascals* movie shorts. He was about sixteen years old when I met him, and he was pretty much finished as a child actor. I guess that's why they moved back to Texas from Hollywood. He now had fame without fortune and I think that's one of the reasons that he and Daddy bonded the way they did. Daddy had done the *Our Gang* movie with him back in 1938, and Spanky had become the son he never had. Spanky was a fun and generous guy, and a life-long friend of our family. (Many years later on one of his visits to our Hollywood home he even gave me his trade mark beanie hat that he wore in the movies. He was such a bighearted person. Unfortunately, years later, I had to sell it to pay off a few bills.)

At different times, Amanda and I would run a lemonade stand in the sweltering heat. In June, July and August this part of Texas had an average high temperature of about 95 degrees. Mind you that was just an average as it would easily go above 100 degrees on any given day. Our lemonade stand didn't exactly make us millionaires, but we sure made people smile as they stopped by and that always made us feel good. Of course, there were days when we drank more than we sold. Hey, a girl has to stay hydrated in that Texas heat, right?

We didn't have air-conditioning as it exists today. We had a special kind of cooling system for our home. It was called "open a couple of windows and pray for a breeze". The inside of our house was not very large. There was a living room, a kitchen and two bedrooms. I didn't get my own bedroom, but I did get to share one with Patty. I didn't mind sharing with my big sister, but I don't think that she was all that keen on sharing with me. Patty and I didn't bond much by sleeping in the same room. She was having her life experiences and I was having mine. I guess the little sister was cramping her style. This room of ours would be a place to play, a place to dream, and imagine, and a place for me to become anything or anyone I wanted. Every once in a while though, reality would come crashing in.

The walls were very thin in our new home. I found that they were the kind of walls that you could easily put a fist through. There was a piece of paper that Mother hung on our bedroom wall that had little gold stars on it for the different chores that Patty and I would complete through the week. Mother had just left the room after putting a new star on the paper, when I could hear some loud, scary noises coming from the other side of the wall. It was our neighbor's yelling at each other. As the neighbor voices got louder, the paper would vibrate and rattle more and more on the wall. At one point, it almost seemed as though the paper was dancing to the sound of their voices.

As the voices continued to get louder and more violent, the paper seemed to become afraid and was trying to rip itself from the wall and run away. The man next door was yelling at his wife at the top of his lungs when all of sudden his fist came smashing through our bedroom wall. The noise of the breaking wall was very loud and both Patty and I stood there stunned. We were shocked to have witnessed such a violent act by total strangers. The paper and the piece of the wall it was attached to were knocked clear across the room. We weren't hit by any debris, but it sure was an eye opener to see how badly the house was made. Mother always said that the house was made out of cardboard and she may have been right. I guess all we needed was some tape, and an empty Corn Flakes box and that wall would have been as good as new.

Daddy wasn't around much in those days as he was always off working or socializing. When he was home, he made us laugh and always tried to make things better when he could. Mother was the one that kept us all from falling apart as a family. She was attempting to change two young ragamuffins into two refined young ladies, come hell or high water. We always had food on the table and never went hungry. "Food, Glorious Food." Some eat to live and some live to eat. I was not an obese child, but I did my share of eating and at times I guess it showed. I was a plump little kid, and so I got ribbed a lot, mostly from the adults. We were living in New York the first time I remember being teased about my weight. Mother and Daddy were invited over to another apartment in our building for a party and they took Patty and me with them. They had the most beautiful piano there, and everyone was drinking, smoking, dancing and singing up a storm. Some of the partiers noticed me running around the place just being a kid and I would hear their comments. "Oh, look at the cute little lard ass." or "Here comes little Miss Piano Legs." I don't think they were trying to be mean to me, or that they thought I was even listening to what they were saying but, I did. I would just take it in stride and let it go with a big smile on my face. It hurt a lot, but I seemed to be able to let it all slide away. For some inexplicable reason I knew that it didn't really matter what they said and just rolled with the punches. Those comments left me with some bruises but never any scars.

Patty was the opposite of me and took everything to heart. She was dark and serious and I, on the other hand, was more like Daddy, (when he was sober), fun and light. I was always looking for a way to make others happy and if it meant taking the proverbial (or literal) pie in the face, then so be it. It's all really a matter of transferring your insecurity.

Envision that someone zings a cream pie at your head. When the pie hits you in the face, it stings a lot and makes a total mess out of your face and clothes. So for the moment, the thrower of the pie has the power. Then by licking your lips, and tasting the pie as it drips from your face, you smile, and say something like: "Mmmmm, Strawberry". People laugh and YOU have now stripped the pie thrower of the power. I never understood why Patty couldn't grasp this train of thought. Time would prove there was a lot about Patty that I would never understand.

One day, when Patty ran off to play with her friends, Daddy came to me and announced that we were going to a Tent Show. I kind of knew what a tent was, but I heard the word "show" and that was the selling point for me. Tent Shows, or Minstrel Shows, had pretty much disappeared before Vaudeville took over. There were a handful of these shows still touring the southern states right into the late 1940's and one had come to our town. The show consisted of music, comedy, dancing, and most of the performers were in blackface. Blackface first became popular in the 1830's and 1840's. A white performer would rub burnt cork on his face to look black. One of Daddy's favorite performers of all time, Al Jolson became world famous performing this way. Today, Blackface is considered absolutely racist and it is unacceptable to perform this way, but back then it was an art form. Daddy seemed to know a number of the performers and got up and did a couple of songs and routines himself. He even got me up for a song and I loved it. (We were not in blackface.)

Our visit to the tent show had me all fired up about show business again. The audience just loved all the performers and the performers seemed to live their lives on a whole different level than the rest of the world. Daddy was a star again that day and it was great to get a glimpse of this amazing, former vaudevillian entertaining the masses once more. It always seemed to me that throughout his life Daddy was unsure, insecure, and somewhat doubtful about so much that life threw at him. However, on the live stage he was a confident dynamo of entertaining wit and musical energy. If he could have, I think he would have lived on the stage his whole life.

Here I am with Patty in April of 1946 living in La Renuion, Texas.

(Cynthia Pepper Collection)

Let me tell you about something that helped shape my life and, by no small miracle, entertain me too. It was something called radio. Long before TV took over it was the radio that tied the country together. During the dark years of 1941 to 1943 when a deranged little German fellow with his bad mustache tried to bully the world into his sick way of thinking and later on into the brighter years of 1944 and '45, when the deranged little man was finally put in his place, it was the radio that held us together. The glory of the old time radio shows is lost on most people today, but I will never forget the mystery of this great machine and the fantastic feelings it invoked in me.

The radio gave us the news of the day and of course the European and World updates on the war. It provided entertainment and gave us the ability to shut down our worries for a short time with its magnificent variety programs. I can still hear them all: *Fibber McGee and Molly, The Life of Riley, The Jack Benny Show,* ventriloquist Edgar Bergen and his dummy Charlie McCarthy (You ask; how did a ventriloquist ever succeed on Radio? I reply; Very well thank you), *The Bob Hope Show, The Great Gildersleeve,* and *Roy Rogers.* There was also *Red Skelton, The Fred Allen Show, Duffy's Tavern, Amos & Andy, Judy Canova, Burns and Allen, Abbot and Costello, The Aldrich Family, Walter Winchell,* and an all music show called *Your Hit Parade.* This program had some young upstart named Francis Albert Sinatra and others singing the hit songs of the day. I wonder if that Sinatra kid ever made anything of himself.

My favorite radio shows were *Baby Snooks* starring Fanny Brice, *Suspense,* which had lots of mystery, *Mr. Keen. Tracer of Lost Persons* and *Ozzie & Harriet,* which attempted to show us how family life ought to be. Mother, Patty and I would literally sit around this big box that was just oozing with a rainbow of entertainment selections, awaiting a zap of magical electricity to bring it to life. We had a Philco Console radio, complete with a phonograph, and it was twice the size of me at the time. Console radios were big beautiful pieces of heavy wooden furniture back then. Mother, Patty and I would be drawn towards this big box with its numerous dials and handsome grill cloth protecting the speakers inside. Once it was turned on (and eventually warmed up), we would just stare at the radio console as if to look past the glossy wood and the woven mesh to envision everything that we heard.

Talk about a workout for the mind. All we could hear were voices, sound effects, and music, but the things that we could see were infinite in our minds. All these programs allowed our imaginations to work out and to run wild with our own perceptions of each different show. What we could envision in our minds could be completely different than what the person right beside us would see from the exact same program. It was pure magic. At times, Mother would even have a discussion with us to teach us lessons from the different shows we had just heard. I miss those radio programs to this day. It's a shame that children today can't experience the magic of radio as we did, but they sure have powerful thumbs… Thank you video games.

Shortly after moving into our new place, I started going to a new school on the other side of Dallas. It was called The Ursaline Academy. I would go to this school for Grades one, two and three. Since

Patty was in an older grade than I, she went to a co-ed school called St. Cecilia Catholic School. She would take the school bus to St. Cecilia's, and by all accounts was doing well in class.

This brings up an interesting story that I still shake my head at. When I was a little girl most parents didn't worry about their kids staying out late and unsupervised. They instilled good solid morals into us teaching us right from wrong... Or was it the radio programs that did that? Anyway, the story I'm about to tell you would have most modern parents of today cringing in absolute horror or at least calling an emergency hot line.

I had just turned six years old, I was attending my new school and going into grade one. I would get to and from school on a streetcar, and a bus. Does this sound normal so far? Sure, you say? Just wait for it. The bus I would take was not a school bus, it was public transit. Oh, I think I heard a few folk's jaws drop just then. I would walk over to the very busy Interstate 30 and catch the bus that would take me through Dealey Plaza Park and on to downtown Dallas. The whole trip would be about four miles long. The bus would stop at the Adolphus Hotel, where I would get off and wait on a busy downtown corner with all kinds of active traffic and people heading to work. I would then board a streetcar that would take me another 8 miles to my school, the Ursaline Academy. I know what you're thinking, "Who the hell lets a five or six year old take a twelve mile ride on public transit to school and then back home again every day?" Well at that time, a lot of people did. Most of the time I rode to school alone, but other days, I rode with my little friend Mary Jo. She was younger than me, so I was the one in charge of getting her to school and home again safely. (Ricky and David Nelson never had this kind of adventure).

I liked the nuns that taught at the school, and I also liked the fact that there was a lot of opportunity for me to participate in plays and musical presentations. I performed whenever I could and I loved it. That December, I performed in Ursaline's production of The Nutcracker Suite. I remember that I must have played the part of a fairy because I was covered in fairy dust; either that or I just dumped a pail of sparkly fairy dust all over myself because I loved the way it looked.

The Ursaline Academy was the closest, if not the only, Catholic all girls Preparatory School in Dallas. The fact that I went to a Catholic school was strange because neither one of my parents were Catholic. I think in their minds they wanted me to go to this particular school so that I would have a chance to grow up as a proper young lady. Also, I think that they were feeling some guilt about not making it to church as much as they thought they should have.

I can just hear Daddy now: "Dawn, I can't go to church today! I have to leave right now if I'm going to catch the first race at Arlington Downs! There's a horse there with my name on it."

Mother's response: "I'll bet I know which 'part' of the horse your name is on, too..."

When the school day was over, I would take the streetcar back to downtown Dallas and the Adolphus Hotel. Instead of jumping back onto the bus to head home right away, I would go into the hotel. The Adolphus was a beautiful hotel and still is to this day. With its beautiful white stone and ornate carvings on the outside walls this building was the jewel of downtown Dallas. They've had the pleasure of catering to some very famous guests through the years including Queen Elizabeth II, The Vanderbilt's, baseball's Sultan of Swat, Babe Ruth and now six year old me.

When I arrived at the hotel stop on my way home from school, I would make my way to the Walgreen's soda shop and eatery located at one end of the hotel. I would head straight to the counter and with much effort I would pull myself up onto a stool and order myself a ham sandwich and a vanilla milk shake. No vanilla milkshake ever tasted better than these did. I went to the eatery almost every day and it was always the exact same order. No wonder I was getting called those plump little nicknames.

The reason I ate there was because Mother had secured a civilian job and was now working at the Dallas Morning Newspaper. She wouldn't always be home in time to make dinner so she gave me the extra money to buy myself some food. On certain days, when the stars lined up, I'd get home and Daddy would be there. I'd run to him and give him a big hug and kiss. I would then make us both one of my all-time great sandwich creations, simply known as a bacon and mustard sandwich. Ok, so my parents gave me a lot of freedom, the ability to make good choices and lots of love and support; but as far as nutritional information goes, not so much.

There were two separate things that happened to me on my way to school that I'd like to share with you. You see Texas in the 1940's was just as segregated as any of the southern states on the east coast of America. Their values were pretty much the same. In Dallas, there were signs over drinking fountains saying "Whites Only". There were signs on businesses that said things like "No Dogs, Negroes, or Mexicans." As a little white girl at the innocent age of six, or seven years old I never really paid attention to these signs. However, I could easily have grown up instilled with these beliefs, but two unexpected incidents occurred that made me challenge those racist values.

One day I was waiting on the Dallas street corner for the street car to take me to school. I stood there with my school books in hand and nothing more on my mind than wondering if the street car would be on time. I noticed a black girl, a year or so older than me, also waiting for the bus. As I glanced at her, she came straight over to me and in a very aggressive tone asked: "What are you staring at?"

Before I could answer or even figure out why she was angry with me, she brought her right hand up and slapped me hard across the face. My books went flying everywhere. As my ears rang and the tears welled up in my eyes I said: "I wasn't staring at you."

I scrambled to pick up my books and when I looked up, she was gone. I was shocked and confused. Why would a complete stranger slap me in the face for no reason? Why was this black girl so mad at me?

Needless to say, over the next two weeks, I felt afraid and had untrusting thoughts towards all black people. At the end of those two weeks of fearsome feelings, I was coming home from school one day on the street car. I had to transfer to the bus that would take me home. When I got off the street car, I walked a few steps and then tripped and fell to the pavement. I had dropped my books and papers all over the ground.

As I was getting up a young black girl, around my age, came running towards me. I thought: "Oh no, I'm about to get slapped again and I still don't know why."

As the girl approached me she extended her hand and said: "Here, let me help you."

I was apprehensive, but I took her hand as she helped me to my feet. She then started darting around grabbing my books and papers. I was once again in shock, but this time it was a good thing. We gathered up all my stuff together and before I knew it she was gone. I think I said thank you. I hope I said thank you. I thought about those two events a lot after that. It's not a skin color or race that is bad or good, it's just people. Some people are good some are bad. Some are confused and some are filled with misguided anger. I learned after that to treat people based on how they treat you.

My sister, Patty, wasn't always a happy child and I think part of her unhappiness came from the fact that she was allergic to animals. She liked animals but couldn't get within three feet of any cute furry creature before her breathing would start to labor and her throat would start to close up. Any kind of cat, dog, bunny, or any other cute and fuzzy living thing was potential grief and life threatening danger to her. I always wondered why she was stricken with this limitation in life and I wasn't. As a matter of fact, I loved animals enough for two or three people. I always wanted a pet of my own. Both Mother and Daddy were big animal lovers, but they had to keep Patty safe. So we couldn't have pets. I'd ask and at times even beg Mother and Daddy for a pet only to be told no. They were out to protect Patty at any cost. Since I couldn't have a pet of my own at home, I would pick up, squeeze, hug and love any friendly little critter that I could find. It didn't matter where I was going, school, the movies, or just playing with my friends, I had to have my animal fix. I guess that would explain why I was always coming home with a case of pinkeye, ringworm, or something equally as bad. Mother was always giving me the devil for picking up strays and getting ill. The Doctor was at our place almost every month for something new that I picked up from spending time with my new found friends. I couldn't help it, I was in love with animals. I was quarantined at home a lot in those days, but the time away from school was a fun bonus.

Armed with pinkeye and self-reliance, I think I may have been the youngest student ever to be expelled from the Ursaline Academy. It happened during recess when I realized that I had just been hit with yet another festering attack of pinkeye. I knew at this point in life that pinkeye was not a good thing for others to be around. I somehow got it into my head that I needed to protect my fellow classmates from my affliction so I decided right there and then to leave and go home. Since it was my responsibility to take my younger friend Mary-Jo to school and back home with me that day, I decided that she needed to go home too. I found her, took her by the hand and we left the playground and caught the bus home. Mary-Jo was good with my decision so we left without notifying the teacher. This was not a good decision on my part, at the time. I guess all hell broke loose once the nun's realized that Mary-Jo and I were missing. Police were called, Mother was called, Mary-Jo's parents were called. They eventually found us both safe and sound at my house, playing together. The powers that be decided a few days away from school would be a good thing for me so I got expelled for a couple of days. Hey, I needed the time to get rid of the pinkeye and catch up on my radio programs anyway, so it all worked out.

Another incident that kept my Mother on her toes and made Patty roll her eyes took place just outside of the Adolphus Hotel. For some reason which I can't recall, Mother and Patty were with me at the hotel's Walgreens for a bite to eat. I'm not sure where we were going but when we finished eating we went out to the street corner to catch the bus. As we were waiting for the bus Patty became aware that she had left her pocketbook back inside Walgreens. Mother told me to stay put and that she and Patty would be back in just a minute. They went back into the restaurant as I sat there waiting for the bus. When they were gone, the bus arrived. I must have figured that they'd be back with enough time to get on the bus so I decided to board and wait for them there. Mother and Patty got back to the bus stop just in time to see me waving at them through the back window of the vehicle as it pulled away. I can still see the shocked look on Mothers face. I don't know why I thought this was a good idea. I was on a bus by myself again and I was not panicky. Mother quickly flagged a policeman down and within a short time a squad car had pulled the bus over. The other passengers were confused when I was led off by the police. Wow, I was now in my very first police drama. The only things missing were the reading of my Miranda Rights and the handcuffs. When the officers brought me to Mother I thought I was in big trouble, but instead of punishment she gave me the biggest hug. I was surprised but happy with her reaction. I guess she got a little scared of losing her little girl that day. She was a great Mom and I really felt her love for me that day. Patty just looked at me shaking her head.

We didn't live in the La Reunion house for more than a year and a half before Daddy took over and managed a supper club called the Log Cabin. It was located just outside of Dallas. It was a dinner club steak house that also had great entertainment. Sometimes Daddy would be part of the entertainment for the night as well as the manager of the club. Later in life I remember him telling me that the club had a seedy underside to it. The club was frequented by a lot of mob guys from that era. Daddy told me that it was his job to greet people at the door and to make sure they were thoroughly entertained and happy throughout the night. I never got to see a show there since I was too young, but we did go for an early dinner there once with the family. The steak I had that day was the most amazing I have ever had in my life. Like I've always said, back then we didn't have much, but we never wanted for much either. Thanks Daddy.

Mother made sure that we got a good serving of the arts via the radio. Every Sunday she would let us listen to a radio program that read the funnies, or comics, to us. When that was done, she would dial into another station that carried the classical music broadcasts from New York. We gained a wider appreciation of classical music by listening to these shows. If there wasn't any classical music on the radio Mother would drop one of her classical records onto the phonograph. As it played, she would describe and explain what it was that we were all listening to. She would have us listen as one instrument or section of instruments would take over at times or play in tandem with the others. Mother explained how certain musical pieces represented thoughts or emotions. She taught us about music dynamics and that playing in an orchestra was a team effort. If they didn't have enough discipline on their chosen instrument the whole thing would just fall apart. "Practice makes Perfect", she would say. I would have no concept of musical imagery and how it could enrich someone's life, as it had mine without these teaching moments that my Mother provided us. She loved classical music and I really miss those music appreciation sessions with her. I can never thank her enough for those shared days.

It was 1947 and the Peppers were on the move again. We didn't relocate too far from La Reunion. We moved into an apartment in Oak Cliff that was just outside of downtown Dallas, but closer to Daddy's work. I hoped this would be the time that I would get my own bedroom. Well, I was wrong again.

The building complex was called the Stevens Park Apartments. It was located close to Interstate 30, the Trinity River and, of course, Stevens Park. It was a small apartment house. Our new place had a living room, dining room and kitchen on the main floor. There was a door from the kitchen that led to the outside covered car park. I'll never forget the coat closet that was in the living room, directly under the stairs to the second floor because that's where we kept my pal Bozo. *Bozo the Clown* was a plastic blow up toy that you could punch as hard as you wanted and he would bounce right back. Daddy showed me how to do it. I guess he figured every little girl should know how to throw a punch just in case they were attacked by a plastic blowup toy. I certainly smacked Bozo a few times in my day and he always came back smiling. Not a bad life lesson to learn. Smacking Bozo was a great stress reliever for a lot of kids back then.

Many years later I met the man that performed as, and owned the rights to, the name and image of, *Bozo the Clown*. His name was Larry Harmon. I met Mr. Harmon when I was attending the Toy Show Convention in New York City in 1962, to help promote my TV show *Margie*. He seemed like a very nice man focused on making Bozo the most famous clown of all time and he sure did that. He was dressed in full Bozo costume when I met him and NO, I didn't punch him to see if he'd bounce back.

Meanwhile, back at the apartment in Texas, 1947. Even though I didn't have my own bedroom I still liked the fact that my big sister was around for protection in this new part of Dallas. Patty was a lot tougher than I was and I might need her protection here in the new neighborhood.

I quickly discovered that the Oak Cliff area was a little nicer than La Reunion and I had very little to fear. There were lots of open areas and green grassy mounds to play on. We would stay out all day and up to nine or ten o'clock at night, sometimes just running, playing hide and go seek, or catching fireflies in jars. The fireflies were like little shooting stars that would shine so brightly in the jar, and then flicker off. I loved how intensely they could glow but then just as quickly fade away. The fireflies couldn't seem to hold that brilliance for very long but when they did it was extraordinary. I would never keep them in a jar for very long as I knew they could never survive that way. I would smile as they flew away because I loved all animals, even if they were bugs.

My next big discovery at that time was the movies. My first experience watching a film was something that, to this day, is hard for me to describe. Mother took me to my first movie house. I remember that the movie was a gorgeous attack on all my senses. I took in the music, the actors, the dialogue, the romance, the comedy, the stories, the chase scenes, depicted by the most beautiful and interesting people in the world. It was all brought to me in glorious black & white film for just ten cents! That was a fair bit of money back then, but Daddy always had a dime handy if I wanted to go. I can recall wondering where these actors were. I first figured that they were behind this big well lit screen that I was watching. That hypothesis fell flat when a close-up of an actor came onto the screen, which made his face much bigger than normal. I had a dream that I'm sure some little girls had at the time and that was to be up on that big screen.

I can't overstate it; I loved the movies and I was going to be an actress! I had fallen in love with the movies even though I had to sit on the arms of the theatre seats. I was too short to sit in them properly and still see the whole screen. The ten cents we paid for a movie back then was worth it as each and every film took me to another existence. I would tremble with excitement as the newsreels went by telling me what was happening in the world with pictures and narration. Then there would be a fantastic cartoon with *Bugs Bunny, Elmer Fudd, Little Lulu, Mickey Mouse* and *Donald Duck*, or a movie short with the likes of *The Three Stooges*. (Like most of the female population, I was never really into the Stooges. It's definitely more of a guy thing.) Then the feature film would begin. Whether it was Columbia Pictures half wrapped lady with her torch held high, RKO Pictures radio antenna on top of the world, Warner Bros. giant initials on a shield, or MGM's roaring Leo The Lion, my heart raced in anticipation as those opening credits went by. I was addicted to the movies. I would escape into these other worlds filled with interesting characters and exotic locales. I remember seeing *The Song of Bernadette* starring Jennifer Jones, *Disney's Snow White and the Seven Dwarfs*, even *Red, Hot and Blue* with Betty Hutton and Victor Mature.

It kind of struck me as odd that men in the fight scenes, most notably Westerns, never seemed to lose their hats. They could fight in the bar and later ride their horses at breakneck speeds, but their hats never fell off. Amazing!

The trek to the local cinema, my new found love, would make the modern person shake their head at me again. Bearing in mind that I was only in grade three, I would walk to the movie theatre from our new home and along the way I would have to cross Interstate 30. Sometimes I would do this trip with a girlfriend, other times I'd just go by myself. I was very young to be out by myself, but it was just a safer era back then for kids to be unsupervised, or so everyone seemed to think at the time. To this day I still love the movies.

From the mid to late 1940's life seemed to be going along normally for the Peppers of Oak Cliff. Maybe not Nelson family normal but definitely Pepper family normal. Daddy wasn't home a lot but when he was it got noisy but interesting. He not only managed the Log Cabin dinner club, but was also part owner. He thought this was his ticket to wealth and would talk of actually buying a house instead of renting all the time. Both he and Mother talked a lot about the day that they would be homeowners. He seemed very happy for a while, but in the long run it didn't pan out for him. He was not a great businessman and would make bad financial decisions time after time. He would spend money as fast as he would make it. After a year or so he lost his investment in the club and was no longer managing it. His dream of buying us a house was also dashed at that time.

Mother, on the other hand, was our rock. She paid the bills, kept the books and made sure the household was being managed with the little money we had coming in. Mother had her civilian job at the newspaper and at home she was the one that kept us all on the straight and narrow. She was tough but always fair. She never gave Patty or me any reason to feel unloved, or to think that she was not listening to our concerns and problems.

Patty was becoming more and more of a tough tomboy every day. She would ditch me every chance that she got. At some point during this time I switched schools. I was now attending St. Cecilia Catholic School. This is the same school that Patty had been going to. It was a co-ed school which was a very different experience for me, after attending the Ursaline Academy all girls' school. At the new school boys and girls studied together under one roof. Now this was both new and exciting for me. This is where I met my first boyfriend. He was a cute Irish lad named Michael. It was nothing more than puppy love. We were both very young so it wasn't anything more than holding hands and playing together, but he sure was cute. I was still performing every chance that I got at this new school too. I can remember being on stage and dancing to the song *Chattanooga Shoe Shine Boy*. I got a great response from the audience so I must have been doing something right.

Along with allergies hitting her from every direction my sister Patty also suffered from chronic asthma. To help out with Patty's breathing problems Mother decided that our family would make some road trips to the Ozarks. There were some great times at the Ozark Springs with its fresh mountain air and rolling hills, sporting the most beautiful Blue Bell flowers that you will ever feast your eyes on. The drive to Arkansas was a problem for me as I would always be lying in the back seat of the car holding my head or my stomach, trying to fight off carsickness. I'm sure that I was the kid that invented the annoying question to parents in moving vehicles, "Are we there yet!?" At one truck-stop restaurant, I absentmindedly left my Raggedy Ann doll at the table when we left. It was probably a result of all that carsickness numbing my brain. After we had journeyed many miles down the highway, I announced that I had left my doll back at the truck-stop. With little hesitation, Daddy and Mother both agreed that there was only one thing to be done. Daddy quickly turned the car around and drove all the way back just to get it for me. It's just another reason why they were both my heroes.

Chapter 6

Fresno To Hollywood

In the summer of 1950 things got a little weird. One day Mother told Patty and me that we were going to live with our Aunt and Uncle for a short time in Fresno, California. I knew that Hollywood was in California, and they made movies and radio programs there, but what was this Fresno place all about? Mother said that she and Daddy needed to get a few things straightened out. Next thing I knew Patty and I were on a plane with Mother winging our way to Fresno. I was still not coping well with my motion sickness. I threw up on the plane ride and let me tell you those little bags do come in handy when you're up in the clouds. Before landing, I thought to myself: "Fresno. Well, how bad could it be? I'd see a new place, make some new friends, visit with my cousins and Patty would still be with me."

I soon found out that Patty would not be with me. I was going to live with our Mother's sister and her family. Patty would be living with our Mother's brother and his family. Both of these families lived in Fresno, but they were miles apart. I didn't see much of Patty for the next year. As a matter of fact, I don't remember seeing her at all that year. I don't remember being too upset about us being apart but as an eternal optimist I do remember thinking of the great adventure this would be. I would be away from my regular family for about a year. Now I had a new family and what a fun year it could be. Hey, maybe now I would get my own room: nope, wrong again. I would be sharing a bedroom once more except this time it was with my cousin Billie. My Aunt Bunny and Uncle Bill were a very generous to let me come live with them and my cousins Billie and Benny. I was now ten years old, going on eleven, and all the while becoming a little less of a kid every day.

I went to Jefferson Elementary School with my cousins for that year and had the best time. Jefferson back then had two single story brick buildings that were built in 1927 and now in need of some repair. Along with my class work I was performing in plays, musicals and any other school entertainment presentations that I could join up with. I still remember performing at the Grade 5 Talent Show. I sang a novelty song that had been written in 1914 called *Aba Daba Honeymoon,* together with a male classmate. It had just become a hit that year performed by Debbie Reynolds and Carleton Carpenter in the movie *Two Weeks With Love.* I'm not entirely sure if it was our performance of the song or the choice of material, but the kids in the crowd went crazy for it. I had the performance bug in me and it was growing bigger than ever.

I was always looking for a way to earn money so that I could go to the theatre and see what masterpieces Hollywood was turning out. On certain days after school, and on weekends, my cousin Billie and I would go door to door in the neighborhood collecting used newspapers. After accumulating a large amount of paper, we would take them to a recycling depot and get paid several pennies per pound of what we'd turn in. We weren't getting rich, but we were staying out of trouble and making a few pennies to feed our addiction to the movies.

When not at school, the movies or out trying to become a newspaper collection mogul I would usually be found at my Aunt and Uncle's home having a social evening. We would play card games like canasta, or listen to our favorite radio programs on the big radio console in the living room. On certain Saturday nights when my Aunt and Uncle would go out to a club for drinks and dancing, my cousins would take the opportunity to scare the hell out of me and so they did. They'd say in a creepy tone of voice: "I think I hear someone coming through the back door." I'd get scared as I let my imagination run wild. They did it just to see me squirm and be scared, and then they'd sit and laugh at my reaction. Kids can be so cruel at times. I was young and gullible enough to fall for most of their pranks. I guess I was a very naive and trusting child and for reasons unknown to me people seemed to like to take advantage of that.

Let's play Find Waldo. Give up? Second row from the bottom, fifth from the right.
(Cynthia Pepper Collection)

Uncle Bill was a bus driver for the Greyhound Bus Company and did a lot of traveling around California. The one thing I loved most about Uncle Bill's job was that he would take me, and sometimes my cousin Billie, to visit my father in Hollywood. Daddy had been working in the movies and doing radio programs in Hollywood while he and Mother sorted out their issues. He had a two bedroom apartment in Afton Place, located near Vine Street and N. El Centro Ave. It was an ornate four story apartment building with lots of interesting people living there. I'm not sure where my Mother was living at this time but as I said earlier they had issues to work out. One particular trip sticks out in my mind. Billie and I arrived in Hollywood after our uneventful journey from Fresno. It had been a couple of months between visits so it was great to see Daddy after being away for so long. Receiving that familiar full hug from him was even more fantastic that day. After my cousin and I got settled into his apartment, he told us that a couple of days before we arrived he had been working on a radio show and singing with Judy Garland. We were pretty disappointed to have missed that show, to say the least. Judy Garland was a huge star and I had watched and loved both of her last two releases, *Easter Parade* with Fred Astaire and *In The Good Old Summertime* with handsome Van Johnston. Daddy said that he'd make it up to us the next day. He said he was working on a new film being shot by Paramount Pictures at the Melrose Ave, Paramount Studios and asked if we'd like to come with him. Boy would we!

We arrived at the studio early the next day. My cousin Billie and I were wearing our matching Sunday Best outfits. We were ready to see behind the scenes of motion picture production, and checkout all the famous Hollywood magic I had heard so much about. It was a beehive buzz of crazy activity. I hardly had a clue what each person's job might be. There were people pushing things, pulling things, lifting things, talking, and yelling in what seemed to be utter confusion to me. This was the set of a movie called *My Favorite Spy* where Daddy was playing the part of an FBI man. At one point he called us over to meet the star of the picture, or as he referred to him: "...an old Army buddy of mine."

As I approached him, Daddy introduced us to Mr. Bob Hope.

Daddy said: "Bob this is my daughter Cynthia and my niece Billie."

Mr. Hope smiled and said: "So you're Pepper's kid huh? Nice ta meet ya both."

I smiled and sputtered: "It's nice to meet you too Mr. Hope."

He laughed saying: "Call me Bob."

Then someone suggested that my cousin Billie and I have our picture taken with Mr. Hope. Like anyone would say no to that? Here we were on a real working Hollywood movie set with a real big time movie star and his pal, my father. This day just couldn't get any better... Then it did.

Daddy was introducing Billie and me to some of the other cast and crew just like a proud Poppa would. Then he asked us to follow him so that he could introduce us to Hedy. As we followed him, I thought to myself the only Hedy I had ever heard of was Hedy Lamarr. Just as that thought occurred to me, I looked up to see none other than Hedy

Lamarr herself coming towards Daddy. She gave him a hug and kiss then looking at us she asked: "Who are these beautiful young girls Jack?"

Oh My Gosh, Hedy Lamarr just referred to us as beautiful. At that point in time, there were very few women in Hollywood that could compare to the poise and beauty of Hedy Lamarr and she called ME beautiful? I don't think that I stopped smiling for the rest of the week.

We stood by and watched all the activity at the movie set for most of the day, but nothing compared to meeting the two stars of the picture. One thing I learned that day was the meaning of the phrase "Hurry up and wait." There is so much setup time required to shoot a scene, and it must be done before the actors are brought in to do their magic. Another thing I learned that day was there is no such thing as Hollywood movie magic, just lots and lots of hard work. I was ready to jump in and work as hard as any of them. By the time we got home later that day, I was on cloud nine. I stayed there for a good month. Thanks Daddy.

I was able to hitch a ride with my Uncle and his bus on certain weekends to see Daddy in Hollywood. The funny thing is that I don't remember seeing much of Mother on those visits, if at all. I'm not even sure if she was living with him at the time. I guess at that age for me, it was all about having fun and looking forward to the adventures the world could provide to a ten year old. Why wasn't I concerned about my Mother at that time? What was she doing? If she didn't live with Daddy, where did she live? My sister Patty seemed to have the same lack of concern for our mother. I didn't really know what was happening with Patty and her substitute family, nor did I give it much thought that whole year. The only thing I heard about Patty was her dreadful bouts with asthma. She had to be taken to the doctor's office a number of times. I didn't worry about her as she was now fourteen years old and very tough. I was pretty sure that she could take care of herself.

Chapter 7

Look Out Hollywood, Here I Come
Room For One More
The Hollywood Ranch Market

In the summer of 1951, I got the news that our family unit was getting back together. Mother and Daddy were living together in Hollywood and wanted Patty and me to live with them. Move over All American Nelson family. The Peppers were back together again and we were going to get it right this time. It was a great feeling to know that I wouldn't have to live off the kindness of strangers or relatives anymore. I was excited to know that I'd be living in Hollywood. I had almost given up on ever getting my own room, but I felt that this time would be different. This was a time for optimism, a time for a change, time for brightness, time for confidence, maybe even time for my very own room! However, as the stage manager once said to the eager understudy of a big Broadway show shortly after the lead actor shows up ready to work a mere fifteen minutes before the curtain is called: "Too bad kid, maybe next time." Yes, I was sharing a room again.

The Peppers moved to the Elaine Apartments located at 1245 Vine St., Hollywood. It was a two bedroom apartment located on the 4th floor at the back of the building. We had a view of some trees and a pool in the courtyard below. From a different window, we had a view of the rooftops of a housing subdivision that faced to the west. Many actors and artists had lived there over the years. The building itself was reported to be owned by Charlie Chaplin, for a time. Some of its inhabitants through the years included Orson Wells, John Hamilton, (the actor that played Perry White in the Superman TV series.), Earnest Borgnine and now Jack and Dawn Pepper and their clan.

For a while things were pretty good for us as a family. Mother went back to giving us music appreciation lessons, plus teaching us right from wrong. She would scold me when I needed it. When I wouldn't finish my vegetables because I was in a hurry to be somewhere else she'd say: "Cynthia Ann Culpepper, you sit back down and finish those Brussels sprouts. Don't you know that there are starving children in Europe that would love to eat them?"

I'd say: "Then let's send them to Europe." I was lucky that I didn't get clobbered for that remark.

Patty and I were getting used to our new schools, and all the social awkwardness that goes along with trying to fit into a new place with strangers. Mother had picked up a job working in a restaurant somewhere on Hollywood Blvd. Daddy was working a lot, acting in movies, television and what was left of radio work at this time. His movie work that year included *Just For You* with Bing Crosby, Jane Wyman and Ethel Barrymore, and *Stop, You're Killing Me* with Broderick Crawford and Claire Trevor. He also worked in *Son Of Pale Face* with Bob Hope, Jane Russell, Roy Rogers and one of my favorite stars Trigger. (Now there was an actor.) Both Daddy and Mother were trying very hard to make things work for the family.

My new school was called Vine Street Grammar School, located at 955 N Vine Street, which was about eight blocks south of the Elaine Apartments. Vine Street Grammar had some very interesting alumni from days gone. The list included Mickey Rooney and a plain looking gal by the name of Norma Jean Baker, who later morphed into the beautiful Marilyn Monroe. Much later down the road Denise Crosby, who played Tasha Yar on *Star Trek: TNG* and Charlene Tilton, who played Lucy on *Dallas,* also attended this school. Vine Street Grammar wasn't too far from Paramount Studios. My mind would be running rampant with thoughts of being an actress on the big screen while I walked to school.

My first few days at Vine Street School were a bit lonely and awkward to say the least. The other kids weren't really talking to me much, as a new student in the class, but I kept a happy face and kept moving forward. One day it was announced that the entire school was going to the auditorium to watch a movie. "Fantastic, I love movies. I wondered if it would it be the new Gene Kelly and Leslie Caron picture called *An American In Paris* that was just released? I didn't think they would show us Bette Davis in *All About Eve* but who knows. Heck I'd even take an old Gable & Lombard flick. Will there be popcorn?" As it turned out, the movies they showed us in the auditorium were designed to enlighten and educate. It was subject matter like "How a Monkey Peels a Banana in Borneo" or "Why Penguins Eat Fish While Wearing Tuxedos."

One particular movie afternoon we were ushered into the movie auditorium and told to take a seat. No one really wanted to sit with me so I ended up sitting by myself. The movie was almost ready to start when a cute girl with brown hair in pigtails came up to me and asked: "Can I sit with you?"

I was thrilled just to have a fellow student talk to me, let alone sit with me. I smiled and said: "Sure."

Her name was Vicki McIntyre, and pretty much right then and there she became my best friend. We were almost inseparable all through grade school. We complimented each other in almost every way. She was a brunet and I was blond. She was Veronica and I was Betty. She was a pistol and I was the target. In class, she would send me notes when the teacher's back was turned to the class and I would inevitably be caught reading the note when the teacher turned back around. Vicki was wild, she was incorrigible and she was my friend.

Vicki lived in a house behind our apartment building with her Mom. Her mother was divorced, and back then that could make other kids look at you like you were a freak. I didn't care about that kind of thing because she was my friend. Since she lived right behind me, we would walk to and from school together every day, along with another good friend Diane Borden. Diane was and still is a beautiful person. She had gorgeous blond hair and warm brown eyes. Diane had the most bubbly personality and we couldn't help but notice how much all the boys liked her. She was definitely the kind of person you'd like to hang around with.

At night, I would sit in my fourth story bedroom window with a flashlight, sending messages to Vicki's bedroom window at her house below. Eventually, I did the same to Diane's house. Since we didn't know Morse Code the messages, I would receive from their flashlights were really about the knowledge and comfort of knowing that they were there for me. They also knew that I was there for them no matter what life would bring and life was about to bring plenty.

Ah, Hollywood! It was the perfect place to live, or was it? Through movies, TV, radio and movie magazines the whole world was presented an image of Tinsel Town that made it an ideal, if not heavenly, place to live and seek your fortune. The streets were paved with gold and there were movie stars hanging out on every corner.

Here's a story that was perpetuated about screen star Lana Turner. She was discovered at fifteen years old while having an ice-cream soda at Schwab's Drugstore in Hollywood. (The truth according to Lana was that it happened at the Top Hat Café across the street from Hollywood High School. She was sixteen years old and it was a Coke she had, not an ice-cream soda.) No matter how you look at it, a young girl from Idaho became a movie star just by going to Hollywood and sitting at a soda counter. How hard can that be? Well, a lot of young people felt that this was easy pickings and headed to the Golden State to become Movie Stars. Unfortunately, not everyone that showed up was as talented or as beautiful as Lana. They would soon find out that just showing up and waiting to be discovered was not good enough to make it in this town.

Both my parents experienced the audition and rejection process in show business. They also knew that it was important to get some good schooling to provide a strong, solid base in acting, so they sent me to Muriel Alts Acting Studio. I loved the acting studio and all the lessons. After school, I wasn't out playing as much as the other kids, but instead I was learning to act. You might say that acting was my playing and it was a big part of my life. One day the Studio was hosting a recital and I was featured in it as a dancer and singer. I was so excited to be performing on stage and in front of a real audience. All the kids were excited.

When I was home rehearsing, Mother told me that she wouldn't be able to attend the show as she had to work that night. Not attend the show? I had worked so hard on my act and I wanted to show her what I could do. I said: "You have to come."

She explained again that she was sorry, but she wouldn't be able to. I was upset. Showing her very little respect I grumbled: "It's not fair!"

She looked me in the eyes and said: "Listen, I have to go to work so that we have money to eat and pay the rent. You need to remember that."

She really knocked me down a peg. She was right, but I was hurt. Maybe I was overly sensitive at the time. She was teaching me humility, but her words really stung.

Patty still had no interest in acting so generally, I got my parent's full attention whenever I was rehearsing or performing. I could share the things that I learned, including the methods of acting and how to go through the audition process, with my parents. I was never comfortable with auditions as a kid. I just wanted to please and to be liked by people, so when I was rejected for a part I took it hard. I was told to have a tougher skin because I had to get out there, get seen, get rejected and hopefully somewhere along the line I might actually land a role and turn it into something fantastic.

Room For One More

I got my first movie part and my first Hollywood reality check at the same time. I had auditioned for a movie part at Warner Brothers Studio and, luck upon luck, I got it. Mother and I were on a bus heading to the studio where I would possibly become a star. It was just the day before we made the trek downtown and picked up my Social Security Card so that I could work legally. The movie was called *Room For One More* starring Cary Grant and his wife at the time Betsy Drake. Oh boy, I was twelve years old and had my first big acting part with Cary Grant no less. I let my mind wander with thoughts of working with one of the biggest movie stars ever. I pictured myself out on the town at the Brown Derby or Ciro's Nightclub with my new dreamy, perfect boyfriend and co-star Cary. Betsy would just have to understand.

The day I was shooting my scene I got a bit of a wake-up call about life in Hollywood and how movie making worked. First of all, I wasn't given a script because I didn't have any lines, and secondly I wasn't exactly doing a scene with Mr. Grant. I arrived in the early morning and was allowed to wander around a little. I walked over to a trailer that turned out to be Mr. Grant's. All of the stars on a movie set had their own trailers as their home away from home. Just then, I saw him heading to his home on wheels. He was even better looking in person than in the movies. My heart started to flutter and I swear it skipped a beat. I was just a few feet away from my dream beau, Cary Grant. He was a handsome, dreamy, breath taking hunk of a man. He was all poise and perfection in a suit. As he climbed... No, not climbed, as he floated up the stairs to his trailer I abruptly heard him yell to a person following behind him: "What the hell are you talking about? That's the most God damned, stupidest thing I've ever heard!"

My jaw dropped. I stood there in shock. I didn't know what to do. Cary Grant can't swear, he's a movie star. However, my own ears had just heard that my perfect Cary Grant had potty-mouth. I ran back to where my Mother was, inside the studio, and half out of breath I told her: "Mother! Mr. Grant said God damn. He cursed. I heard him." She told me to calm down and not worry about it. She said we'd talk about it later.

After my shock and confusion about Mr. Grant's comment, I was taken to the costume department where they dressed me up in mittens, a winter hat, and a warm winter jacket. I should mention that this was July in California. I was starting to sweat and generally feeling very overdressed for that time of year. I was taken to a place on the set that looked like a pretty winter's day. I was placed on the set behind a fake concrete wall with potato flakes for snow and painted cardboard for icicles. I quickly realized that they didn't use real snow or icicles to make movies and that the huge lights made things even hotter. Another little girl and two boys about my age, dressed in winter clothes and just as sweaty as I was, were placed behind the fake wall with me. The director, Norman Taurog, came over to us to explain what he wanted us to do in this scene.

Mr. Taurog had been a child actor in the 1920's but as an adult he found more success behind the camera as opposed to in front of it. He had directed *Boys Town* with Spencer Tracy, *Broadway Melody* with

Fred Astaire, and *Skippy* with Jackie Cooper, which he had won an Academy Award for Best Director. The studios knew he was an expert at directing light comedies and musicals, especially the ones where children were featured. In his 1981 autobiography *Please Don't Shoot My Dog,* Jackie Cooper wrote that, during filming, Taurog threatened to shoot his dog if the child actor could not cry for the scene. Jackie cried, they got the money-shot and no animals were harmed in the making of the film, but what a cruel thing to do to an innocent kid.

Meanwhile, back to my big scene… As we stood there sweating in our winter clothes, Mr. Taurog was very nice as he told us what he wanted us to do in the scene. He explained that we were orphans from the orphanage and we were in the playground, peeking over the wall as the ladies on the other side of the wall walked away. One of these ladies was Betsy Drake, but I didn't pay much attention to her as I was focused on my part in the scene. Since there was just a fake wall and a fake window for us to see I knew my great imagination and acting classes would be helpful here today. Then I thought: "Wait a minute… Where were the cameras?"

I couldn't help but notice that there weren't any cameras in front of, or even beside, us. Mr Taurog told us to crouch down behind the wall and when he gave us the signal we were all to slowly come up from behind the wall. The camera would film us from behind as we looked towards the fake building and windows. "Behind us? The camera is behind us?" This was not making a lot of sense to me. How was I going to use my acting skills if the camera couldn't see my face? All those lessons so that the camera can shoot the back of my head? Well, I was going to use all my acting face lessons even if the camera couldn't see me. As the director finished directing us he also added: "Oh, by the way kids, stop sweating."

Then he called for make-up. "Make-up? What do we need make-up for, the back of our parkas?"

Of all the directions to give to someone, stop sweating would be by far the toughest one to pull off but I was up for anything. As we waited, a lady came over and started putting more powder on our faces. While we crouched down and waited for the call for action more lights were turned on, and that made it even hotter. I still felt like a star because of all the lights, the quiet that fell over the studio after some guy yelled: "Quiet On The Set!" and the crew that was focused on us and every little thing we were doing.

We shot the scene six or seven times and with each new shot I would try a different expression: happy, angry, sad, confused, and scared. They were all lost on the camera from behind. I heard Mr. Taurog yell: "Cut! That's A Lilly! We're Moving On." All the big hot lights instantly went out as people started to take the fake wall away and sweep up the potato flakes. I almost fainted from heat exhaustion right then and there. I was also left feeling a little empty because all that focus was instantly gone. The other kids in the scene with me were whisked away by their parents. People just walked by me as if I wasn't even there. Just moments ago it seemed that the whole world was focused on me and what I was doing then instantly no one seemed to care. I was as important as the fake wall or discarded potato flakes. When Mother came over to get me, I tried to explain this to her. She said: "You did very well Honey, but that's what it's like as an actress." As I peeled off my soggy, winter jacket and waterlogged mittens I asked what she meant. She explained: "This is what the business is like. When you do your scene you are important and everything is about you but once they're done with you it's over and they move on. It's all part of the process." At the time, I had no idea how well she was predicting my future in Hollywood. I felt better that Mother understood how I was feeling. She seemed to know the front side and the backside of this business. As we took the bus back home, I wondered if Daddy understood the business as well as Mother did.

After my first movie experience, I was ready for more acting jobs, but I also had other things in my life to turn my attention to. Like school and learning about "monkey's eating habits in other lands". There were my two great friends Vicki and Diane that I did everything with. We'd spend so much time going to movies or sitting in my bedroom playing and discussing handsome movie stars, and boys in general when we did our homework. We would also spend hours upon hours hanging out at the Hollywood Ranch Market.

The Ranch Market was conveniently located at Fountain Ave and Vine, just across the street from our apartment. This place had it all. On the north outside corner of the building, they had a snack bar. I think that's where I first got hooked on fountain sodas. To this day I prefer a fountain soda over soda from a bottle. Right above the snack bar was a huge clock sign that read "Everybody Shops At The One And Only Hollywood Ranch Market." Above that again were the words, "We Never Close". In the 1950's it was almost sacrilegious for any business to be open all of the time, but then again we are talking Hollywood. We loved this place as kids because they never closed.

There was always some kind of excitement going on at the Ranch Market. The store inside the building boasted: "A Corral Full Of Bargains", and it was. Most of Hollywood's famous and non-famous alike shopped here when they couldn't find what they wanted at any other place, and at any other hour. Vicki, Diane and I would end up lying on the floor of the Ranch Market reading comics and movie magazines for hours. I guess they knew we didn't have any money so they just let us hang out. Like I've always said about growing up a Pepper; "We didn't have much, but we didn't want for much either." Both Mother and Daddy had odd hours back then so I kind of had a free reign to do what I wanted. I could go wherever and do whatever I liked after school, and the Ranch Market was a great hangout. The Steve Allen Theatre, located at 1228 Vine St right beside the Ranch Market and right across the street from our apartment was another great place to spend some time and enjoy the magic of Hollywood. We saw a couple of his shows, but just watching the people around the theatre was fun too. Steve Allen was a strange man but very funny. He also understood the world of variety entertainment better than most others.

Even though Vicki was my best friend and we spent a lot of time together I did have other friends that I hung around with at the Elaine Apartments. We were just discovering boys and the boys were discovering girls. Sometimes we would play Spin The Bottle, or Peaches and Cream. You've never heard of Peaches and Cream? Well, let me tell you how silly it was. Two girls would be in a dark closet as two boys would be on the other side of the door. The boys would quietly decide which one of them would be Peaches and which one was Cream. Then one of the girls would decide if she wanted Peaches or Cream. The other girl in the closet would get the other one. The boys would come into the closet tell us who was what and then the necking would begin. It never lasted long and left us all giggling. The boys my age, in the apartments, were pretty good, clean kids just growing up and having fun. One such kid was my cute red-headed friend Jimmy Boyd. We would play in the courtyard at the Elaine Apartments and get into all kinds of mischief together. He was a great kid and very funny. He was eight months older than me, but we got along famously. He'd bring his guitar out and sing at the drop of a hat when we were all together. Jimmy was originally from Mississippi, but his folks had moved to California to try and make a better life for them. None of us had any way of knowing at the time but Jimmy was about to become a huge singing star.

Jimmy got his first big hit song when he auditioned for the Al Jarvis Talent Show on KLAC-TV. It was a local talent contest with the winner being booked as a featured act on TV. Jimmy auditioned for Jarvis and appeared on the show that night. He won the contest, which lead to a regular spot on Jarvis's TV show that also featured a young Betty White. One thing lead to another and in 1952, when he was just thirteen, he was asked by Columbia Records to work with a new guy named Mitch Miller the new head of A&R. Jimmy went to Columbia Records and recorded a song called *I Saw Mommy Kissing Santa Claus.* That record went to #1, selling more than two and a half million copies in the first week it was released. The following year it was released again at Christmas and went to #1 again. It's a song that still sells to this day with reported sales of over sixty million copies since its initial release. Needless to say, Jimmy and his family moved away to a much better neighborhood and the next time I'd see him was on TV. It couldn't have happened to a nicer guy.

The Elvis Connection #1

In the 1960's Norman Taurog directed no less than nine Elvis movies. I told you he was good at the light musical comedies. He directed: *Blue Hawaii* (1961), *Girls! Girls! Girls!* (1962), *It Happened at the World's Fair* (1963), *Tickle Me* (1965), *Spinout* (1966), *Double Trouble* (1967), *Speedway* (1968) and *Live a Little, Love a Little* (1968).

Earlier I had mentioned meeting Ginger Rogers when she was making a TV pilot called *Vacation Playhouse: A Love Affair Just for Three.* Her co-star was Cesare Danova. Cesare would later co-star with

Elvis Presley in *Viva Las Vegas.* He played Count Elmo Mancini, Ann-Margret's other love interest in the film.

As time went on, Jimmy Boyd tired of recording novelty songs and really wanted to try this new thing that was gaining popularity in the mid 1950's called rock & roll. Jimmy had heard of a guy named Sam Phillips in Memphis, who seemed to know how to make rock & roll. Sam had a studio called *Sun Records* and Jimmy wanted to record there. This is the same studio that helped launch Elvis' career. After much deliberation, Jimmy decided to concentrate his efforts into TV, movies and furthering his education. Who knows if things had been different I might have been making *Kissin' Cousins* with Jimmy.

The other Elvis connection occurred in 1960 when Jimmy married, my soon to be friend, Yvonne Craig. (This was before her role as *Batgirl* in 1967) Unfortunately, their marriage ended in 1962. Yvonne appeared in *Kissin' Cousins* with Elvis and me. Disney was right; it is a small world after all.

Chapter 8

Scary Incidents At The Elaine Apts Jr. High

There were a couple of incidents that happened to me while living at the Elaine Apartments that I've never talked about publicly. I'm talking about them now because I've come to realize that kids should never be afraid to discuss things with their parents and must learn not to keep the darkness bottled up inside.

Vicki and I were playing around the apartment complex one day when we decided to go up to my apartment. We got onto the elevator and a man followed us in. I hit the fourth floor button as Vicki and I were talking and being goofy with each other, but the man was quiet. I noticed that he didn't push a floor button so I guess he wanted the fourth floor too. Vicki didn't notice, but he was staring at us during the ride. When we reached our floor, we got out of the elevator and started to walk towards my apartment at the end of the long hall. For some strange reason, and to this day I don't know why, maybe it was instinct or just a scary vibe he gave off during that short ride but I looked back and saw this odd man get off the elevator too. He was looking at us in a way that gave me the creeps and then he started to follow us. I picked up the pace as Vicki kept talking and laughing. As I looked back again at the man, I noticed that he had picked up his pace too. Was he chasing us? How absurd and yet how odd. I wasn't afraid and I thought it was strangely funny in a way. When we started walking a little faster again so did he. Now the race was on. I gave Vicki the nod to run with me down the hall and she got the hint. We were in a foot race with each other and some stranger behind us but for some reason we both thought this was funny. The man was not too far behind and running after us.

We arrived at my apartment, pushed open the door and went flying past Mother and Daddy, giggling and out of breath. After closing the door, Mother asked what was going on. We just laughed it off, ran to my bedroom and slammed the bedroom door shut behind us. Vicki and I sat on the bed looking at each other laughing and feeling our hearts pound in our chests from the excitement. A few seconds later there was a loud knock at our front door. We immediately stopped laughing and froze. We stared at each other for a second or two and then we both jumped up to open my bedroom door. We opened it just a crack and peered through in time to see Daddy open the front door. There stood the man from the elevator. When the man saw Daddy he immediately said in a cool, calm voice: "Oh, I'm sorry. I must have the wrong apartment."

Then he turned and walked away. Vicki and I quickly closed the bedroom door and started to laugh again. I think we were laughing out of nervousness more than anything. We were so young and naive.

Daddy took a minute and put two and two together and came into the bedroom.

"Do you girls have any idea how stupid that was?" Daddy looked very upset.

I quickly shot back: "Oh Daddy it was nothing at all."

He bellowed back: "Nothing at all?" "You think it's nothing at all?"

He yelled to Mother: "Dawn, did you hear that? She say's it was nothing at all."

I couldn't figure out why Daddy was so upset. I didn't see the problem. We were chased down the hall, not him and it was just silly laughs to us.

He continued: "If you had read a newspaper at all you would have known that there has been a guy in the area, grabbing and molesting little girls just like you two. What if that was the guy? Do you have any idea how lucky you two were today? Just think about it. It was just stupid dumb luck that nothing bad happened to you." What a silly thing for two young girls to do!! Granted, we were innocent and trusting to a fault but we were not stupid. When I think of how badly things could have turned out, I get chills. I guess the 1950's were not as innocent as some of us thought. We never saw that creepy man ever again but I was certainly looking over my shoulder a lot for the next few weeks.

Another incident that took place at the Elaine Apartments scared me for a long while, to this day really. I'm a very modest person and this occurrence had a lot to do with it. I've not spoken about this incident because it happened at a time when I was young and didn't really know how to properly handle the situation. I had no idea how to react, or deal with it, so I buried it. It's an ugly incident to have to relive, but I'll try. A short time after the creepy guy chased us down the hall, my life went back to the normal innocence of being a little girl. I was attending school, acting classes, and playing with my friends. I had great friends as a kid and a lot of freedom as a latchkey kid. For those that don't know, a latchkey kid is a child who returns from school to an empty home because his or her parent or parents are away at work. It can also be a child who is often left at home with little or no parental supervision. Patty was a rebellious teenager doing her own thing after school, Mother was working odd hours as a waitress in a Hollywood restaurant and Daddy was either working or off doing whatever Daddy did when not at home. I never knew, from day to day, if anyone would be home when I arrived.

This particular day was just a normal, nothing day. I had just walked home from school with my friends. We talked about getting together after dinner, and I said good-bye. I then entered the Elaine Apartment complex. As I turned left at the courtyard, I could hear the birds in the trees singing brightly. I got into the elevator and pushed the button to go to our fourth floor apartment. Just before the elevator door closed; a man that we all knew at the complex got into the elevator with me. He was in his mid-thirties and was someone that was well known to my parents and everyone that lived at the Elaine apartment complex. I don't want to cause any of his surviving family any pain, (I know what you might be thinking, why should I care? My answer is, I'm just wired that way) so I will just refer to him as Mr. Smith.

As the elevator doors closed, he turned towards me. I was about to say hello when he began to talk to me. He was saying strange things and then he started to touch me. Before I even knew what was going on he was pushing me against the elevator wall and fondling me with both of his hands. I tried to push his grimy disgusting hands away but he was too strong and they were all over me. I said: "Don't!" but he just kept touching me. I was in shock and I tried to get away from him but I couldn't. His hands were down my pants and almost everywhere else. I prayed that the elevator doors would just open so I could try and run away, but they didn't. I watched with tears in my eyes as the elevator numbers moved slowly past the first, second then third floor I wanted to scream out, but I couldn't. I could barely breathe as this pig of a person kept grabbing me. It seemed to take forever to get to my apartment floor. When the elevator arrived at the fourth floor Mr. Smith stopped touching me and told me to never tell anyone about what had just happened and he threatened me.

I was completely stunned. I wasn't even sure about what had just happened. I went down the hall to the apartment with tears in my eyes, unlocked the door and went straight to my room. No one was home at the time so I fell onto my bed and I cried. I had been violated by someone that my family and friends knew and I couldn't tell anyone about it. I couldn't tell a soul. It would be my dirty guilty secret all these years. I was taught to trust adults so now what was I supposed to do? Was this my fault? If I had told Daddy, he would have killed the man. I'm not just saying that as a passing idle phrase. My Father would have literally killed the man. I knew that would take Daddy away from us forever and I wasn't going to let that happen so I just shut-up about it. I buried the memories so deep into my being that in time even I couldn't find them. Denial was easier than looking for answers at the time. I wasn't old enough to understand that it wasn't my fault. If you ever have anything even remotely close to this kind of abuse happen to you I encourage you to talk to someone. Get it out in the open where it cannot harm you anymore. I made certain that I was never alone with, or ever near, this guy again, so there was never a repeat of this monstrous behavior. I'm sure this person has had to answer for his sins by now and I can only hope he got what he deserved.

Jr. High

In 1952, I graduated Vine Street School. I was so sad to be leaving all the relationships that I had made, but I was moving on to new adventures. It turned out that the new school I'd be attending was not that far away and most of my friends were headed there too. I would be attending Joseph Le Conte Jr. High School, located at 1316 North Bronson Avenue. The school was about ten blocks away from our apartment. I walked everywhere in those days, yet it seemed so far away compared to the distance to my last school. I complained to Mother about the walking distance to my school and she gave me the Story. You remember the Story. I'm sure most of you got it from a parent at one point. My Mother said to me: "Too far? You think your walk to school is too far? Well, young lady when I was your age I had to walk ten miles to school in three feet of snow and it was up hill both ways! So don't complain."

It wasn't until I realized that Mother had grown up mostly in Fresno, California that has an annual average snowfall of 0.1 inches. That's one tenth of an inch or as I like to say the width of two ukulele strings side by side. The things we say to motivate our kids.

It was time to attend the new Junior High school, which coincided with those strange transitional rites of passage into one's teenage years. Or as Rod Serling from *The Twilight Zone* might have said, with his strange TV theme music playing in the background: "I submit to you a time and place not of this world. The times are the in-between years; the place is Hollywood, California. You are not cool but then again not entirely uncool. You're not in grade school, but you're also not in High School. Where are you? You are in school purgatory or as I like to call it, The Jr. High Twilight Zone."

My new school, Le Conte, (to be cool you dropped off the Joseph part of the name), was dubbed "The Home of the Stars." Many of the students that attended Le Conte went on to become famous later in life. Notable alumni included Yvonne De Carlo, Betty Grable, Nanette Fabray, and later on would include Carol Burnett, Stuart Whitman, Yvette Mimieux, Jody Foster, and Charlene Tilton. Oh boy, if the halls could talk at this school.

For me Jr. High was a rush of fun and education on so many different levels. I was still performing in any school production that would have me, including the Girls Glee Club, and the Talent Show where I would sing and dance to my heart's content. I didn't always win the parts that I tried out for because the competition was getting tougher. Let's face it, most of the kids going to Le Conte Jr. High had parents that were in show business at the time, and a lot of kids were driven to succeed. All I knew for sure was that working on the stage felt like home to me, sometimes more than my own home did.

On my way to school each day, I had to pass Gower St. and the Columbia Studio. (It's now called the Sunset Gower Studios). I would dream that someday a director would come running out of the door from the soundstage, take one look at me and yell; "That's her! I want that girl in my picture!" In the 1930's, this area got the nickname of "Gower Gulch" because many of the extras in Western movies would dress in their cowboy costumes at home, then walk south to the Paramount, Republic, and RKO studios, which were all located just off Gower Street. Now that would have been something to see on the way to the office every morning.

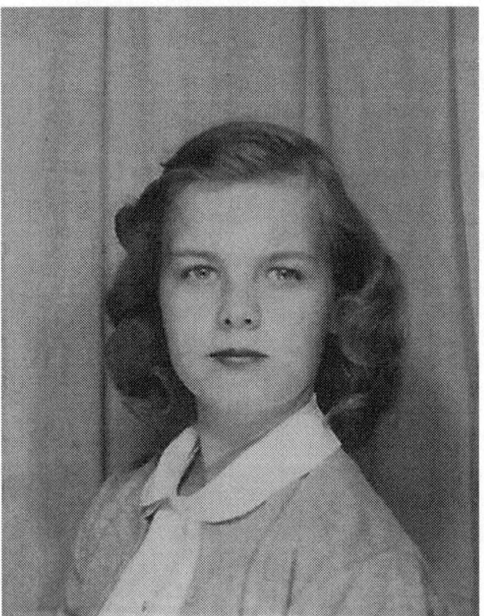

Jr High School – Looking very dramatic at such a young age.

(Cynthia Pepper Collection)

During my second year at Le Conte we moved from the Elaine Apartments to what was to be a short term dwelling located at 5177

Fountain Ave. Mother had quit her job at the restaurant and had moved on to the world of retail sales by securing a job at The Broadway Hollywood department store. Mother was our financial rock. A friend Mother had made at the Broadway said that she lived in a great place. She would let Mother know when an apartment in her court on De Longpre Ave became available. I don't know why we didn't just stay at the Elaine Apartments until the other apartment was ready, but I was happy to move away from the elevator creep and start a new chapter in my life.

The short term apartment we were moving into was a lot smaller than the one we had at the Elaine Apartments, but we would make it work. One positive thought I had was that I'd get another roll of the dice possibly to get my own room. Here I go…the dice are out and rolling and "Oh-Oh, Snake-eyes!" I crapped out and wound up sharing space with Patty yet again. As in the past, I didn't mind sharing a room with her, but the fact that we would be sharing a Murphy bed together was stretching the situation for both of us. For those of you that don't know what a Murphy bed is, it's a space saver bed that is built into the wall. When you want to go to bed you open the two doors on the wall, and the bed slowly folds down from its hidden storage in the wall to the floor. When you get up in the morning, you fold it back up into the wall and close the doors. No fuss no muss, but wait: it gets even better. To top off this disappointing turn of sleeping events, the Murphy was located in the living room. Yes, you heard correctly, the living room. Patty and I didn't even have a bedroom in this apartment. Things were getting more and more crowded for all of us. I found myself really missing the Elaine Apartment.

The Murphy bed was a pain to deal with at times. The Three Stooges, Charlie Chaplain and several other slap-stick comedy acts would include, at some point, episodes of mayhem with a Murphy bed in their films and it was always hysterical. Who, other than some crazy fictional movie characters, would have such a foolish bed in their living room? Oh, that's right, the Peppers. There wasn't a lot of comedy with our Murphy pull out as Patty still had some bad bouts with her asthma. I really felt awful for her when it would flare up but sharing an asthma attack in the same bed was taxing for all of us. My heart always went out to her during her bad episodes and some night's sleep was hard to come by for both of us.

Patty was four and half years older than me so she ran with a completely different crowd. There was not a lot that transpired between us other than the sleeping space that we shared. I guess I didn't know what having a loving sister was supposed to feel like, and maybe that's why I've always felt closer to my friends than my sister. Patty didn't have a ton of time for me, but that was ok because I was doing my own thing now anyway.

From our temporary apartment window, we could see the units we were waiting for. They were located just one street away. We probably looked like helpless drooling animals with our heads hanging out of the window. We could see what we wanted, but we were not able to get to it, as our master was saying: "Stay. Stay... Good Doggies." We were told that the apartment was to become available soon, but "soon" quickly turned into a year. It was a rough year for my parents. I noticed that they were drinking and fighting a lot. I guess it was mostly over money issues as I knew they both still loved each other.

Daddy finally won some acting work in Hollywood. From 1951 to 1953 he was in the movies *Silver Canyon* with Gene Autry, *My Favorite Spy* with Bob Hope, *Off Limits* with Bob Hope and Mickey Rooney, and *Trouble Along The Way* with John Wayne and Donna Reed. It reads like a great list of credits but a lot of his parts were small, unaccredited and didn't pay anything close to the stars' salary. He had lines and at times would even sing and play different musical instruments in these pictures but with very little acclaim. In 1954, he was in *A Star Is Born* with Judy Garland and James Mason plus he did an *Adventures With Superman* TV episode with George Reeves. He just couldn't land anything better than a sub-supporting role and I think it was eating him up inside. He knew all of these people personally and they knew that he was a top performer, once upon a time. His lost fame must have been eating away at him through those years.

Daddy and Mother loved to socialize with their friends. On the weekends, if they weren't hosting a small party they were usually going to one. This was fine for me, "the latch-key kid", as I sure had a lot of freedom most of the time. I would hang out after school with my pal Vicki and our boyfriends. Yes, we had boyfriends by then, with the operative word being friends. Nothing much of a sexual nature ever happened. Sometimes Vicki's Mom, Jeri would take pity on us and drive us and our dates to the Drive-In Theatre. What a great sport her Mom was. She was a hoot. She was a wonderful character and I still talk to her to this day. She's now well into her ninety's.

Back in my day when a girl was going "steady" with a fellow you'd wear his ring around your neck to show everyone that you were taken. Mind you, going steady was a fleeting thing at that young age. You could be going steady for a month, a week, or even a couple of days. It wasn't a big commitment on either person's part.

I was going "steady" with a very cute, athletic boy named Chris. (I'll leave his last name out to save him some embarrassment.) My relationship with him may have been one of the shortest, but I remember this one incident that happened between us. We were going to the afternoon show at Hunley's Movie Theater. Hunley's was a great theater that a lot of us went to when the latest and greatest films came out. It was a bit of a walk from my place, but I didn't complain because my Mother would start telling me her tough snow-walking story again; "… Uphill both ways." We arrived at the theatre just in time for the newsreel and cartoon short that preceded the feature film. We got all we needed, and could afford, from the concession stand and found our seats. We were sitting together eating popcorn and drinking our sodas as the film came on the screen. I wanted to see the stars acting skills. I could learn some tips just from watching them. I had already been in a film, but I was sure that roles involving peeking over walls were a dead end for me. I would learn as much as I could and be a leading actress one day. Shortly after the credits went by and the opening scene began to play Chris seemed to get a bit restless. I didn't pay a lot of attention to his behavior as I was getting caught up in the world that was being offered on the big screen. He shifted in his seat nervously for a bit, and then he did the famous arm stretch that went up in the air and behind my back. I could sense his fingers walking along the back of my movie seat and stopping as his hand reached my other shoulder. I didn't object, but I didn't really know what was about to happen either. Out of the blue Chris said, in a rather loud voice: "Well, here goes nothing." Then he pulled me towards him and kissed me quickly on the cheek. I was in shock. First of all, his kiss ripped me away from my emotional investment in the film that we were watching. Second, what does "here goes nothing" mean? Should I be insulted or thankful for the kiss? Should I be happy or angry? Should I have made a snappy comment like: "You were right, it was nothing." We went back to watching the movie. He was less fidgety for the rest of the film, so I guess the whole thing was good for him. I was just confused. Was that it? How should I respond? Is that what making out at the movies was all about? Will I ever catch up to the plot of the movie that I missed? We didn't go steady for too much longer after that.

One day, out of the blue, Daddy and Mother announced that we would be moving again. "Goodbye and good riddance Murphy bed." I swear I should have been born into a career military family because we moved just as much as they did. "Army Brat Cynthia A. Pepper reporting for moving truck duty, Sir!" The year long wait was finally over and the Peppers were on the move again. I think I now know what people in the Witness Relocation Program go through. Our next pack up and go was a simple one. We were off to 5144 De Longpre Ave located right behind the building we were now living in. The new place was a small two storey unit built back in the 1920's. No more elevators or molesters that ride them.

There were seven similar buildings that housed fourteen bungalows in this apartment complex. It was more like a small house than an apartment, but my parents were still renting. They were not exactly the most modern of apartments, as they were built in the 20's, but the style was typical for a home in Hollywood at that time.

When you walked into the courtyard, just a few steps past the fountain; you would find our new place. It was the middle apartment on the right. As you walked through the front door into the apartment, you would end up in the less than average sized living room. There were stairs to the right that lead up to the bedrooms. As you moved further into the living room by about two feet, you would bump into Daddy's easy chair. It looked a lot like Archie Bunkers favorite chair from *All In The Family*, and it was just as worn. Across the room from Daddy's chair were three TV sets. They sat one on top of the other, with only the top one in good working condition. The other two TV sets just served as a stand for the working one. TV sets were expensive back then, and even if they didn't work, no one liked to throw them away.

Moving two more steps from the TV's, and you were standing in the living room, which quickly merged with the dining room. The kitchen was small, barely large enough for a small eating table that was pushed up against the wall. It was a very cramped kitchen. Just outside the kitchen door was a small back porch. Nearby was a very tiny half bathroom with a sink and toilet. If you go onto the back porch, you will find another door that leads outside to the small driveway. The upstairs of our new home was only accessible by the front door. When you go upstairs, the first room you would encounter was the upstairs bathroom with shower/tub, sink and toilet. The next room was the bedroom that I, (yes you guessed it), would be sharing with my sister. At least the Murphy bed was long gone. Mother and Daddy's bedroom was located about five feet further down the hall. It was very snug indeed.

My hopes and dreams for my own private space were once more in the wind. It really wasn't that big of a deal as it was all I had ever known… But still. Our bedroom had two twin beds and one small closet for us to share. Both of the bedrooms had a roof deck to sit out on. Even though the place was small, there was a lot more breathing room here than the last place.

I still hadn't abandoned my idea of having a pet. I was looking for a dog, a cat, anything that I could love. Mother and Daddy finally gave in, but they kept Patty's asthma in mind. That's how we got Spunky, our pet parakeet. He was colorful, full of life and very affectionate for a bird. He had full reign of the apartment and would go wherever he wanted. Flying or hopping up the stairs or kitchen floor. Things were going pretty well for Spunky that is until the day he flew into a frying pan full of cooking bacon. Mother rescued him as fast as she could, but his one leg had been burnt badly by the hot grease. She iced his little leg, but his foot was too badly damaged. Spunky survived, but his one leg was now a stump. He still had full reign of the apartment, except now you'd see him hopping on the stairs or kitchen floor with just one leg. He got pretty good at it too. At night, he would go to his perch and sleep by leaning up against the cage bars. I was truly living in a houseful of survivors.

When we first moved into the apartment the landlord actually provided a maid service. That didn't last too long as he wanted to up the rent to cover the cost of the service… Good-bye Maid Service. I forgot to mention that we had a piano in the living room that was given to Daddy by one of his cronies. That big, black, wooden box of strings and ivories must have been 50 years old at that time, and took up a good chunk of real-estate. It was the focal point of the living room and, boy, did that thing get good use. It was said that Rudolph Valentino used to live in these same apartments at one time before he was famous. As a matter of fact, there are two statues erected in his memory in the very tiny De Longpre Park, not too far away from the apartment. If you go to the park don't blink or you'll miss it. How romantic it was to think that maybe Rudy played on his piano in this very room. Well, a girl can dream can't she?

I took piano lessons as part of Mothers' music appreciation sessions. Now you know where the maid service money went. I would practice on the piano when I could, but its main function was to make music at the parties that my parents hosted. These parties were very casual, (usually chili and rice boiling in the kitchen), but they were epic in regards to the size of the gatherings, the talent that was there and, the fact that they lasted until the wee hours of the morning. Heck, a few of these rowdy sessions ended up lasting a couple of days. A bash like that made it hard for a young girl to get any sleep at all.

Daddy and Mother always made sure to invite all the neighbors to these epic parties. This way, the neighbors wouldn't complain about the noise, and they never did.

The parties were an opportunity to gather all of the old superstars of the Vaudeville era in one place, our living room. Some had come out of the demise of Vaudeville with a decent life and were still working in show business. Others were down and out, looking at their last dollar, with no place to go. Mother and Daddy were always generous in making every single one of their guests feel welcome. I didn't understand the extent of their generosity or their zest for life, since I was so young at the time, but I wish I had. Oh, the questions I would have asked about life on the Vaudeville stage. There were great singers, musicians, jugglers, magicians, dancers and actors performing in my living room. I've forgotten most of the folks that would come to these social gatherings, but I do remember, Scatman Crothers, Uncle Willie, George Spanky McFarland, Jack Albertson, Paul "Mousie" Garner, and Arthur Lake, who was famous for playing Dagwood Bumstead in the *Blondie* series. He was a very interesting and funny man. These folks brought a lot of the merriment with them and I miss them all.

To get the music started, Daddy would play our piano. He had so many old buddies attending the party that could fly up the keyboard as Liberace and come back down as Duke Ellington that he would eventually give it up to one of them.

These were just some of the musicians that played with Daddy's good friend Spike Jones. Now that guy was crazy. Eventually, Daddy would bring out his ukulele and show them how it was done. Daddy was like a human jukebox because he could pull so many old tunes out of the air.

Of course, Mother brought her own wonderful personality and essence to these shindigs. She was a grand dancer, but not a great singer. I can still remember her preparing food in the kitchen as the entire household was singing and laughing. She would be laughing and dancing around the kitchen, half Cyd Charisse and half Julia Child. Someone would yell: "Hey Dawn! Gives us a tune!" The group would cheer her on for a song. She would dance gracefully out of the kitchen with a whisk in her hand and regale the crowd with one of the worst renditions of *Rock of Ages* that you have ever heard. After eight bars of this ear piercing performance, the partiers would quickly have a change of heart and plead for her to stop. She would laugh, give them a spin and a high kick, and head back to the kitchen with a round of applause.

Unlike Mother, Patty had a lovely singing voice. She definitely took after Daddy in the singing department. Every now and then she would let loose and sing a song or two at these parties and the small audience would give her big applause. My voice was never as good as hers. Patty never wanted to pursue a career in singing, or music in general. I wish she had because she would have been great.

Mother and Daddy really came alive as people and performers during these celebrations. As always, there would be no lack of booze. The air would be a dense blue fog with cigarette, pipe and cigar smoke wafting about the rooms. One of my jobs was to go around the room and empty the ashtrays and believe me that was a full time job at these grand social gatherings. On the subject of smoking, you have to remember that at this point in time smoking was considered cool and socially acceptable. What someone smoked would tell a lot about that person. If you smoked a pipe, you were intelligent, if you smoked a cigar you were tough, if you smoked cigarettes you were sexy.

Smoking was even recommended by doctors. Remember those ads on the radio: "…that's right folks more doctors smoke Camels than any other cigarette…" And ads on TV: "…four out of five doctors recommend Lucky Strike…." Even the Flintstones had an animated commercial about smoking Winston's. Salem cigarettes even had a TV ad with lyrics that went something like: "It's a wonderful world of softness, it's a wonderful world of freshness, and it's the wonderful, wonderful, world of Salem cigarettes." Man, have times changed. Can you imagine hearing that kind of ad now?

With all this advertising pressure, it's no wonder that later I took up smoking as a young woman. Peer pressure can be a powerful thing at a young age. I always tried to keep it hidden from Daddy because he thought that a lady shouldn't smoke. Hypocritical, sure but hey it was the 1950's. I'm so glad that I quit smoking later in life but like most people of my generation, I wish I had quit sooner.

Here's an interesting recipe. You take the rowdy nature of these parties, add a teaspoon of past history from the guests, stir them together with an ample serving of alcohol, and voila, you have yourself the perfect Drama Soufflé. Invariably, someone would imbibe a little too much, become obnoxious, and try to pick an argument with anyone who would listen. This would generally result in someone crying, or stomping out of the house or maybe both. For some of the partiers it was a negative ending to such a wonderful start, similar to a lot of their careers.

At the end of these parties, I would almost always fall asleep in my room upstairs in a state of confusion. Was this where life in show business would lead? Does every performer end up so broken? I was always perplexed listening to the sounds of the richly talented people partying below my bedroom. Why would they even get together if they knew there was the slightest chance that it would end up in such disarray?

There was always so much fun and celebration for this brotherhood of performers. Maybe they clung to each other so tightly out of love, or maybe out of fear. They were fearful because the world they had known and excelled in was all gone. It was changing into something they could no longer be a part of, or adapt to. The contact they shared at my parents parties helped to keep their spirits alive. It's a fact that the Vaudevillians helped make the developing industry of Hollywood movies and TV a huge success. Hollywood needed professional singers, actors, dancers, and comedians, to put in their movies. Vaudeville was Hollywood's pool of talent to fish from. However, not all were able to master the new media and attain the big payoff. Some called the camera a one-eyed monster, and moved on to the unemployment line. Sometimes, I would wake up the morning after one of these gatherings, and come downstairs to find some of the party guests asleep in the living room. Mother and Daddy never said no to an old friend that wanted to stay for the night, or even the month. I think it was around this time that Daddy would answer the phone by saying: "Hello, House of Good Sheppard." He did love to help people when he could, but sometimes it turned out to be a mess.

The same kinds of parties were happening with other showbiz people that lived in the affluent Hollywood Hills area, but with a much bigger budget of course. I'm talking about the actors, performers, and studio executives that were really making it in Hollywood. These were the people that had found the big payoff. The folks in the hills were in a totally different tax bracket, yet they came from the same kind of showbiz background, and had the same need to stick together. Daddy was always traveling between these two worlds. He would spend time in Beverly Hills with Lou Brice, Fanny Brice's brother. He was also good friends with Marion Davis' sister Rose, who lived in The Hills.

Daddy would either be on a movie set working, or on the phone at home calling his agent and looking for work. The rest of the time, he would take off to San Diego to be with his buddies Jackie Gleason or Phil Harris for a long weekend of drinking, playing the ponies, and God knows what else. To use an old time word, Daddy hung out with the "swells", he just didn't have any 'swell' himself.

When Daddy finally came home to us after his wild weekends, he'd try to smooth things over with Mother. They would both have a few drinks and that would unleash a torrent of anger that included a drunken knock down, dish throwing and screaming slugfest. Their fights would eventually bring the police by for a visit. Many times, Patty and I sat at the top of the stairs and listened to the reality show that came to life below us. I could picture the entire play as it unfolded. It was like a radio program but with better sound quality, no commercials and no censoring of the colorful language. The show would almost always follow the same script. It would generally start with many accusations followed by yelling, and cursing. Next, the pushing and hitting would start and things would break. Then the threats started and there would be the eventual call to and arrival of the local constables. It was like an exciting weekly radio drama right in our own home. Let me say this, you didn't get this kind of a story line or performance from the *Ozzie & Harriet Show*.

I can joke about it now but back then when the drama ended I would just go to my bed and cry myself to sleep. Interestingly, as often as they fought, Mother and Daddy never directed any harsh words or physical violence towards Patty and me. They saved it all up for each other.

It was around this time that my sister became somewhat mean spirited towards me. Maybe she blamed me as the cause of our folk's frequent fights. Patty may have been jealous of my relationship with Daddy. She may have thought that my relationship with him was closer than hers, which it wasn't. He never played favorites with us. I once asked Mother if Patty was jealous of me on some level. She just said; "Patty had the exact same opportunities that you had, but she decided not to take them. She decided that it wasn't for her so she has no right to be jealous now." Maybe Patty thought of entertainment as my thing and didn't want to compete. Regardless, but it doesn't explain why she was becoming increasingly sad and angry at the world in general.

Sometimes when Mother had to work a late shift and Daddy was away working on location, or out with some of his pals. It would just be Patty and me at home alone, for the night. I was never sure if it was her growing mean streak, or just the fact that boredom set in, but she would love to think up ways to scare me in the new apartment. She would accomplish this very easily: for Patty it was almost like fishing. I was so gullible. I was an easily hooked fish, a Betty Bass.

It all started one quiet night. It was mid-evening and the sun had just set. We were lying in our twin beds listening to emergency calls on our radio as it had a local police scanner built into it. As the darkness began to shroud the city and our little neighborhood, Patty looked up with a start and whispered to me: "Shhh... Did you hear that?"

"What?" I'd ask, listening intently to the hallway. (She was now baiting the hook).

"That noise, silly. There was a noise on the stairs."

"I didn't hear any noise." I said dismissively.

She turned off the scanner and put her finger to her lips: "Shhh, there it is again. I think it's getting closer." (The fishing line had been cast into the water).

I started to tremble as I asked: "What is it?"

Pausing for just a moment, Patty said: "I'll bet it's that guy I read about that sneaks into homes looking for brown haired girls your age to kill." (The fish has taken the hook).

I was horrified as I scrambled to remind her: "Well you've got brown hair too!"

"Yes but I'm the wrong age. He's looking for younger girls, he's looking for you." (The fish is now being reeled in. Betty Bass is now in the net).

By this time, I was very frightened and would try to hide under the covers, under the bed, under anything I could. Eventually, she would laugh at me and tell me she was just joking and how scared I looked. "You should have seen your face." Some nights it was the same story but with a new twist. I believed everything she said and it would take me hours to fall asleep due to my vivid imagination. I'd have nightmares about it all. She knew all my buttons and she loved to push them.

Another night when our folks were away, Patty got a little more physical with me than usual. We were playing nicely enough when she decided to start a pillow fight. I didn't swing my pillow at her too much because I didn't really want to have that battle right then. I knew how that kind of thing could get her asthma to flare up. I said:

"Patty, stop it I don't want to fight with you." She seemed to take what I said as a challenge and kept on pounding me with her pillow, with even more energy and more laughter. She was obviously having fun. I yelled at her to stop but instead of stopping she pushed me backwards onto my bed and jumped on my stomach and chest. She was too strong for me to push her off so I just looked up at her and yelled at her again to stop. She just kept laughing.

She pressed her pillow down hard against my face to the point where I couldn't breathe. The pillow covered both my mouth and nose which made it impossible to get a breath of air. The harder she pushed down on the pillow, the more I fought back. She just laughed at me as I panicked. I thought this was it. I was about to be killed by my crazy sister. I was trying to scream, but the pillow muffled any noise I would try to make. It was like being underwater and not being able to get back to the surface. Out of sheer panic I made one last grand effort to save myself by thrashing from side to side. I finally broke free and tried to catch my breath. As I sat up gasping for air, trying to get my wits about me, I asked her: "What the heck do you think you were doing?"

"Oh, sorry, did I hurt you?" she replied sarcastically.

I don't think she realized that the pillow fight had gone too far. Then she just ignored me, and, with no apology, treated the whole incident as if it was a big joke and no big deal. She made me feel that I was overreacting to the whole thing. Was I? Patty thought this was great fun, but I didn't.

I'm sure the whole incident was just a couple of minutes long, but it felt like an eternity. I was shocked and confused; shouldn't an older sister be protecting her younger sister? Over the years, I've often wondered if she just wanted to scare me or did she really try to kill me? Was she trying to share the pain of her breathing issues by showing me what it was like to have asthma? Could she have just explained her pain to me without the physical demonstration? Or was it just some simple fun that got way out of hand? To this day I don't know how to explain why my sister did what she did. However it certainly helps to explain why I'm claustrophobic. Maybe this was her way of feeling some power or control in her own life. I never spoke to Patty about the pillow fight after that night. I've never mentioned this incident to anyone, not Vicki, and not even my parents, but maybe I should have. My relationship with Patty seemed different after that and I wondered if we'd ever be close on any level.

I became more anxious to have good, solid friends in my life since my relationship with my sister was no longer close. In 1954, I had a number of great friends, but as I've always said: "There's always room for one more." That one more was a girl named Diane Phillips. She had just moved from the East Coast to live with her Mom in Hollywood. She was a year older and lived in one of the units at our new place on De Longpre. As a matter of fact her mother, Mrs. Phillips, was my Mother's friend from the Broadway Hollywood that gave us the line on the new apartment. (Now I had two Diane's in my life.)

When Diane and I met, I was fifteen and she was sixteen. She was fun, sweet and honest. Many times she would knock on the front door and Daddy would yell for her to come in. He'd be sitting at the piano in his underwear, working on a song. Diane would just take it in stride. She'd say hello and then ask where I was. It never fazed her. When it came to my family, Diane was always a good sport. Diane and I had a great time during the summer of '55. We would go to dances and double date together. Whenever we went to a coffee shop, we would write messages on the napkins and leave them behind. We would giggle at the thought of someone finding the messages and thinking they were real. We would write things like "Grace Kelly was here.", Or "Debbie Reynolds was here and the Aba Daba coffee was really good."

I was Debbie and she was Grace. It was all just simple fun for a couple of bored Hollywood teens.

Mind you, we did have one incident that almost got out of hand. Diane and I decided that it would be fun to trek up the Hollywood Hills and see how the other half lived.

As we walked up the steep roads, we marveled at all the beautiful mansions and luxurious living all around us. Security back then wasn't like it is today. At some point, we became very hot and tired. Then we saw a big backyard with a beautiful "empty" swimming pool sitting in the middle of it and with no owners in sight, there was only one thing to do.

We quickly scaled the fence and pulled up a couple of lounge chairs and rested by the pool. We were Grace & Debbie, lying by the mansion pool, discussing our next big movie projects and whom we would be dating next. Just then there was a big commotion up at the mansion behind us. A couple of people came out of the house yelling: "Hey this is private property! You're trespassing. Come here!" Diane and I jumped up out of our lazy lounging positions and ran like the wind to the fence. I don't remember climbing back over the fence, but it seemed like I just cleared it in a single bound. I found that I could run a whole lot faster scared then they could angry.

Diane and I ran down the hill laughing our heads off at the thought of almost getting caught by the angry rich people. The following day the newspapers reported that the police were searching for two girls that had illegally trespassed on the property of Mr. Rock Hudson. They were looking for two girls with light brown hair, possibly dangerous. Diane and I were stunned. We were now two criminals on the loose. Of course, we didn't tell anyone that it was us and nothing ever came from it. Who knew that we were the original *Thelma and Louise*.

As a teenage girl, birthdays are important. Every birthday gets you closer to being an adult, and that seems to be what teenagers want. Since my folks didn't have a lot of money, presents were affordable and practical gifts. Daddy was not always there for my birthdays, but Mother always made sure I had a happy time when they came around. When Daddy could, he always tried to make them memorable for me. My fifteenth birthday would prove to be just that. On September 4th, 1955, Daddy was away visiting his very good friend Chill Wills at the Warner Brothers studios. Mr. Wills was working on the set of the movie Giant with Elizabeth Taylor and Rock Hudson. (Thank God Daddy didn't know about the incident with us and Mr. Hudson's pool)

I was at home when the phone rang that afternoon. "Hello?" I said nonchalantly.

"Hi honey. Happy Birthday!" (It was Daddy)

"Hang on someone wants to talk to you..."

Before I could say anything, Daddy was gone and I could hear that the phone was being passed to someone else. Finally a man on the other end spoke:

"Hello. Is this Cynthia?"

Wondering exactly what Daddy was up to I answered: "Yes, this is Cynthia."

The voice on the other end of the phone then said: "This is James Dean. Your Dad said it was your Birthday today. Is that true?"

I stammered back: "Yes…"

He continued: "So how old are you?"

My lower jaw was now resting on the kitchen floor, but I managed to say: "Fifteen."

He responded with: "That's great. Well, I just wanted to wish you a very Happy Birthday."

I said: "Thank you." He said goodbye and just like that, he was gone.

I don't really remember if I talked to Daddy again or if I just hung up the phone, but that was the longest and most memorable fifty-five second phone conversation I'd ever had. I was somewhat in shock but can you blame me? I was just talking with screen idol James Dean on the phone. The conversation happened so fast and just like that, he was gone.

There were so many things I could have asked or discussed, but I guess I was just dumbfounded. It was a missed opportunity on my part.

On September 30th, just twenty-six days after that wonderful Birthday phone call, James Dean was driving to Salinas for a car race in his new 1955 Porsche 550 Spyder. Along the way, he was involved in a fatal car crash… And just like that, he was gone.

He was only 24 years old.

When the summer had ended and the fall came around I felt somewhat melancholy. My friend Diane was going into her first year of High School and I still had a year to go in Jr. High. I knew that I would miss her every day. This would be my final year at Le Conte Jr. High, but I was looking towards the future and couldn't wait for this new year of school to end. Diane, on the other hand, was excited about her new school. I knew that in a year I'd follow her scholastic footsteps to the same high school. Not to just any High School mind you but to the most famous high school in California, or in the USA if not the whole world, Hollywood High School.

Chapter 9

Hollywood High

In 1956, I was fifteen going on sixteen, (sounds like a song). My musical tastes included songs from the 1920's and all the Big Band music I could get my hands on. I wasn't a fan of Country and Western music at all. Daddy had written a few songs that Gene Autry had recorded, but I still wasn't a fan.

My girlfriends had all fallen head-over-heels for a new singer after hearing his latest record on the radio. It was called *Heartbreak Hotel*. I first heard it when I was at a girlfriend's place, and it came on the radio.

"Oh Cynthia, listen to this guy. He's a dream."

"I don't like Country and Western much." I replied.

She said: "No this is different."

As the song played, I was shocked and amazed by the sounds that I was hearing. *Heartbreak Hotel* was a strange piece of music that was bluesy, sad and yet somehow sexy at the same time.

When it finished, the DJ came on the air and blasted: "Hey guys and gals that was the Hillbilly Cat himself all the way from Memphis Tennessee with a new disc riding up the charts with a bullet. Elvis Presley with *Heartbreak Hotel*..."

I remember thinking, Elvis Presley? What kind of name was Elvis? My girlfriend handed me a teen magazine with his picture on the cover. His look was sexy and mysterious. He had the hair of Tony

Curtis, the deep eyes of James Dean, and the pouty lips of Brando. He sure was a doll, but all I could think about was who in the world would name their kid Elvis? Today the name Elvis is synonymous with Rock & Roll, but in 1956, it was all brand new. This innovative singer really seemed to have something that captivated us, and I loved it. To use a term of the day; he was dreamy. I couldn't help but wonder how long this guy, or even Rock & Roll music, would last. For now both were just what the doctor ordered. I bought the 45 rpm recording of Heartbreak Hotel. I played that recording so much for the next month that I wore out the grooves on the record. I then bought another one and wore it out too. The B side to the record was Elvis' recording of the song *I Was the One* which was also worn out. My parents must have loved me for all that.

Mother was still working at The Broadway Hollywood. Daddy had already finished work on an episode of the TV show *Cheyenne* with devastatingly handsome star Clint Walker. He had also started work on two other unaccredited roles in the movies. The films were *Any Thing Goes* with Bing Crosby and Donald O'Connor, and *That Certain Feeling* with Bob Hope, Eva Marie Saint and George Sanders. These roles were unaccredited, but was still work, and he was bringing some money into the household, minus the Horse Track losses of course.

To get by financially, I worked a number of different jobs. I started taking in ironing from families around the court where we lived. A lot of people did that back in the 50's to make some cash. It was repetitious work, but I liked it. It freed up my mind so that I could allow my imagination to be elsewhere, such as on stage or a movie set in the future. Daydreaming? Sure, but with daydreams come hope and hope flows eternal.

A bunch of my girlfriends and I eventually got a job at the Five and Dime store located on Hollywood Ave. I was working at the costume jewelry counter helping customers. The old man that owned the place would stand up on the balcony at the back of the store most of the day watching all of us and everything that was going on. I don't think there was anything perverted about it. As a matter of fact, I think he was the security system for the whole store. If someone decided to pull the old five finger discount, he knew about it. We called him old eagle-eye. When you think about it, he was a human security camera.

There were some jobs that I was just not cut out for. One of them was a job in a print shop, where I worked for six months. Daddy knew the owner and set it up for me. It was the perfect job for a young actress as the owner loved show business people and would allow us time through the day to go to auditions if need be. It was a decent job and I liked stocking the shelves and helping customers find what they were looking for. I was doing very well at my own pace in my own space. Then one day one of the girls needed to go to a last minute audition, so management decided to put me on the cash register in her place. They didn't have anyone else to do it at the time so they thought this would be a good thing. I warned them that this might be a bad idea and as it turns out I was right. You see it's not that I didn't know how to make change, I just panicked. I got confused. I was just not adding things up right in my head due to the responsibility of the cash register combined with the intimidation I felt from customers. I ended up costing the store about seven or eight dollars after just half a day because I gave out too much change. (This was big money back then.) They took me off cash duties and put me on the printing press in the back. Now this job I liked. I was on my own, no cash interactions with customers, and low stress. I felt so bad about costing them money, but I DID warn them. That's when I first knew, that handling money was not my forte.

Hollywood High was, and still is, located at the intersection of North Highland Avenue and West Sunset Boulevard. It was built in 1905, which was about 6 years before Hollywood's first studio was open for business. The school was nicknamed the Star Hatchery in 1936. It was called that because that's when Mickey Rooney, Judy Garland, Alexis Smith, Lana Turner, and Nanette Fabray were all attending Hollywood High at the same time. The list of famous alumni is a very long one, but I'll include it just so you understand how prolific this school really is Meredith Baxter, Carol Burnett, Keith Carradine, Robert Carradine, Lon Chaney, Jr., Cher, Linda Evans, Mike Farrell, Laurence Fishburne, James Garner, Alan Hale Jr., John Huston, Jill St. John, Chuck Jones, Sally Kellerman, Swoosie Kurtz, Alan Ladd, Carole Lombard, Richard Long, Joel McCrea, Heather Menzies, Ann Miller, Yvette Mimieux, Ricky Nelson, David Nelson, Sarah Jessica Parker, John Ritter, Jason Robards, Sharon Tate, Charlene Tilton, Tuesday Weld, Rita Wilson, and Fay Wray just to name a few.

My class picture from Hollywood High School

(Cynthia Pepper Collection)

There's a feeling of fear and excitement that comes with your first day at a new school. Will I be liked, will I fit in, how do I find my classes? For me, these fears were soon replaced with joy. Vicki and Diane Phillips were also going to school here so I had the confidence of having my friends close by. I found the school to be everything that I had hoped for, and more. The girls all wore cute skirts with bobby socks and Mary Jane shoes. The dress code said that those skirts had to be below the knee, or you were sent home to change. The school staff was very strict on that. The girl's outfits were topped off with a matching blouse and, occasionally, school sweater. Their hair was usually looking fine in a ponytail or a page boy cut. The guys wore a nice, pressed white shirt, maybe a tie and khaki pants or Peggers. The penny loafer was the shoe of the day for the guys. What can I say about the guy's hair? It was either a brush-cut or the slicked down

Brylcreem or Vitalis look. Some guys had so much grease in their hair that Texaco could have bought their oil from them.

There was an incredible school spirit and attitude that seem to permeate the hallways of Hollywood High. You couldn't ignore the fact that so many kids who graduated from this school went on to make it pretty big later on in life. Now it was our turn. The school colors were crimson and white. The school teams were called the Sheiks, (named after Rudolph Valentino's famous character the Sheik and his silent movie by the same name). Even the school motto was motivating: "Achieve the Honorable". To say that I was inspired to attend this school would be an understatement. I knew that attending Hollywood High didn't ensure success in the world of entertainment, but it sure didn't hurt.

It was a beautiful school with lots of green grass and trees. It was very rural. We would spend most of our lunch time sitting on the grass on the Highland side of the school. During class, I concentrated on getting decent grades and after class I would audition for any school production that would let me in. I excelled in subjects such as typing, drama, music, English and dance. I did just enough in every other subject and maybe a fraction more, to get a passing grade.

If you really wanted to socialize at HHS you would try to join a group, a clique, a club or pledge to one of the sororities. There were the Alpha, Beta, Lambda, and Theta clubs, but I became a Delta Girl. Delta Psi Deltas Rule! It felt great to belong to a club and to be accepted by others. Vicki had pledged to another sorority, but Diane was a Delta sister. Sure, Hell Night was a crazy initiation for the new pledges, but it was worth it. My friend Joyce Browne pledged at the same time as I did. The pledges are all invited to someone's house and at some point in the night you had to go into a semi-dark candle lit room. Then we ate gross, disgusting things and drank some green slime from bowls. It was all I could do to keep it down. By the end of the night, I was accepted into the Deltas and my list of friends had gotten a whole lot longer.

They were not just my friends now, but my Delta sisters. It's a solid bond and a great comfort knowing that people will back you up when you need them. All the sororities had their own tree and bench where they would gather for lunch every day in the quad. In retrospect, I'm sure it was an elitist thing to do, but, hey, all the kids were doing it. It was a very territorial thing to be involved in a club and not just anyone would be accepted. Lots of girls were turned down. Linda Evenstad was not one of them.

I'll never forget the first time we laid eyes on Linda Evenstad. She was stunning from every direction. Seeing her on that first day at school was right out of a romantic comedy. She came strolling through the grounds with her smooth blonde hair blowing in just the right way. She used all the body defining modeling skills she had acquired at some Hollywood school of runway-walking. She was a swan, an absolute swan. All the girls looked at her and in amazement said: "Who is that?" as all the boyfriends would turn and follow her wherever she would go. She was excruciatingly shy in spite of her dazzling looks. Her parents had put her into drama school to bring her out of her shell. It must have worked because she later changed her name and went on to massive success in show business. Yes, that would be Linda Evans. I'll never know how that shy girl was able to climb out of her defensive covering and blossom into the world. She was able to climb so high, in fact, that she landed starring roles on TV's *The Big Valley* with Barbara Stanwyck and later on *Dynasty* with John Forsythe and Joan Collins. I guess great talent can just knock the shy right out of you.

Mike Farrell was another person that always had it going on; he's a real sweetheart. No wonder he was able to find a ton of work in TV. He worked hard for his roles and he deserved it. They were great shows, and his work lead him all the way to one of TV's most successful productions, *M*A*S*H*. What a talented guy he is.

Most people at HHS seemed to be accepted into just one group, and that was their place. It was the crowd they would stay with throughout their high school life. I, on the other hand, seemed to transcend these different groups. I'm not really sure why or how, but if I had to guess I'd chalk it up to my personality. I could hang with my fabulous Delta sisters, and then spend some great quality time learning my craft with my drama classmates. It may also have had something to do with my newly found space and privacy at home. I think I was becoming more comfortable and adventurous as an individual now that I had my own room. Hang on, I have to do this right: "And so it was written that in the fifteenth year of this young girl's life she would finally know the word 'privacy' as she would now have her very own room with which to reside." I know that was a bit much, but when I waited so long to finally get my own bedroom I tend to get a little excited. Did we renovate the apartment to make it bigger? No, the family just got smaller. At nineteen years of age, my sister decided that it was time to strike out on her own life's path. Patty would finally leave the nest and soar far across the lands, across the oceans and into the heavens to seek her independence… Ok, so she and a roommate named Carol just moved into the apartment across the court from ours. I think that it was a mere forty feet from our front door to theirs, but did I also mention that I now, for the first time in my life, had my own bedroom?

Attending Hollywood High School created a bond that continues today with my friends from school. My great friends included people like Dick Rippey, Joyce Browne, Jim Farrell, Kerry Cotton, Mickey Beauchamp, Diane Phillips, and Vicki. There was even a girl named Taffy.

Her full name was Taffy Paul and she was both a Beta and Lambda girl. I guess it was inevitable that we would give her the nickname Taffy Pull. I hope she's forgiven us for that one. She was a smart, fun, and very down to earth girl. Taffy got into a little trouble one night with regards to the sororities. It caused quite a stink at school; this is how I remember it happening.

A Beta sister, Carol Wells, was throwing a slumber party at her parent's home for the sorority. Some guys from a bunch of other clubs came over to crash the party. Her parents would have none of that, so they told everyone to go home: the party was over. It was a rainy night, and people jumped into whatever car could take them home. Taffy ended up in a car with five boys that had been drinking a fair bit of beer that night. As they drove past HHS, some resentment towards the Beta's erupted within the car. Someone started saying: "How dare they do this to us. They can't treat us this way. We should do something. We ought to go cut down that Beta tree. That'll show 'em."

A small saw was then conveniently found in the car and that's what caused all the trouble. The boys jumped out of the car and with Taffy looking on in complete amazement they did exactly what they said they would, they cut down the Beta tree. This was a knee-jerk reaction to being thrown out of the party. As Taffy said; "It was all fun and games until we had to go to school the next day."

There laid the tree. Cut down and looking so sad and dead in the quad. It was a tree that had been planted by the girls' Vice Principal, Big Bertha, and she was very upset. The Police came quickly to the school. Then they rounded up Taffy and the gang of tree cutting gangsters, paraded them out of the school, into the squad cars, and whisked them away to Juvenile Hall. This was a bit excessive for cutting down a single tree, but the Vice Principal was angry and, hey, it was the Delta's tree. The tree cutters were sentenced to some community service and were eventually allowed to return to school. Taffy laughs about this whole silly incident now. It certainly didn't hold her back from her goals in life. In 1962, she got into the movie and television business as an actress in a very big way. Oh, did I mention that she changed her name? What was it again…? Oh yes: Stefanie Powers. No more Taffy Pull for her. Later in life she became heavily involved with the preservation of Africa's plains and wildlife by becoming the president of The William Holden Wildlife Federation. I think that she's more than made up for the tree, don't you?

The Nelson Family had been on the radio since 1944, and on television since 1952. They became synonymous with the 1950s ideal American family: a standard that we all tried to live up to. It was a lofty goal that no family could ever achieve, not even the Nelsons. Ricky Nelson attended HHS at the same time as I did, but he was running with a different, rougher crowd. He had been black-balled by the Elksters, which was a sport loving fraternity, so he joined up with a greaser car club called the Rooks. These guys were nasty. They'd drive along Hollywood Blvd at night just to harass and get physically tough with anyone that crossed their paths. Ricky had been brought up in the lap of luxury as a kid, so he didn't have a good handle on life, or any direction at that point in time. He was rebelling and figured the Rooks were the guys to do it with. After being arrested a couple of times his father, Ozzie, stepped in to get him back on the straight and narrow. Ricky's singing career got an indirect kick start from Elvis Presley. It happened when he was a cocky sixteen year old attending HHS. His girlfriend at the time was smitten with Elvis, and Ricky told her that he too was about to make a record. After his father had pulled a few strings with Verve Records, a date was set for him to record some songs. On March 26, 1957, Ricky recorded the Fats Domino standard *I'm Walkin'* and *A Teenager's Romance,* reaching #4 and #2 respectively on Billboard's Best Sellers in Stores chart. Well, that was certainly one way to impress a girlfriend. She didn't last too long after that, but we all know that his music career sure did.

HHS was never in short supply of talent or technical equipment. There were always great in school productions and school spirit was high. The stage, lights, and sound equipment were all top notch. There was never a short supply of people to put on a professional looking production.

Good looking guys were another thing that was never in short supply at HHS. This was kind of important for a young lady coming of age. One of these good looking fellows was Ivan Haas. When we first met he was seventeen years old and one grade ahead of me.

Ivan was born in the city of Prague, Czechoslovakia. During World War II food was in extremely short supply. His formative years there were not fortified with the right nutrients and vitamins that a young boy needs to be healthy. He became a diabetic at a very young age due to this terrible diet. Ivan and his parents escaped to the United States during the war searching for a better way of life.

Ivan had beautiful blue eyes, fantastic light brown hair, his own car, and an independent spirit that was the envy of most of the other guys in school.

I first noticed Ivan at the school choir rehearsal. I thought he was cute. He had a personality that was a cross between James Dean and Elvis Presley. We were all singing our parts when I noticed that he was looking at me. He gave me a quick smile from across the room and so I shot him one back. After rehearsal, a group of us went to a place called Coffee Dan's which was located at Highland and Hollywood Blvd. Coffee Dan's was a cool hangout for the in-crowd of Hollywood High. Ivan and I struck up a conversation over a couple of sodas and that was it for me. He eventually nicknamed me Tink, which was short for Tinker Bell from *Peter Pan*. He said that much like Tinker Bell; I was short and magical. From then on I was smitten with my Ivan.

This is the only picture that I have with Ivan and me together.

(Cynthia Pepper Collection)

Within the school there were different cliques, groups and clubs. Everyone seemed to fit somewhere, but not many could fit everywhere. There were sororities, jocks, artistic people, geeks, and the tough kids. Ivan was one of the tough kids. These were the kids that, between classes, would hang around the Highland side of the school, just off campus, smoking and generally trying to be dangerous. They'd have their smokes rolled up in their sleeves and would constantly play with their cigarette lighters or a book of matches. This group was full of the classic teenage angst. They never caused a lot of trouble but were always posturing as if to say: "Man, we could snap at any minute, so back away." The tough kids didn't judge each other unlike many of the other groups around the school.

Ivan liked this group and felt he belonged with them. Ivan had a tough, edgy persona, but there was another side of him that very few others saw. The real Ivan could be located about an inch below his tough guy image. He was sensitive, smart, funny, and a good, moral human being. His home life, on the other hand, was far from perfect.

His parents, Bebe and Hugo, were divorced from each other, but both lived in Hollywood. Ivan lived with his father, Hugo Haas.

After escaping the Nazis in World War II the Haas family arrived in Hollywood to create a new life for themselves. Hugo Haas had some success back in Czechoslovakia as an actor, and director. He quickly transitioned into a successful Hollywood actor, and director and he also wrote a lot of the Hollywood B movies popular at the time. However, he was not a very successful father with Ivan. He didn't really devote a lot of time to his son. I used to go to Ivan's house a lot after school. Many times Mr. Haas would have a young starlet upstairs interviewing or auditioning or going over a script, or… I think you know where I'm going with this. I could sense a very intense, dark side to Mr. Haas. A lot of that came out in his movies. One of his better accomplishments was to get his family safely out of Czechoslovakia as the Nazi's were invading his country. Mr. Haas' father and brother were both killed in the German concentration camps, so it was to be expected that he would have a dark, serious side. It was pretty obvious meeting him in person but, this darkness was reflected in the movie he wrote and directed in 1955 called *Hold Back Tomorrow*. It starred John Agar and Cleo Moore. It was very gritty, very dark, very Hugo Haas.

Ivan found it particularly embarrassing that his father would be upstairs with some young girl while we were downstairs in the living room watching *Dick Clark's American Bandstand* or some other TV show we were into at the time. One particular day, as we were watching a new show called Mr. Adams & Eve starring Ida Lupino and Howard Duff, Mr. Haas came down the stairs with Miss Universe. No kidding, it was her. I chuckled to myself and thought I could understand why he's divorced now. Mr. Haas was not the most handsome man in the world, but I guess Hollywood power can work miracles at times, Universal miracles to be exact. I was always proud and happy that I avoided the Hollywood casting couch during my entire career in the city of broken dreams.

Ivan had so much going for himself, but the one thing going against him was his diabetes. Every day he would have to give himself a shot of insulin. There was no one to do it for him so it was just a part of his life and he got used to it. He had to be careful to regulate his blood sugar at all times. I always admired him for being able to keep it under control and go on with his life. There was never a "poor me" attitude from Ivan. He would come to our house a lot as his father was always working on a set and his house was often empty.

My father would always ask: "What do you see in that kid and why is he always dressed like a bum?"

I would counter with: "He's not dressed like a bum he's wearing blue jeans and a white t-shirt just the same as the other boys."

Daddy retorted: "That's what bums wear."

"No Daddy that's the style now." I said.

He countered with: "I don't agree."

"Well, it's true." I snapped back, defending my boyfriend.

Daddy just leaned back smiled and said: "Well I guess that's what makes horse races." Daddy could always turn a phrase and that one was his favorite. I knew deep down that Daddy liked Ivan, but he was just watching out for his little girl.

One day Ivan and I drove to Santa Barbara to see the fellow with the funny name in his debut movie Love Me Tender. Sure, I loved Elvis' look and his voice, but he was now a singer, turned actor, and we were curious to see if he could act. It was an hour and a half drive up the beautiful coastline to see a handsome guy on the big screen in glorious black and white.

It was wonderful to have my soul mate right beside me in living color. It was official that we were going steady because he gave me his ring to wear around my neck. We never did anything other than kiss and make out, as they say. Ivan would have gone further, but I was saving myself for marriage because that's what you did back then. We both thought that we would marry each other one day and that nothing on God's green earth would happen to ruin our plans. Or so we thought. Oh, by the way, the singer turned actor with the funny first name... It turns out that he was a pretty good actor after all.

My last summer with Ivan was spent doing what kids did in the late 1950's to have fun. We spent time with friends, made out, drove in very fast muscle cars, made out, hung out at the coffee shop and burger joints, made out, hid people in the trunk of the car to get them into the drive-in for free, and then later... made out.

Since Ivan was a year older than me, he graduated before I did, in 1957. We had a great summer together. The new school year was quickly approaching and Ivan announced to me that his mother Bebe had decided that he would be going to Europe to continue his schooling. I felt like I'd been kicked in the gut by a mule with both hind legs. It was like I couldn't breathe. Even months after he'd left I was still searching for air.

I told him that I didn't believe him; this had to be a cruel joke. He said: "No Tink, it's true." When I asked why he had to leave, he couldn't give me a reason. His mother had made the decision that he should continue his schooling back in Europe. She thought it would be a better education for him. I told him to refuse to go. I was so angry with his mother. He wasn't even living with her. There had to be a better way. He could go to College here. He could come live with us. Mother and Daddy would surely see that it would kill me if he left. He said it was set and he had to leave.

It took me a long time to be able to inhale and exhale normally again. I didn't see him off at the airport. I couldn't handle it. I didn't want to say goodbye. I couldn't hold it back so I just cried all that day.

I kept trying to find a reason for it all. I had a sadness that I'd never had before. Eventually, I was just numb. Unlike the movies, there was no last minute reconciliation or change of heart. There was no taxi that arrived at my doorstep that had Ivan jumping out and into my arms vowing to stay. It was just a vast emptiness that seemed to be never ending.

People had come and gone in my life in the past, but this was different. I felt hollow inside. It wasn't a child's pain but an adult's pain. I ultimately came to realize that life was not one big Ozzie & Harriet episode after another and that growing up was not as simple as radio and TV shows may have made it out to be.

When I went back to HHS for the new semester, my heart was still broken as I was still missing Ivan very much. I didn't want anyone to see it so I slowly found myself being even more social if that was possible. I threw myself into acting and the arts even more than before.

The drama teacher at HHS was John Ingle. I found him to be a very handsome man and a terrific teacher. I learned a lot from him and his methods of acting. He taught at HHS from 1955 to 1964, and then he later taught at Beverly Hills High School. Some of his other students included Nicholas Cage, Swoozie Kurtz, Richard Dreyfuss, Julie Kavner, David Schwimmer, Albert Brooks, and Barbara Hershey just to name a few. You know the age old saying: "Those that can, do... And those that can't, teach." Well, John Ingle threw that old saying out the window forever when he showed us all how to work. After he had retired from teaching, he started using his skills as an actor. He did a lot of TV work on different shows. You'd probably know him best on the soap opera *General Hospital* as Edward Quartermaine. Thanks for still teaching us in your retirement John.

In 1958, I graduated from Hollywood High. Our commencement was a huge gathering held at The Hollywood Bowl. We looked so stylish and smart in our academic regalia. It was all very formal and organized to the nine's. I wished Ivan could have seen me. You can't go to prom alone so I was lucky enough to go with Peter Virgo Jr. He was a fantastic guy and a good friend. His father, Peter Virgo, was an actor and appeared in a number of movies such as *Spartacus* with Kirk Douglas and *What Ever Happened To Baby Jane* with Bette Davis and Joan Crawford. Peter Jr. also went into acting and has appeared in a number of shows including the *Star Trek* TV episode called: *The Paradise Syndrome*. I thought he did a great job on that show.

We had a fantastic time dancing and celebrating into the wee hours. I can still remember getting home later that night with my whole life ahead of me and thinking: "Ok, Now what?"

The Elvis Connection #2 - Hollywood High

Although Elvis did not go to HHS, there is a pretty interesting connection. Hollywood High School Graduate of 1948, US Postal Master General Anthony Frank made history on January 8th, 1993. He helped produce the most popular stamp ever done up to that point in American history. It is the now famous Elvis Presley Stamp. It was released on what would have been Elvis's 58th Birthday. There were two pieces of art work in contention. One was the younger 1950's Elvis and the other was the more mature 1970's Elvis. For the first time ever, the U.S. Postal Service allowed the public to vote and choose which art work they preferred for the stamp. The people had their say, and the younger 1950's Elvis stamp prevailed.

Chapter 10

A Working Actress in Hollywood
Getting My Feet Wet
The River of Work
Mother & Daddy

Well, there I was with all my acting, dancing and singing chops and nowhere to ply them. At this point, I had even mastered tears on demand if the scene called for it. My close friend and actress Beverly Washburn had mastered this crying skill long before I did. As a young girl she was able to land some great roles in the movies *Shane, Old Yeller,* and *The Greatest Show on Earth* with this in her bag of acting skills. I certainly recognized how useful this could be if I were ever called upon to cry in a scene. (No one would ever have to threaten my dog to get a good cry out of me.)

When you are young, you tend not to understand how your actions and decisions will affect your future. You live in the present and look after your immediate needs. At this point in my life, I was consumed with becoming an actress. My ambitions were evident during a dinner out with Mother and Daddy at a swanky restaurant. Normally, we wouldn't even be able to afford to breathe the air in a place like this, but we were invited out by Daddy's good friend Henry English and his wife Vickie. They had been family friends for years but traveled in a slightly higher economic state than the Peppers.

Uncle Henry, as I called him, at his insistence, founded and owned Red Ball Freight Line in Texas and had become quite wealthy as a result. They lived in a huge house in Texas with maids and a valet, yet he and his wife were the most down to earth people you'd ever want to meet. They both had a lot of fun in life and didn't mind treating others to some of that fun too. It was just part of their nature.

As we sat around the table after eating a magnificently prepared meal, the men lit up their cigars and were talking about everything from sports to politics to music and everything in between. At one point there was a quiet gap in their conversation. Uncle Henry turned to me and asked: "Cynthia darlin', now what's going on in your young life?"

"Well, Uncle Henry..." I said: "I graduated from high school a couple of months ago and I guess I'll have to get a good job now."

He smiled and said: "What kind of job would you like to get?"

I quickly answered: "Well I'm going to be an actress. I've studied a lot and have had a couple of jobs already. Nothing too big but I know that I can be good at it. I know that I've still got a lot more that I can learn."

He took a long puff on his fat cigar and asked: "So where would be the best place for you to go to learn more about acting?"

I said: "Well the best place for me to go would probably be The Pasadena Playhouse. They have the best theatre arts course in California."

"Oh, I see." He said leaning back in his chair. "So why are you not going there now?"

I was a little embarrassed and said: "... Well, Uncle Henry, I can't afford to go there."

After another long, thoughtful pull on his cigar, he smiled at Daddy and said to me: "What say I give you a choice. I can give you the money to go to this Pasadena Warehouse..."

"Playhouse..." I said interrupting and correcting him at the same time.

"Right, Pasadena Playhouse. I can give you the money to go there, or I can give you your own car. Which would you like to have?"

I was dumbfounded. "For real?" He shook his head yes.

I thought about it for a second or two and answered: "I'll take the car."

Well, he let out the biggest laugh you ever heard. It practically made the restaurant shake with delight. He then said: "Ok, little lady the car it is." Mother just looked at me with a confused expression.

I said to her and everyone there: "Well the Playhouse would be great but if I had a car right now I could get to more auditions and possibly get working faster."

Maybe the Pasadena Playhouse would have been a smarter choice in the long run. After all, it had worked wonders for Raymond Burr, Ernest Borgnine, and Eleanor Parker so why not me? The question will have to remain unanswered as I was going for the car.

Uncle Henry completely agreed with my decision and a week later the car was delivered to our house, just for me. It wasn't a new car mind you, but the radio worked and it would get me around town just fine. Thank you Uncle Henry.

I was young, naïve, and scared but eager to get out there and audition towards that elusive role of a lifetime. Before you can even get an interview with the people that make the casting decisions in Hollywood, you need an agent. Daddy suggested I meet with his agent Sam Armstrong, who was also representing one of my hero's in the business, the wonderfully talented Mitzi Gaynor. After seeing my short resume and what I could do, Sam took me on as a client and I was off to the races, kind of. Sam was a former vaudevillian with an act called *Armstrong & Phelps: The Boys From Hollywood.* I think they were a song and dance act, but I'm not too sure. He had a lot of contacts in the business and that was a must for a good agent. His daughter is actress Jackie Rusell. She starred opposite Walter Matthau and Inger Stevens in *A Guide for the Married Man* in 1967. We would eventually work on a lot of the same shows but on different episodes.

Acting jobs were tough to come by in the beginning because I still had a lot to prove. I had to convince the producers and directors that I was good enough. There were many days when I had to convince myself that I was good enough, but no matter what was blocking my path I never lost sight of my dreams.

After numerous auditions, a couple of paying offers came in from the acting world. I was thrilled to say the least. I was able to do a number of live theatre pieces including a part in the San Bernardino Light Opera production of the musical *The King and I* with Marni Nixon in 1958. Oh man, I was working in a show with Marni Nixon, how lucky was I?

You've not heard of her? Well, let me introduce you. She was, and is, the world's greatest ghost singer. Whenever an actor or actress couldn't sing a part in the movies, they hired a ghost singer to come in and dub their singing voice onto the soundtrack. Prior to 1958, Marni had lent her voice to Margaret O'Brien in *The Secret Garden*, Jeanne Crain in *Cheaper By The Dozen*, and sang part of a line for Marilyn Monroe in *Gentlemen Prefer Blondes*. She also sang for Deborah Kerr in *An Affair To Remember* and again for Ms. Kerr in the 1956 movie version of *The King and I*. In the live production we did in San Bernardino, Marni was front and center as Anna and she was great. I found her to be a classy and gracious lady to work with.

After the show closed, Marni went on to become the singing voice of Natalie Wood in *West Side Story* and later as Audrey Hepburn's singing voice in *My Fair Lady*. She was also in *The Sound of Music*. Not just her voice this time, but herself as an actress. She played Sister Sophia in the movie and what a great job she did. Audiences could finally see the lady with the voice they knew so well.

The River of Work

In the Hollywood of the late 50's and early 60's there seemed to be a never ending flow of show business opportunity running right down the center of Hollywood Blvd.

It was like an energetic, streaming river filled with TV shows, movies, producers, hot properties, investors, directors, actors and almost any other kind of an entertainment prospect you could imagine. Let's just call it "The Hollywood River of Work".

Money, not water, kept everything afloat. You couldn't just wade into this river; you had to be invited. The trick was to dance, sing and hold up a big sign at the side of the river and maybe you'd get invited in. Sometimes people would just dive in head first and naked without knowing how deep or how shallow the river was. They would generally hurt themselves, or they would get tossed out of the river pretty fast, not knowing who they were anymore.

Others would bundle themselves up as a cannonball and jump high in the air, making a big splash in the middle of the river. Sometimes the river liked a big splash, sometimes it didn't. The one sure thing was that if the river did like you, you could float from project to project for either a short while, or for a very long time depending on the currents.

I wanted into that river and was doing everything I could to get invited in. Auditioning was the path to the river.

I would now like to introduce you to auditioning 101 as it was known in the late 1950's Hollywood. Auditioning for a role could be grueling and demeaning at times. For those that have never experienced it, here's what you could expect at an audition.

Hollywood casting directors would put the word out that they were looking for someone for a particular role in a TV show or a movie. The word went out to all the Hollywood agents. Your agent would find out what the casting directors were looking for, then would call you and say: "You'd be perfect for the part."

Even if you were not perfect for the part, they would say it anyway as they liked to hedge their bets on you so that would get their commission. The agent was gambling that by some miracle the casting people would love you so much that they would forget what they were looking for in the first place, and give you the part. I think it was called wishful thinking.

Your agent would arrange an audition for you. The audition would usually be booked on the day that you needed to be at your day job, so you would call in sick. (The audition will not move for you, you must always move for the audition). Sometimes, it was booked on your only day off, when you had a lot of other very important things planned to do. It's called Murphy's Law. (I think Murphy was once a casting director.)

Let's assume for a moment that you were right for the part.

On the audition day, you would arrive at the place of the audition and immediately notice that there were a lot of girls in a small cramped waiting room that look just like you. Some look exactly as you do, right down to the exact same shade of lipstick. That's ok, don't panic you're in the right place and you at least have a shot at the part.

Now if, on the other hand, the waiting room is full of girls that don't look like you at all, then you are either in the wrong waiting room or your agent is desperate for a commission and is sending you on anything that comes across his desk. Either way, you should just leave as you don't have a shot at the part.

Once again, assume you are in the right place... In the waiting room, you are handed some paper with printed words that you must quickly memorize. These words are called scripted lines, or sides, and usually come with a small and sometimes useless description of the character you'll be playing. It may read: Elsie Roberts (She is of medium build. She is blond with one earlobe longer than the other.)

As you are trying to decide which earlobe is the longer one, you begin to memorize and work on your sides, and so is everyone else. Some people are yelling, some are laughing, some are crying, and since it's all about choice some are trying a thousand different ways to say the same line. Like: "Excuse me sir, is that your monkey?" "Ex-Cuse ME sir, is that YOUR mon-KEY?"

You must, somehow, learn to block them and their noise out so that you can now do the exact same thing that they are doing.

Once it is your turn to enter the actual audition room you will be greeted by any number of strangers sitting behind a big table. They look horribly bored and totally unimpressed to meet you. You must smile at them anyway; treat them like old, lost friends. Try to look thrilled to be there, and enthusiastic to win them over. (See the acting process has already started.)

Unbeknownst to you is the fact that they had already made their minds up about you before you walked into the room. They were going to make you jump through the hoops anyway.

It's all good practice for you, or so your agent will tell you later when you don't get the part. If there is only one person in the audition room and he asks you to sit down and make yourself comfortable on the big comfy couch while he mixes you both a couple of drinks, you should run like hell. They will not be using you for the part. However they may try to use some of your parts for other things, so again I say; "run like hell."

When you get home from the audition, your agent will call you and ask how you did and you'll say that you think that you blew it. He will tell you; "That's not possible as you are too talented for that to happen." Just when you think he will give you more praise and love, to help heal your fragile, bruised and battered ego, he says that he has another call coming in and he has to go. As you hear a click on the other end of the line, you can't help but wonder how different that click may have sounded if you actually had one earlobe longer than the other.

You will then wait a very long period of time to see if you get a callback. A callback means you did something right at the audition and they want to see you again. (You will never know what you did right, so don't ask.) If your agent calls you about the callback, you get to return to the audition room and do it all over again for the same people that are trying to remember you from the last time you were there.

This time there will only be about five or ten girls in the waiting room that look like you. Some are still wearing the same shade of lipstick as you. This time at least four of them are wearing the same outfit that you are wearing.

Since there are only five or ten girls in the waiting room, your odds just got a whole lot better.

After this, you will go home again and continue waiting to hear from your agent.

Should you actually get the part, your agent will call to let you know the great news. However, that will be about a month or two after your audition and you will have forgotten all about it by then. Just act like you know what they are talking about.

The best quote I've heard in the past from a number of actors is: "The most important thing for an actor is honesty. And once you learn how to fake that, you've got it made."

When auditioning, I was the kind of person that wanted to, please people and to have them like me. There was one line that I've always wanted to use but could never find the right fit during the audition. It might work best in a scenario like this:

I would walk into an audition room with a bunch of pompous "Studio Suits" that are still wet behind the ears, sitting behind a long table. They didn't do their homework to know who I was. Each one of them has a picture of me and a copy of my resume. They are all looking very important and humorless, when one of them looks up and asks the same old question that they always ask: "So tell us Cynthia, what have you done lately?"

I would then answer: "About what?"

I've always wanted to answer that way, but I just don't think they would get it.

The rejections I got from auditions were hard for me. It's difficult not to take them as a personal affront. It's just the way I'm wired. Still I had to get out there, get seen, get rejected and hopefully somewhere along the line, with a whole lot of luck, I just might land a role and turn it into something fantastic. That is how the system works.

My first few roles in Hollywood were less than fantastic, but I was working and that was the main thing. The income from each and every job was much appreciated by a young girl that ironed clothes for a living.

The first television part I got was on a show called Divorce Court. As you can guess, it was a show about cases that involved divorcing couples. The actors would reenact the day in court from some real life cases. On my episode, I was cast as the daughter of a couple that was getting divorced.

They gave us our characters and a loose outline with key points that we had to hit, but the rest was up to us. Not too scary for a little girl's first TV experience now was it? It was explained that they could stop filming if they had to, but they'd rather continue right through.

I loved my day in court and the producers were happy with my performance. It gave me a lot of confidence. I thought: "If I could do that without much of a script, and without stopping the recording process, think of what I could do with a full script and the ability to stop tape."

My resume was slowly building which meant that I had a toe in the river of work, but would that be enough to keep me and my career afloat?

Mother & Daddy

Since I was still living at home at this point, I want to explain what my life was like as a young woman. First of all I've never felt like a "young woman". I'm not sure why but I've always felt like a young girl, an ingénue if you will.

I've met many women that had an air of sophistication, or even sexiness, about them. In my mind, I've always felt more like a girl. I know that's an odd mindset. I think that's why I've always had a playful nature as a person and so have most of the characters I've played through the years. I thank Mother and Daddy for that mindset. It's a lighthearted one and I enjoy it. Its childlike at times but not childish.

As an actor, you have to be playful, fearless, and willing to attempt almost anything. Mother taught me to enjoy life, to love, and to play within the rules. Daddy taught me to enjoy life, to love, and to play without the rules… To a degree. He also told us to; "Do as I say and not as I do."

Mother, on the other hand, would attempt to lead us by example. One of her favorite, philosophical sayings that she would impart to me was a line from Shakespeare's, Hamlet: "…to thine own self be true." I've always thought these words to mean: be truthful in life, in your work and to yourself. The other lessons that both my parents taught me were sharing and the value of friendship. Hey, I shared a bedroom for the first fifteen years of my life, so I know sharing.

This philosophy of shared love and friendship was always demonstrated at our house during the holidays, those times when families would gather together like Easter, the Fourth of July, Halloween, Thanksgiving and certainly Christmas. Mother and Daddy made sure that our family spirit was extended to all. I'll tell you about Christmas in particular, but it was the same for all the holidays.

The spirit of giving at our house was never more alive than in and around December 25th. There would always be a number of showbiz friends of Mother and Daddy that would be down on their luck, with no place to go during the holidays. They would always be invited to come spend that time with us. We would be up early opening our presents, and later in the day our guests would arrive for dinner and lots of merriment. During the year if we had a couple of extra dollars at any time we would buy gifts for them. We never knew who was coming, but there were always gifts waiting for them.

Mother would take the gifts that we accumulated through the year, put them in a big pillow case, and hand the pillowcase around. We called it the grab bag. Each one of our guests could reach in and pull out one gift. The pillowcase would keep circling around the guests until all the gifts were gone. There were about ten gifts for each person. It wouldn't be anything expensive because we were also just getting by. There would be useful items like socks, ties, stationary, pens, and t-shirts. On the surface, the gifts may have seemed trivial, but oh how their eyes would light up when they saw their new presents. The gifts allowed them to feel like they were part of the family, albeit a dysfunctional family, but a family none the less. Later, we would share our dinner with these one-time greats of the entertainment world and have a heck of a celebration afterwards.

I know that we all have to shoulder some blame when life doesn't go our way, but no matter the fault it was just a sad thing to see happen to anyone. The one great thing I learned from these wonderful, shared Christmases is that no matter what your lot in life, try to find the happiness of each day share it and embrace it. Now you know why my father answered the phone "Hello, House of Good Sheppard." At times, it really was that kind of house.

Just so you understand, and as I mentioned earlier, not all of these get-togethers ended in perfect harmony. The good and virtuous intentions of these celebrations could go south very quickly. The equation I like to work with is that History + Alcohol combined with something we will just call "the stress factor" = Drama. I wasn't immune to this result myself. It could be from a house guest, but there were times when it came from my sister Patty.

When it came to booze, both my parents drank a lot but I could take it or leave it. Mostly I left it. Thank God the taste for alcohol gene skipped me, but it certainly didn't skip Patty. She loved to drink. Just like Daddy. She would eventually become a functioning alcoholic later in life.

At some of these parties, she would get on a toot and say snide and hurtful things to me. I really didn't know what these random comments were stemming from. I'd try to defend myself, but she just wouldn't stop. There were times when I would be the one crying and leaving the party in a hurry. People would say; "pay no mind, it's just the alcohol talking", but I knew that there had to be some basis to her words and feelings. Mind you, these incidents didn't happen all the time, but enough to really hurt me. They would leave me wondering what I might have done to her, for her to resent me so much. Alcohol doesn't create feelings that are not already there, it just brings existing problems to the surface.

Sometimes she would bring her roommate Carol to the parties. They had been living together in the same court as us. After Patty got a snoot full, she would sometimes attack Carol in front of everyone. This became very embarrassing for everyone. I never understood why she was so angry at me, or Carol, or even the world for that matter. If I asked her what the problem was, she'd just say: "You'll never understand. You don't know anything."

I know that I was naive about certain things at that age, but I wasn't stupid. I wish I could have found a way to communicate with her, and to get closer to the sister that I wished for. I had hoped that she could find a way to communicate without animosity, but she never did and that's the way it was. It is difficult for most people to accept the things they cannot change, and Patty was no exception.

Chapter 11

I'm Getting Married In The Morning

After my live TV experience, I went back to my normal life of drama classes, dance instruction, auditions and odd jobs to pay for my lessons. Unknown to me my "normal" life was just about to get a whole lot more interesting.

After high school, Peter Virgo and I had broken up as a couple but remained friends. I had been dating another fellow named George, but I never thought of it as anything too serious. When he went back to Ohio, I figured that we were over as a couple and that I was available to meet and date other people.

I was still thinking of Ivan and wondering if he would ever return. I knew in my heart of hearts that he wouldn't be back in my life anytime soon. A friend of my Mother's that lived in the same court as we did, suggested that I go out with her friend's son. I thought that it was a bad idea but then I figured: "What the heck. What have I got to lose?"

All I knew about my blind date was that he worked in production at the Warner Brothers Studio and that his name was Mervyn Edwards, but everybody called him Buck.

We met for our first date and right away I was smitten. He was three years older than me, nice looking, funny, with a bit of an edge to his personality. He loved to party, but he also loved to entertain others. He was very attentive towards me and I liked that.

We had the movie business in common so the conversations flowed nicely. He had been in the movie business since he was a kid. His father, who had passed away some years earlier, had been the prop master at Warner Brothers Studio for nineteen years. His father's best friend, and Buck's god-father was movie director Mervyn LeRoy. (*Gone With the Wind* and *Wizard of Oz*.) When he was a kid Buck worked as a go-fer for his father, out of the prop trailer. Eventual he got his own job working there.

After a few more dates Buck, really grew on me, as did the thought of marriage. I think I fell in love with the notion of being a bride, a wife and maybe someday, a mother. Now I could find out what love was really about. You see, I was still a virgin and was so incredibly curious about what came next in a physical relationship, but I would never act upon these feelings out of wedlock. It's certainly an antiquated notion now but very much alive back then. You have to keep in mind that there was no sex education class in school, and my parents never had "the talk" with me or Patty. Civilized people just didn't talk about that kind of thing back then. All I knew at the time was that Buck was the guy for me.

One night, at a restaurant somewhere near Hollywood and Vine, Buck looked at me and with a serious face asked: "Will you marry me?" There was nothing particularly romantic about it. At least he didn't preface the question with; "Well here goes nothing." There were no flowers, or an engagement ring in the bottom of a champagne flute, and he didn't drop to one knee. It was just a straight forward question, so I gave him a straight forward answer: "Yes."

In the words of Chubby Checker, "here comes the twist." Remember George? Oddly enough, about a month after Buck and I were engaged, George, the guy I had been dating before Buck, came back from Ohio. He was shocked to find that I had moved on. I got the feeling that maybe he wanted to marry me too. I explained that I didn't feel the same way towards him as he did for me. Also, he had left without giving me any indication of a future together.

I know that I hurt him that day, but that's what happens when you break up with someone? George was a great guy and I felt terrible for him as I could see that I had broken his heart. I cried that night, knowing that I had hurt someone because I don't like to hurt anyone.

It was almost like something out of a sitcom script. I went from having no fellows to marry and now I had two.

At that moment, I felt good about my decision to be with Buck. However, as time went on I did wonder how different my life would have been with George.

It was a whirlwind courtship filled with the kind of fun and adventure that I was looking for. After six or seven months of being swept off my feet with parties, dinners, movies and generally having the time of my life, Buck and I were married on April 17th, 1960. I was nineteen and a half years old, and now a married woman.

My wedding dress was designed and made for me by a wonderful man named Howard Shoup. He had made gowns for *The Jazz Singer, The Eddie Cantor Story, The Young Philadelphians, Ocean's Eleven* and now for me. He would go on to be nominated for five Academy Awards later in his life but on this day he won the Pepper Award for making me feel so beautiful in his design.

We were married at the Methodist Church in Glendale, CA. I can still remember my proud Daddy walking me down the aisle, (or were we dancing?) to give me away. It was a great ceremony and a fantastic reception. The band was playing, the alcohol was flowing and there was just too much fun happening in one room. I'm sure that Daddy got up at one point and did a song or two with the band. Mother was dancing and showing the rest of us how to do it. I was too busy socializing with all our guests to really take it all in. The whole event went by in a flash.

We didn't have a lot of money for the honeymoon so our plan was to just drive down the coast to a hotel in Carmel. However, we spent our first night at the beautiful Beverly Hills Hotel. It was a gorgeous, ornate place with all the services that you could imagine. All the stars went to The Beverly Hills, (with or without their spouses.)

Well, the big exciting night was here at last. We were in our hotel room and with our heads still spinning from the reception and champagne we began to make love.

Finally, all my questions would be answered.

"Are there fireworks? Will I be floating around the room on a cloud of warmth and love? Do the Heavens open up as the Angels sing…?"

Then finally the big moment had arrived… And then it disappeared.

I thought: "Is that it? Is this what I'd been waiting for all these years? Did I just miss something? Cut! Print! That's a Lily!"

After our honeymoon, I learned more disappointing news. Newlyweds don't get to live in a beautiful castle in the sky right away. We did move into a place that was a little in the sky, but it was no castle. It turned out to be an apartment above Buck's parent's garage. Talk about living with the in-laws. We did have our own space, but it was still a little too close to the in-laws for me. I got along pretty well with Buck's stepfather Jim, but his mother, Estelle would prove to be a little less in my corner than I was first lead to believe.

I spent days decorating that tiny apartment the best I could with what little we had, went to auditions and dreamed of the day that we would be moving out. Maybe we'd never have a castle but we could at least strive for something with less gas and carbon monoxide seeping through the floorboards.

In 1960, I got the part of a Malt Shop Girl on a new TV show called *The Many Loves Of Dobie Gillis*. The episode was titled, *Dobie Spreads A Rumor*. It was shot at 20th Century Fox Studios. The show starred Dwayne Hickman as Dobie Gillis and Bob Denver as the strangest beatnik that you'll ever meet, Maynard G. Krebs. (Bob would later become known to the world as Gilligan on *Gilligan's Island*, but that was still a few years away.)

Both Dwayne and Bob were great guys to work with. The set was professional but also a lot of fun to work on. There was no live audience to play to, except the crew, so the laughs were flown in later in editing. Sometimes you had to pause a bit before your next line to allow room for the laughs to be put in later. It was the way most sitcoms were done at the time and I got into the groove of things pretty quickly. Dwayne and Bob were both very funny people so it was a great experience.

The character of Dobie was described as such: "Dobie Gillis is an average teenager living in an average Central City..."

Well, if that was the case then Dwayne was the oldest average teenager I'd ever seen. When the series started in 1959, Dwayne was already 25 years old. The series ran until 1963 at which point he would have been 29... and you thought Dick Clark was the world's oldest teenager.

My next two jobs came in the form of dramatic roles and both were for the same program. The TV show was produced by Warner Brothers and called Bourbon Street Beat. The show starred Van Williams, Richard Long and Andrew Duggan. Bourbon Street Beat was set in New Orleans and it never ceased to amaze me how much Stage 14 of the Warner Brothers Burbank Studio could look so much like New Orleans. Now that was Hollywood magic.

Van Williams was just your run of the mill drop-jaw gorgeous Hollywood heartthrob. Trust me when I say that he was even better looking in person. You may remember his big claim to fame that would come about six years later when he starred as Britt Reid on the TV series The Green Hornet.

The first episode I was in on Bourbon Street was called: The Deadly Persuasion. I played the part of the applicant. (What was I applying for? I don't remember.) It wasn't a really big role, but I must have done something right as they had me back in less than a month to play another character with a bigger part.

The second episode was called: Interrupted Wedding. This time I played the part of the bridesmaid and I had plenty to do in this role. I was able to apply a lot more of my skills with this character, but I was still learning a lot as I went along. I watched the crew, the director and the other actors making it all work. I was like a sponge. It was starting to feel like I was up to both ankles in the river now and it felt warm and good.

My next job was on the hit TV series *77 Sunset Strip* starring Edd Byrnes, Roger Smith and Efrem Zimbalist Jr. This was filmed at the Burbank Warner Brothers Studio.

The show was about a couple of wisecracking private detectives that had an office at 77 Sunset Strip in Los Angeles. Right next door to their office was a very expensive and flashy restaurant where Kookie, (Edd Byrnes) worked as a hip talking valet. Sometimes Kookie would help the P.I.'s solve crimes. He was the coolest character on TV in those days.

The episode I was in was called: *Attic*. Lee Van Cleef had a bit part in this episode but would go on to be one of the great movie villains of all time in movies like *The Good, The Bad, and The Ugly* and *For A Few Dollars More*. He was a very good actor because when he was not in character he was such a nice guy on the set.

Edd Byrnes was the one that really stole the show as Kookie. He is a great example of what a little stage business with a comb can help create when in the right hands. His hip patter and style made him one of televisions first teen idols. He and Connie Stevens even recorded a song called *Kookie, Kookie, Lend Me Your Comb* that became a very big hit. In later years, I was glad to see him make a comeback when he played Vince Fontaine in the movie *Grease*.

This was turning out to be a very good year and I was thrilled with the amount of work I was getting in my chosen profession. I was up to my knees in the warm river, and it was all happening so quickly.

I finished off 1960 in a very scary way… Well, TV scary that is. I was on a TV show called *Thriller*: It was a crime-drama-horror show for lack of a better way to describe it.

It was shot at CBS Studio Center, Studio City, LA. The episode was called *The Fatal Impulse*. It starred Boris Karloff, Robert Lansing and Whitney Blake. I played the part of the receptionist. (A bit of trivia: if you watch the elevator scene you'll see a young Mary Tyler Moore as one of the women in the elevator.)

I can still remember standing in the unemployment line with Mary not long before that episode. I don't think she's had to stand in that line for a long time now. Like I've always said to visitors that come to Hollywood; "…a good place to see the stars in Hollywood is at the airport and the unemployment line."

I was jumping from TV project to TV project and in between I was trying to be a good wife by making Buck his dinner at night and breakfast in the morning. I tried the best I could to make our 'apartment above the cars' into a decent home. As if life wasn't busy enough, I had also enrolled in LACC - Los Angeles City College. I was taking psychology and drama. I was doing it all, except sleeping.

Bucks mother, Estelle, wasn't exactly making things easy for me. She was the family matriarch and could be quite domineering. Her new husband, Jim, was a good man and an obedient spouse. She was always interfering in the domestic side of my life. She strongly suggested that I not only iron Bucks shirts and pants but also his underwear, socks and undershirts. I'm not making this up. Estelle was a feisty Mexican lady and could be passionate about everything including un-ironed undergarments. How silly was that?

She also said I should iron the bed sheets, towels, and pillow cases. Guess what, I did them all. I was a new nineteen year old wife / homemaker and I wanted to do a good job. I was lead to believe by her that this was all part of the job. Mind you I didn't remember my mother doing any of this. I guess that I was so new to married life that I allowed myself to be intimidated by her. Since she lived so close to us, a surprise inspection could happen at any time. I figured it was easier to do what she said rather than risk the confrontation that we would have if I didn't. Just go with the flow. Swimming upstream was tough enough in the Hollywood river without adding stress at home. If you've ever been uncomfortable with an in-law, then you know what I'm talking about. Feel free to insert all and any mother-in-law jokes here.

Buck and I appreciated the cheap rent we paid for our garage rooftop paradise, but I was praying for the day that we could make enough money to get our own place. I dreamed of a space of our own without any influence or interference. Buck was bringing in a regular paycheck, but it was not a very big one, and my paychecks were sporadic to say the least. Just when it looked as though we were going to spend our whole lives living above automobiles, the miracle of all miracles happened.

Chapter 12

My Three Sons

One lovely morning my Agent Sam called to say that there might be some steady work for me. He said that it looked like a really choice part on a new sitcom that was picked up by the ABC Network. It starred Fred MacMurray, Tim Considine, Don Grady, Stanley Livingston, and William Frawley. It was called *My Three Sons.*

The general synopsis for the show went like this. Fred MacMurray played the widower Steve Douglas, who has to bring up three boys all by himself… Almost by himself. He does get help from his housekeeper Michael Francis "Bub" O'Casey played by William Frawley. The sons were Mike Douglas played by Tim Considine, Robbie Douglas played by Don Grady and Chip Douglas played by Stanley Livingston. There was another family member that would often steal the scene and his name was Tramp; he was the lovable family dog.

In 1960, a show on TV about a single parent family was a pretty progressive project. But the groundbreaking owners of Desilu, (Desi Arnaz and Lucille Ball) were just the right people to bring the subject to light. *The Andy Griffith Show* would be the second TV sitcom they would do it with. *My Three Sons* had been on the air for a couple of months when my agent, Sam, called. He said that they were trying to put a family together to be the next door neighbors to the Douglas's and that they wanted me to audition for the part of Jean Pearson. She was the teenage daughter of the family next door and was to be the love interest of the oldest son, Mike. Best of all it was a regular part, not just a one shot appearance.

Since we only had one car at the time, a sporty MG, I drove Buck to work as I did most days and then continued on to the set of *My Three Sons* at Desilu Studios. I pulled up to the gates and gave the security guard my name. He looked up my name on a huge list that would dwarf Santa's list in December and said: "Oh yes. Welcome Miss Pepper."

He then proceeded to give me directions to my meeting place. After parking on the lot I was escorted to the trailer of the director, Peter Tewksbury, for the audition.

Mr. Tewksbury had directed a number of TV shows before this one including *The People's Choice* starring Jackie Cooper and Patricia Breslin and *Father Knows Best* starring Robert Young and Jane Wyatt. Needless to say, I was a nervous wreck about meeting Mr. Tewksbury. The possibility of getting a large part in a TV show that had the legs to go on for a long while also had me nervous and excited. This would be the biggest part that I had tried out for to date.

When I was ushered into his trailer I was greeted by Mr. Tewksbury, and his assistant, with a big smile and a handshake. As he spoke he reminded me of what I thought a powerful older man should look like and behave. I thought that he was around my father's age, but the opposite of my father in many ways. Daddy was always scatter brained when it came to business whereas Mr. Tewksbury looked like he was organizing a big, yet complicated party, and he was doing it well. He looked and acted as a man in charge.

I figured that my audition for this part was just one of many because I was sure that every actress in town wanted the role. Well, it's not like they're just going to give it to me on the first reading, right? I kept my new marital status to myself as I was auditioning to play a teenager and I didn't want to be perceived as too old for the role. During the reading, my emotions were all over the place, but I was able to keep my excitement down to a dull roar on the outside. I felt like I had the entire three ring circus of Barnum and Bailey performing in my stomach. I didn't know how many girls they looked at before I auditioned, but after reading a number of lines from a script, and answering a few of his questions, Mr. Tewksbury looked at me smiled and said: "Well… I think we have our family."

He was referring to the Douglas's next door family, the Pearson's. After hearing him say those words, I was as high as a kite.

Usually at the end of an audition they say something like: "Thank you, someone will be in touch", or "Don't let the door hit you on the way out", or my favorite "Don't call us, we'll call you." This was beyond my wildest expectations. Right then and there I had a new name, Jean Pearson.

With so many fantastic thoughts racing through my mind I quickly jumped into Buck's MG and started my drive home. On the way home I was thinking about my new role, how this would help our financial situation, and how happy Buck would be to hear the great news. Maybe we could get out of the tiny apartment, away from the in-laws and that O' de La'Garage smell. I was so excited, in fact, that while I was driving home I almost ran over a guy at a stop sign. The operative word here is almost. I slammed on the brakes and screeched to a stop in plenty of time, but it shocked the heck out of both of us. As the rattled pedestrian walked across the street, I rolled down my window and with a big smile on my face I yelled: "Sorry!" He just looked at me and yelled back: "Lady, are you crazy?" He was right for asking because I was crazy, crazy with happiness.

I thought that I would feel uncomfortable during my first day on the set of My Three Son's because I was the new kid on the block. On the contrary, every actor, and crew member made me feel right at home. The show was a joy to work on and a number of people from that cast and crew have remained friends to this day.

The atmosphere on the set was influenced by its star, Fred MacMurray, and it was a very conservative feel all around. William Frawley, best known for his role as Fred Mertz from the *I Love Lucy* television show, always tried to lighten things up when he could. Bill, as we called him, was a very good friend of Daddy's. He called Bill up before my first day on the set and told him to watch out for me, and he sure did. He watched everyone that approached me on that first day, and he personally made sure that I felt welcomed by the cast and crew. I enjoyed going to lunch with Bill every day at a little restaurant across the street from the studio, aptly called Lucy's El Adobe Cafe.

(This was not owned by the Arnaz's in spite of its name.) Bill was a very down to earth guy, much like Daddy, and he had lots of great road stories to tell. We would vary our choices from the menu each day, but Bill always had a few nips with lunch before heading back to work. He had the same love of distilled spirits that Daddy had. However, he never got drunk or out of control. He and Daddy always said that the Irish are able to hold their liquor well. I guess he would now be called a functioning alcoholic, but back then he was just called Bill. I miss Bill and our time together. I would give almost anything to have just one more lunch with him.

Fred MacMurray was a big movie star at the time and carried a lot of weight around the studio. I think calling him frugal would be an understatement. Every day he would bring his own lunch from home in a brown paper bag. Some folks referred to him as "the thrifty multimillionaire". He would come to the set, do his work and leave. He wasn't one to stick around, or to get chummy with anyone in the cast or crew. I personally found him to be a nice man and very professional, but he was just there to do the job and get back to his real life. He even had it built into his contract that he only had to work about thirteen weeks a year on the show. This kind of contract was unheard of at the time. This meant that all his scenes, in every episode, would be shot first so that he could get back to his life on the ranch with his family, and the cattle he was raising. It was the perfect situation for him, considering the chance he was taking. As an established movie star, and with TV being the small screen of Hollywood, he wanted to keep his career options open.

When he was gone, the rest of the cast would find themselves working with stand-ins that would say Fred's lines off camera so that they could do their scenes. At one point, they even had a stage hand holding a long mop in front of the actors so that they could get the correct height of Fred's head and it would look like they were making eye contact. This was very helpful for the other actors on the show, but can you just imagine the kind of acting chops it would take to make a scene work while talking to a mop? For a chuckle the next time you see a rerun of the show and the scene is with Fred, but it's a close up of another actor talking to Fred, just picture a mop. I guarantee it will make you smile.

If I had to use one word to describe Fred, it would be "polite". According to TV Guide, Fred's character, Steven Douglas placed 7th in TV Guides "50 Greatest TV Dads of All Time". This was better than Ozzie Nelson's showing in the 21st position. All I can say is that was some good TV fathering for only thirteen weeks a year.

I had a lot of scenes with Tim Considine. Since I was playing his girlfriend on the show, the public would always speculate whether we were an item or not. I'm here to tell you that we were not. I was a happy newlywed and Tim was very happy with his girlfriend. Buck and I would often double date with Tim and his girlfriend, which must have kept the press guessing. Tim was very professional and so very nice to me. We hit it off right from the start.

Tim Considine was a joy to work with on My Three Sons.

(Cynthia Pepper Collection)

Tim was a very successful child actor with a lot of past work at Disney under his belt. *(The Adventures of Spin & Marty, The Hardy Boys*, and *The Shaggy Dog*.) We were both 20 when we started working together. He had a lot of drive, but was also very generous as an actor and as a human being. Tim's grandfather was Alexander Pantages, founder of the Pantages Theater chain that helped propel Vaudeville to popularity back in the day. I think that a lot of Tim's drive might have come from his grandfather's legacy.

Once they had aired a couple of my episodes, the producers asked Tim and me to make a public appearance at a stock car race in Texas. I didn't feel like a huge celebrity or anything special, but they asked me to do this and I thought: "sure I'd love an all-expense paid trip back to Texas. I'll come along for the ride and watch Tim with all his fans." When we arrived at the airport in Texas, a man in a nice suit welcomed us and said: "Your ride to the race track is waiting for you so we have to go now."

"Now?" I asked. "Can't we go to the Hotel first to freshen up?"

"No," he said with a smile. I thought to myself; that's ok I can freshen up a little in the car along the way. He then led us from the plane back towards the tarmac.

I asked: "Isn't the airport terminal that way?"

"Yes." He confirmed, "But the helicopter is this way."

"Helicopter?" I said in amazement. "No one said anything about a helicopter!"

As we piled into the chopper, I thought that this was a first for me, and prayed to God that I would be around later to talk about it. As we approached the stock car track I asked: "Where are we going to land?"

The pilot responded with: "The racing track. I'm going to put us down right on the track."

"Of course you are." I retorted.

When we arrived at the track, the stands were filled with thousands of drag racing fans. Tim and I weren't sure what it was that we'd be doing and I was feeling way out of my element. We were told that we would be driving in a stock car around the race track. We each got into a separate car and were then driven around the track. With all the windy modes of transportation that day, planes, choppers and automobiles, I knew that having a good hair day was right out of the question. I'd only been on the show a few weeks so I was sure that no one would know my face, let alone my name. As we drove around the track, they announced over the loudspeaker system that we were from the *My Three Sons* television show and the crowd cheered a deafening cheer of delight. I had never heard a crowd noise like that in my life and that was after the loud helicopter ride just a few minutes before. A few seconds later they announced our names and the noise that came from the crowd seemed twice as loud as the first one. I yelled to my driver: "What do we do?"

The driver just smiled back at me and said: "Start waving."

I started waving and the crowd cheered again. It is such a humbling and indescribable feeling to experience that appreciation and love from so many strangers. After that they rushed Tim and me to a tent for a quick interview with the press. What an amazing, crazy, fun day. I was so glad that I got to share it all with my friend Tim.

I didn't get to know Don Grady as well as I knew Tim because most of my scenes were with Tim. I liked Don a lot and he was a multitalented guy. He had a lot of experience in acting before becoming Robbie Douglas. He was a child performer at Disney working with the original *Mousketeers*. Yes, he was with Annette Funicello and the gang. He was a fine actor, very professional, and his skills didn't stop at acting. He was also a writer and a musician. He would eventually go on to write two episodes for *My Three Sons*, and also compose music for the show. Later in his career he would write music for two of Blake Edwards films *Switch*, and *Skin Deep*. He even wrote the theme music for the *Phil Donahue Show*. An interesting bit of trivia about Don is that, in 1967, he was in a band called *The Yellow Balloon*. He played the drums and sang. So as to not take away from the band or their music he would always wear a disguise of sorts at their appearances. Their big song was a sun-shiny hit called *Yellow Balloon*.

Stan Livingston was the perfect child actor to play Chip. He was just about the cutest little blond headed boy I had ever seen. He was a fun loving kid on and off the set, but also very precocious. He could hit his mark and deliver his lines better than most child actors his age. I was 20 years old and he was 10 when I first met him. He had some great lines portraying an innocence that only an inquisitive little boy could deliver. He had already gained a wealth of acting experience having been in a couple of movies including *Please Don't Eat The Daisy's* with Doris Day and David Niven, *How The West Was Won* with Debbie Reynolds and *The Adventures Of Ozzie and Harriet*. After *My Three Sons,* he went on to write, direct, edit and produce other projects. He's now a very well-known and sought after artist with his own art gallery. Stan is a very talented guy and he is one of my closest friends to this day.

Here's some more trivia, did you know that Stan and Fred McMurray were the only actors to appear in every episode of the *My Three Sons* series? After 12 years that's a lot of camera time. Physically Stan logged a lot more "On Set" time than Fred did but I don't think Stan would trade that experience for anything.

I'm proud of Stan, and his real life brother Barry Livingston, (he played Ernie Douglas), for making it through life as child stars in Hollywood.

We all know the horror stories about child actors that have fallen by the wayside, but the Livingston brothers are one of the exceptions. They were able to make it through that Hollywood river of showbiz without getting towed under, and both went on to become productive and terrifically talented people.

One day, while we were working on the set, it was announced that one of the shows sponsors, General Motors, would be there to meet with the cast. I wasn't sure if this was good news or bad. The show was doing well in the ratings so I was pretty sure we weren't about to be canceled. When the people from GM arrived at the end of the working day, we were told how grateful they were to be the sponsors of such a great and successful show. As a reward for our hard work, we would each be getting a new car. I was stunned. Did I hear them correctly? I guess I did as they handed out keys to the cast. I was never so happy to have a driver's license in my life. A new car! We later found out that the cars were not ours to keep but that we would have the use of them for a year. I was still thrilled. A free car for a year is fine by me. Now Buck wouldn't have to loan me his MG anymore. I wouldn't have to drive him to work every morning and pick him up at the end of the day. He'd be as thrilled as I was, at least for a year.

Things were sure improving in my life and career at this point. I was a happily married woman working at my dream job. I was grateful and loving every minute of my life. Things, however, were not as good for my folks. From 1956 through to 1960 the strain was getting worse at home for my parents.

Mother's job at the Broadway Hollywood made her the only consistent breadwinner. My father's income throughout the year was pretty small and what he did make was not in the bank for very long. He still had a hunger for the ponies and a need to socialize with his much more successful friends. It took a good stack of cash to keep up with those fellows. I'm sure his friends like Jackie Gleason, Bob Hope and Phil Harris would cover some of his expenses while he was with them, but Daddy would have still tried to cover his own costs. He had his pride.

Daddy was hired for a number of movie acting jobs like 1956's *Anything Goes* with Bing Crosby and Donald O'Connor, *That Certain Feeling* with Bob Hope and Eva Marie Saint, and 1957's *Man on Fire* with Bing Crosby and Inger Stevens. He also worked on *Beau James* with Bob Hope and Vera Miles, 1958's *I Married A Woman* with George Gobel, *Once Upon A Horse* with Dan Rowan & Dick Martin, and 1959's *The Five Pennies* with Danny Kaye, Barbara Bel Geddes and Louis Armstrong. It's obvious now that if it weren't for Bob & Bing he might not have had any work at all in the movies through those years.

I think that Daddy found the business very frustrating and he longed for the days of live performance. He preferred it when the audience was right in front of him and not in a camera lens. He didn't really work at getting better at his craft, nor did he try to find ways to improve his position on the studio lots. He wasn't very proactive when it came to his career. He was happy to hang out with the crew between shots. He always felt that the crew was the real spine behind the Hollywood magic and they deserved better recognition. He would stick up for the crew and the little man on the sets of these working films, much to the detriment of his own career.

Daddy was working as an extra for most of his roles, sometimes with lines but a lot without. He would play a ship worker, politician, a bystander, club member, roulette croupier, or taxi driver, but all of these were mostly unaccredited acting parts. If he were working today, he would be known as a professional "background artist".

In 1958, Daddy did get a credited part on a TV show called *Fury*. It was a thirty minute western action show geared towards kids. *Fury* always had a good lesson and moral at the end of each episode. Daddy played the part of Jake Farris. The episode was called *Palomino,* and it starred Peter Graves, Bobby Diamond, and the number one star of the series, Highland Dale. If you find the name Highland Dale a bit odd for an actor, you won't once you know that it's the name of the horse that played Fury. You can see why Daddy was frustrated. After such an illustrious career, he was now getting billed way below that of a horse. I have to admit Highland Dale's resume was pretty outstanding. He starred or co-starred in *Black Beauty, The Return Of Wildfire, Wild Is The Wind, Black Eagle* and even performed on the TV series *Lassie.* At that time, the horse's resume was looking better than our entire family's put together.

Business Schmizness

The year of 1960 had been a very good year for me to get to know Hollywood and for Hollywood to get to know me. Buck and I celebrated New Year's Eve, 1961 in style. We were both on cloud nine. Our bank account was growing and we could afford better things now like an upgraded car, fancier clothes, larger parties and better apartment. We were moving, and I was so thrilled not to iron bed sheets and undergarments anymore. We left the cramped accommodations above my in-laws garage and moved to a nicer, yet tiny, place at 10975 Bluffside Dr in North Hollywood. It was not the biggest place, but it was all ours.

I was working regularly on a successful TV series and bringing home a regular, decent pay. We were paying $84 a month for our new apartment. I know that the amount sounds pretty cheap by today's standards, but it's all financially relative.

To show you what I mean here's a quick look at the cost of living in 1961:

Average Yearly Salary - $ 5,315.00

Average Monthly Rent - $ 95.00

New Car Cost - $ 2,275.00

A gallon of gas - .25¢

A Loaf of Bread - 21¢

I was making about $400 a week from the TV show and I think that Buck was bringing home about $95 a week from his job. We were enjoying our position in the middle class demographic of Hollywood. For me, the job was never about the money. I liked what money could get us, but in the long run I was just happy to perform and be liked. That is why Buck controlled all the money.

Buck paid the bills out of our account. All I had to do was to keep the money flowing in and he kept an eye on what flowed out. He never once displayed any worry or concern about the fact that I was making more money than he was. He was quite comfortable with it. I was so uninterested in the money side of work that it would be a few more years before I learned how to write a check. In retrospect, this may not have been the smartest thing to do.

From November of 1960 to June of 1961, I had completed eight episodes of *My Three Sons.* Jean Pearson was becoming very well-known across the country as the girl next door. Every "All American" boy wanted to date her. I was starting to get a lot of fan mail, which is one way the studio gauges how well you're doing. Sometimes it was addressed to me via the studio, and sometimes it was addressed to my character Jean, but it always made its way to me. By the looks of things, I would say that my career was really doing very well.

Things, however, got a little strange in my home life.

I started to notice that Buck was changing. He developed a dark sense of humor that I hadn't really noticed before. We had been invited to a preview of a new movie directed by Alfred Hitchcock called *Psycho.* It starred Anthony Perkins, Vera Miles and Janet Leigh. Obviously this movie has become a classic but at the time it was not well known. Buck and I jumped in the car and drove up the coast for the preview. That movie scared the heck out of me and Buck knew it. The classic scene where Janet Leigh is stabbed to death in the shower was so well done that I still get shivers thinking about it. The eerie stabbing music in the background really enhanced the entire scene. After the movie, we drove back home and I was still shaking over the shower scene. We both thought that it was a great, yet very disturbing, movie. I told Buck how much it affected me and how hard it was to get some of those disturbing images out of my mind.

The next night I was going through my bed time ritual in the bathroom, which included a shower. I was about half way through my shower when out of the blue the shower curtains were quickly peeled back. There was a figure of a man dressed in black, wearing a mask, holding a knife, and making the eerie music sound while moving the knife towards me in a stabbing motion. I screamed bloody murder as I tried to keep myself from falling backwards. For a few terrifying seconds, I was on the verge of hysteria. The guy then pulled off his mask revealing his face. It was Buck. I stood there dumbfounded, shaking and crying as Buck was doubled over in a fit of laughter at what he thought was the funniest joke in the world.

As I was drying off still mortified as to how a person could do this to another person, let alone the person you married. I asked: "Why would you do that to me?"

He said: "Oh, cool off. It was just a harmless joke."

"I know it was a joke, but it was far from harmless." I said trying to find his sympathetic side.

I'm pretty sure that my heart stopped working for about 20 seconds back in the shower. Buck couldn't see how his gag had bothered me, and I was upset that he didn't seem to care. I saw a mean streak in him that I hadn't been aware of before. He'd always been an aggressive person, but he usually cared about me and my feelings. This all felt so different.

Another incident took place after a hard day of work on the *My Three Sons* set. When I got home Buck was already there reading a magazine and waiting for his dinner.

As I took off my coat, I said: "I'm pretty tired from my day so I don't feel much like cooking. If it's ok with you, I'll just make us a couple of TV dinners."

"Ah huh." was what he grunted back.

I put the Swanson TV dinners into the oven then I got changed into some comfy clothes. It had been a particularly long physical day on the set for me so I was very tired. When the dinners were ready I pulled them out of the oven and with one dinner in each hand I started over to the table where Buck was already sitting. As I approached the table, one of the dinners slipped out of my hand and splattered all over the floor. I was devastated and upset at what had just happened. I looked at Buck with apologetic eyes waiting for him to say something nice to help me feel better. He just stared at me with a look of derision, grabbed the other TV dinner out of my hand and said: "Well I got my dinner I don't know what you're eating tonight."

Without a smile or another word, he ate the dinner. I was now more in shock at his response than I was with the accident that I had just had. As I cleaned up the mess from the floor I just kept wondering who this guy was and what had happened to my loving husband.

The Elvis Connection #3 - 1960

I have three connections here.

The first connection is the man that gave me a job on *My Three Sons*, Peter Tewksbury. In 1968, he would direct the MGM movie *Stay Away, Joe* starring Elvis, Burgess Meredith, and Joan Blondell. Mr. Tewksbury must have done a good job for MGM because they hired him again the following year to direct Elvis' next film *The Trouble With Girls*. This movie had a great lineup or co-stars including Marlyn Mason, Sheree North, Dabney Coleman, and Vincent Price.

The second connection is from my one appearance in *The Many Loves of Dobie Gillis*. I worked with a great Chinese character actor named Guy Lee. He was in the Dobie Gillis episode I was in, as well as a couple of others. He appeared in a number of movies and TV shows through the years such as *Gidget Goes Hawaiian* and *Bonanza*. In 1962, Guy Lee played the part of Chen Yung in the Elvis movie *Girls! Girls! Girls!* with Stella Stevens. This was also one of the Elvis movies directed by Norman Taurog. (My very first director when I was just a little girl in *Room for One More*.) The Hollywood world is a small one at times.

The third connection I'd like to make concerns Mary Tyler Moore. She is a very generous person and extremely talented actress. Her Academy Award nomination in 1980 for *Ordinary People* proved that. However when you're first starting out in this business you're hungry for anything that will get you in front of the camera. That is how she ended up in the elevator scene on the TV show *Thriller* with me.

What's the Elvis connection? - In 1969, she starred opposite Elvis Presley in Universal Pictures *Change of Habit* with Barbara McNair and Ed Asner.

Chapter 13

Margie

The *My Three Sons* shooting season ended in June and I had no reason to believe that my contract wouldn't be picked up for the following season when the show went back to filming in September. Shortly after wrapping *My Three Sons* for the season, my agent Sam called to let me know of an audition for a brand new TV sitcom that he had lined up for me.

You see, actors have that dreaded feeling that the last show they just finished could literally be their last show, ever. With that feeling in mind, I thought I would hedge my bets and go to the audition.

On the day of the audition, I was feeling pretty anxious. Since I was already working on a successful TV show I should have gone into this audition with a lot more confidence than in the past, but I didn't. The audition took place at the 20th Century Fox Studios. The show was to be called *Margie.* It was loosely based on the movie by the same name that was released in 1946. The movie had starred the beautiful Jeanne Crain, who was also in the movie *Cheaper By The Dozen*.

For the TV version of *Margie,* they were looking for someone to play the teenage lead named Margie Clayton. The plot was as follows; Margie lives in a small New England town in the 1920s and attends Madison High School. She lives with her parents, Harvey and Nora Clayton and her brother Cornell Clayton. They were even going to use some silent film era tricks and effects like speeding up the film on certain occasions for comedic effect, or using "intertitles" or "titles" as they were called back in the day. In the days of silent films, titles were the graphic device they would put in between scenes to help the audience understand what was going on as there was no dialogue. Even though the characters in *Margie* would be heard by the TV audience, they would throw in a black screen now and then that would have the words "The plot thickens..." or words to remind the audience to "Pay Attention". Once again this was done for comedic purposes.

As my audition continued, the one thing that came across in the interview was my love and knowledge of the music and times of the 1920's. I don't know if I was influenced by my parents, but I just loved Ragtime Blues and the early Jazz music of that era. Musicians like Paul Whiteman, Louis Armstrong, Fats Waller and Al Jolson provided the musical genius of the time. They also had dance steps to go along with the music. These dances had the craziest names like The Shimmy, Buzzard Lope, Turkey Trot, Monkey Glide, Chicken Scratch, The Bunny Hug and of course the most popular dance at that time, the Charleston.

I knew that I was up against at least two hundred girls for this part so the casting department had a lot of work to do and, so did I. Lucky me, I got a callback. Mind you, they were very thorough casting this part. This was not as easy as my audition for *My Three Sons*. Auditioning for *Margie* was starting to feel like a full time job. Over a period of about a month, I would have to go to a number of different interviews, screen tests, and personality tests. They eventually whittled down the two hundred actress hopefuls to twenty-five and I was one of them. Then I had to go in for several callbacks and screen tests. The screen tests were fun as I would dress in costumes that they had prepared for me and a hair piece that gave me pigtails. I hadn't had pigtails since I was a little girl in Texas. They were a big part of Margie's persona as they helped to give her a younger look.

After one last callback and a film test with character actress Hollis Irving, who would later play Margie's Aunt Phoebe, I went home to wait. I was very excited about the prospect of getting this project. I now had a 25 to 1 shot at getting the part. Daddy would say; "That's a long shot, but I always bet on the long shot."

I started to really fixate on how great it would be to actually star in my own TV show. Ok, now I was feeling anxious. I wanted the part so much that eventually I had to put it out of my head, or I'd get an ulcer from worry. I had moved it to the back of my mind when one day the phone rang and the voice on the other end said: "Hello Margie."

I said: "I'm sorry you've got the wrong number." And I hung up the phone.

I stood for a moment in shock then sat down by the phone just staring at it. I was trembling as I thought to myself: "That was too much of a coincidence."

I stared at the phone for what seemed like an eternity trying to will it into ringing again.

The phone rang. I answered it before the first ring was even half way through ringing. I could barely spit out the words: "Hello?"

Then I heard the same voice from the call before. It was my agent Sam. In a big, happy voice he said: "Cynthia, don't hang up. You got the part. They want you to play Margie."

I shrieked with joy. I'm sure the neighbors heard me all the way down the block. I said: "What about *My Three Sons*?"

Sam said: "You let me worry about that."

After a couple of weeks of contract negotiations and a little nail biting on my behalf, the part was mine.

I found out much later from the producers, one of the reasons why I was chosen to play Margie. They said: "We were looking for a rather plain, 'Girl next door' actress. Certainly she should not be glamorous or sexy." Voila, I fit the bill! At first I was a little hurt but I got over being sensitive and insulated real fast.

It was now official I had my very own TV show on ABC called Margie. Actually, what I had was a pilot to film. A TV show pilot is a sample of the show. You get one shot at the show then it gets shopped around which gives you more time for nail biting.

I felt bad about not being able to see and work with all the great actors and crew from My Three Sons again, but having my own TV show was a once in a lifetime opportunity. How do I say no to that? I knew they'd understand.

The Pigtails. Margie dressed as a Hobo from the episode, "Margie the Jinx".

(Cynthia Pepper Collection)

Buck and I had a good summer together in '61. He was a little more like the guy I remembered before we were married. I was preparing for my role and dreaming of our future together. It was just a mere year and a half ago that we were trying to figure out how to make the rent and wondering how much would be left for groceries. All of that would change now. Our social calendar was filling up quickly as we attended numerous parties and had quite a few of our own.

We had also joined something called Hollywood Life. It was a young Christian group that was an offshoot of the Hollywood Christian Group that was started by actress Jane Russell. Most people think of her as the voluptuous sex symbol from Howard Hawks' *Gentlemen Prefer Blondes* with Marilyn Monroe or Howard Hughes' *The Outlaw* with Walter Houston, but she had a very dedicated spiritual side to her as well. Hollywood Christian Group would meet for a weekly bible study at her home and was attended by some of the biggest names in the industry. Roy Rogers and Dale Evans would frequently attend. One day they all decided that the younger Christian actors and actresses of Hollywood needed a place to study too so the Hollywood Life group was created.

Buck and I joined the Hollywood Life group as we thought this could be a positive thing in our lives. We could broaden our minds spiritually and meet and mingle with lots of the new up and comers in Hollywood. Spiritual networking if you will.

These meetings would be held at different locations every week. Sometimes the meetings were held in people's homes, theaters, or at a retreat. One of the retreats was up at Big Bear Lake. We had a professional hypnotist there and he hypnotized me as part of his presentation. I didn't like the feeling I had when I was brought out of it. I don't like losing control like that which is probably why I don't drink to excess to this day.

We met a number of other actors and people in show business at these gatherings, including Christopher Riordan, and Claudine Longet. We also had some great guest speakers such as Pat Boone, Elmer Bernstein, and Stephen Boyd. These social gatherings had such a great atmosphere. In the beginning, we loved being part of them. As time went on I started to see some dissention and back stabbing in the group. This seemed, to me, to be the opposite of being a good Christian. Buck and I lost interest and eventually drifted away from the group.

Oh, how Buck loved to entertain. He could drink, smoke and schmooze with the best of them. He was a man's man and could be quite the charmer when he wanted to be. When I think back, there were times when his personality really reminded me of Daddy. Buck and I weren't exactly part of the "Hollywood Elite Set" but we were now part of what I like to call the "Hollywood Could Eat Set." We didn't live in Beverley Hills but by the same token, we didn't need to scrimp and save just to get by.

The *Margie* pilot was to be filmed at 20th Century Fox Studios, Culver City. Keep in mind that even though I had won the part of Margie Clayton the producers still had to sell the pilot to a network before any of us had a TV show to work on. Once a network bought the pilot, the 20th Century Fox Studios would be our home for as long as the series stayed on the air.

It wasn't lost on me that 20th Century Fox had a long history of great actresses. The list included Marilyn Monroe, Betty Grable, Dorthy Dandridge, Jayne Mansfield, Gene Tierney, and their very first big film star, a talented little girl named Shirley Temple. I had a good feeling about working here, nervous, but still good.

Before we started filming the pilot episode, I got to know the cast and crew that I'd be working with. The producers were Hal Goodman and Larry Klein. Before doing *Margie*, they had written for *The Jackie Gleason Show*, The *Red Skelton Show*, and *Playhouse 90*. They would also go on after *Margie* to write for *The Carol Burnett Show, Flip* (the Flip Wilson Show) and the *Tonight Show Starring Johnny Carson*.

The music for *Margie* was supervised and conducted by eventual Oscar winner Lionel Newman. He would go on to supervise and conduct music for other TV shows like *M*A*S*H, The Green Hornet, Lost In Space, Batman, Peyton Place, Julia* and *Trapper John M.D.* He is also the brother of Alfred Newman and the uncle of song hit-maker Randy Newman. Randy wrote the music scores for movies like *Meet The Parents, Toy Story, Monsters Inc,* and *Cars*. The Newman family and musical genius are synonymous with Hollywood.

Margie had a great group of cast members. Penny Parker was cast as Margie's best friend, Maybelle Jackson. Tommy Ivo played Margie's boyfriend, Haywood Botts, and Dick Gering was Maybelle's boyfriend, Johnny Green. Margie's brother, Cornell, was played by two actors; first there was Billy Hummert, and later, Johnny Bangert. Aunt Phoebe was played by Hollis Irving. Margie's parents were played by Dave Willock and Wesley Marie Tackitt. Overall it was a fantastic cast and a fun set to be on.

Dave Willock was a friend of Daddy's. Dave had been in Vaudeville with his partner Cliff Arquette. You may know Mr. Arquette better by his famous alter ego's name, Charlie Weaver. Once again, Daddy asked his friend to watch out for and take care of me on the set. Daddy was always trying to protect my interests.

Shortly after we filmed the pilot, ABC decided that the show was worth buying. This was great for me as I'd gotten to know a few of the executives at ABC from working on *My Three Sons*. It seemed like a logical and comfortable fit for me. I was now up to my chest in the Hollywood river of work, and it was feeling good.

I would now be bringing home about $500 or $600 a week and it looked like the sky was the limit. We started to get into a spending habit. If we wanted something we just bought it. The pay went up, but the expenses were going up too. I realized that much like Daddy I didn't have a great head for business. I was talked into getting some people onboard that did have experience with the business side. I already had an agent, so I went out and got a Business Manager and a Personal Manager. I was told by both the studio and other actors that I needed them. I didn't want anything to do with the business side, I just wanted to act. In hindsight, I would have done it for free.

A promo pic of Margie moving to a new broadcast date on ABC TV.

(Cynthia Pepper Collection)

It was going to be a busy schedule and a lot of work, but I couldn't wait to get started. Our week went as follows: Monday – Tuesday the cast would do a read through of the new script with the director and writers attending so they could make any last minute revisions if necessary. On Wednesday, we would block the show. Blocking not only put the actors in the right place on the right cue line, but also helped place the lights, audio and cameras in their correct spots. Thursday and Friday we would shoot the scenes and Saturday and Sunday we would have a break from shooting until Monday.

As the lead actor on the show it was up to me to set the tone and I certainly tried to make it an enjoyable one. However, I was very new and very shy at being the star of the show.

This will help you understand where my head was at for the first few weeks of filming.

I'd get up extra early, about 4:00 am so that I could wash and set my hair at home. Then I'd drive to work. I didn't do this because of vanity; I did it so that I wouldn't be a bother to the hair and makeup people on the set. I thought it was my responsibility and that I was helping. Our hairstylist was Margaret Donovan. She was a tough gal and told it like it was but we got along famously.

She always had great stories and Hollywood gossip for me in the morning. She had done hair and makeup on some great movie productions with stars such as John Wayne, Robert Mitchum, Lauren Bacall, Gary Cooper and Burt Lancaster, Bette Davis, Humphrey Bogart, Henry Fonda, Errol Flynn, Barbara Stanwyck, and Marlon Brando. Her stories about working with Marilyn Monroe were epic.

I can still remember all the hard work and effort it took to attach my uncomfortable three quarter length hair braids every morning. I hadn't had pigtails since I was a little girl living in Texas, but they were the signature of Margie's look. It gave me more of a teen look at the time.

One morning Maggie confronted me and asked: "Cynthia, why do you set your hair before you come to the studio? Are you trying to put me out of work?"

"Well, I don't want to bother you as you have other things to do, and I just wanted to help out." I answered.

As she looked at me with a half-smile and she said: "Honey, what's the name of this TV show we're doing?"

I said: "*Margie.*"

"Right," she said. "And what's the name of the character that you play on the TV show?"

I said: "Margie."

She said: "Well that makes you the star, and the star doesn't have to do her own hair and makeup. That's why we're here. So stop it, ok?"

"Ok," I said sheepishly. She was right. So from then on I got to the studio at the regular call time and let her do her work with my hair and makeup. It gave me more time to sit and learn my lines, and it also gave me another hour of sleep time. Thanks Maggie.

Along with Maggie helping me to understand the tricks of the trade, I also owe a lot to a cameraman that came to my unsuspected aid.

My costar Penny Parker had done a lot of TV work before she signed on to *Margie*. She had worked on *My Three Sons* and *Make Room for Daddy* among other shows. Somewhere along the line she had learned to be a smart little scene stealer.

At first I didn't even know that she was doing it. She would attempt to make herself the center of attention in each scene she was in, even if she didn't have any lines. An example of this is that she always had a long thin scarf in her hands during most scenes. As the scene started, she would begin waving and flicking this cloth around as we were doing lines. A lot of the time it was near my face. It's hard to do your lines with that distraction flying around your head. I was new at being the lead in a show and I didn't know how to handle it. I asked my TV show mom, Wesley, what she thought about her. She said: "Oh Cynthia, she's from New York and you know those New Yorkers."

Penny was from New York and definitely had a different attitude towards acting, but Wesley's words didn't help. I still didn't know what to do about the upstaging.

One day Penny and I were shooting a scene in our high school hallway. The scene required us to walk down the hallway together talking, then stop on a mark and deliver the rest of our dialogue. We had to do the scene a couple of times to get it right. After a couple of takes, I was called over by our director of photography Richard Rawlings. Dick had a lot of experience in the business. Before *Margie,* he had worked on the TV shows *Bat Masterson, Highway Patrol,* and *Sea Hunt*. He would later go on to man cameras for *Wagon Train, McHale's*

Navy, Gilligan's Island, The Wild Wild West, Kung Fu, Charlie's Angels, Dynasty and that's only half of his credits.

While our director was busy with another issue, Dick walked me to a quiet area of the set and said: "You're too nice."

"What?" I asked.

He continued: "Don't you see what she's doing to you?"

I said: "No."

He explained: "When the two of you are walking down the hallway towards the camera she keeps stopping a good foot short of the mark. This then forces you to have to stop and look back at her to deliver your lines."

I must have had a confused look on my face because he went on...

"You see if you turn away from the camera her whole face is in the shot, and only half or a quarter of your face is there... And who's the star of the show?"

Here was another person having to remind me that I was playing the lead in this production. How many more will be reminding me? Was I that naive?

He added: "What's with that scarf that she keeps flappin' in your face? Just a suggestion but you might want to do something about that too."

Dick was right. It was now or never. Did I want to be upstaged for the rest of the series? The time to act was now.

The director, Don Richardson, called for us to take our places to shoot the school hallway scene again. This time I was determined to make it right. The director yelled "action" and we started down the hallway towards the mark as we delivered our lines. Just before we got to our mark I stopped and took a short step back as I was giving my line. Penny had to stop walking and now look back towards me to keep the scene going. As she regrouped she started flipping her scarf around. As I started my next line I gently took her hand pushing it and the scarf downwards and out of the scene. As she gave her next line, the scarf came back up flapping like a hungry seagull. Once again, I gently pushed her hand back down. She finally got the hint. I'm proud to say, that scarf and Penny never got in my way again.

Here I am with Hal Goodman and Larry Klein. They were the producers of Margie. I was being honored by "Television Today" with the "Most Promising New Female Star of Tomorrow" award.

(Cynthia Pepper Collection)

As an actor, high self-esteem is a huge plus when performing on any stage let alone starring in your own television show. I, unfortunately, suffered from low self-esteem. I think for most of my career I've been able to keep that ugly monster below the surface of the water, but every now and again it would rear its ugly head. It did overwhelm me during the shooting of an episode of *Margie* called *By The Sea*. The synopsis for this episode was as follows: During an outing at the beach, Margie pulls out all the stops in an effort to get a cute lifeguard to notice her. This was a location shoot that was to take place at Paradise Cove in Malibu.

After reading the script for this episode, I was dreading the fact that I had to wear a bathing suit. For most of my life, I've had body image issues. They probably steamed from being called all those chunky little names as a kid. As much as I was able to deflect anything that was thrown at me, these slights and insults obviously piled up in my unconscious. Now the physical act of putting on a bathing suit and parading around in front of the cast and crew, let alone the millions of viewers that watched the show, was just too much for me to handle. Embarrassment is a huge and useless emotion, but it was all over me that day.

I went into wardrobe thinking I would be all right. How bad could it be? I would get through this. Since the show was set in the 1920's the bathing suit couldn't be all that revealing. Then I saw the bathing suit. It was not all that revealing, but it was revealing enough. I was beginning to feel uneasy. Then the fear took over as I put it on. It was a one piece knit with a scoop neck and wide straps on the shoulders. It ended between my thighs and just above the top of my knees. The bathing suit covered a lot of my body but my biggest fear was how big it made my hips look. Since it was a knitted outfit it clung tightly to my body and very little was left to the imagination. I can look back now and see how silly my fears were, but it was crushing at the time.

I came out of wardrobe with it on. Every step I took made me feel more and more self-conscious. I walked past some of the crew and went straight to my dressing room where I locked the door and refused to come out.

The director called at me to come out, but I refused. Some other cast and crew tried to get me out, but I wouldn't budge. Finally my TV mom, Wesley, came to the door.

She asked: "What's wrong honey?"

Through my tears, I said: "I can't wear this thing, I look awful in it."

She said: "Let me see. Maybe I can help." I slowly opened the door and she came in. After looking me up and down, she said: "Oh honey you look fine."

I said: "No I don't. My hips and my backside are just too big."

Wesley was so sweet and comforting as she adjusted the shoulders of the bathing suit and said: "It doesn't make you look fat at all. It's quite fetching. I even heard two of the crew say how cute you looked in it."

I said: "I look ugly."

She said: "First of all one day down the road you'll look back at this and see how silly you're being and besides you're the star of the show right? Do you think the director is going to make you wear something that would make you look ugly and, therefore, make the show look bad? Not a chance."

As she continued to talk, I slowly came around to her way of thinking. I was still not comfortable doing those scenes, but she was right. I was being silly. After all, I was barely weighing in at 100lbs soaking wet. We see ourselves differently than others see us.

The moral of this story is to leave your personal issues at the door when you work in showbiz and to remember that your mother, if she is a real mom, or a TV mom, is always right.

Margie from an episode called "The Vamp".

(Cynthia Pepper Collection)

I had mentioned earlier that I had met Ginger Rogers in the 20th Century Fox wardrobe department. You'd be surprised at the number of people you'd meet while changing costumes for the next scene. One day I was sent to wardrobe for a fitting for my show Margie, and whom do I meet but Ann-Margret. She was a year younger than me and had just been signed to a seven year contract with 20th Century. I knew who she was because of all the buzz there was about her at the studio. I didn't think she had a clue as to who I was, but I was wrong. I started to introduce myself: "Hi Ann, I'm Cynthia..."

"... Pepper!" She said quickly. She added: "I know who you are."

She then gave me a hug. I was completely surprised that she knew who I was.

She smiled and asked: "Are you working on your TV show?" I answered: "Yes I am. How about you? What are you dressing for today?"

She explained that she was working on a film called State Fair. It was directed by Jose Ferrer and costarred Pat Boone, Bobby Darin and Alice Faye. She explained that she auditioned for the part of Margy, the good girl, but she was cast as Emily, the bad girl. Then she shocked me by saying: "You know a lot of people say we look alike and I think we do."

All I could think of was, "In my dreams!" Ann was stunning. Her skin was perfect. Her smile and even the way she moved had "star" written all over her. We finished up in the dressing room and went our separate ways. Neither one of us knew that we would both be working with Elvis in just a couple of years. Her relationship went much deeper with him than mine did. After all, she was already being dubbed the "Female Elvis".

"Dying is easy. Comedy is difficult."

- Actor Edmund Gwenn

Chapter 14

The Show Must Go On?

There's an old show business adage that has been around for centuries, and it states: "The Show Must Go On!" Whoever came up with this saying needs a good smack upside their head. (It was probably a promoter that had a sick entertainer, but didn't want to return the money to his ticket buyers.) However, most entertainers try to wear this as a true badge of honor no matter what, and I was no different.

One working day, like every other working day, my alarm went off at 5:30 am. I got up and prepared for my day. As I drove to the studio I sensed that I wasn't feeling 100% healthy, but I forged on, because "The Show Must Go On!"

As the day progressed, I could feel myself getting sicker and weaker. The makeup department called out for extra supplies to help put some color back into my face. The director asked if I was ok and I said: "Yes, of course. Let's do the next scene?"

I was out to show them I was tough. I could take it no matter what. One of the crew found a thermometer, and we checked my temperature. Just as I thought, I was running a high fever. It was obvious to me, and most around me that I had the flu. Then I remembered: "The Show Must Go On!"

It was now almost 9:00 pm as the director announced that this would be the last scene of the day. I had been on set with this flu for the last fourteen hours. What difference would another hour make? I was feeling nauseous, but I was sure that I could deal with it for another hour.

The last scene for the day was an interior shot of a car. Tommy was the driver as I sat beside him in the passenger side. Penny and Johnny were in the back seat. The car was really just a shell that had some seats and a steering wheel. It was designed to look like a Model T, jalopy from the 1920's. I don't recall what the scene was about or any of the dialogue, but I remember feeling the sickest that I had ever felt in my life. To make matters even worse, the shell of the car was balanced on two long arms. Two crew members, out of view of the camera, would rock and bounce the car to simulate real vehicle movement. We rehearsed the scene without any car movement. Then it was time to make TV magic. As the car started to bounce, I announced that I thought I might throw up.

The actors in the vehicle yelled: "Stick your head out the window if you have to do it!"

The guy rocking the car on my side of the vehicle yelled: "No! Barf inside the car, not on me!"

My last thoughts were: "...the show must go..." as I threw-up inside the car.

The following morning still sick with the flu, but getting better, my alarm went off at the usual 5:30 am. As I turned it off, and rolled over for another few hours of sleep, I made up my own show business adage: "The Show Doesn't Always Have To Go On!"

As time went on, we had more and more episodes under our belt. The cast and crew were getting more comfortable with each other, and things became even more fun. Don't get me wrong, the set was a well-controlled working environment. However, when time allowed, there were many practical jokes going on between the cast and crew. This would offset some of the boredom that set in during the downtime between scenes. These jokes always seemed to be instigated by other people, not me. I was far too shy at the time, but I was often the victim of these practical jokes and I still don't see anything practical about a practical joke.

Playing Margie had me in a number of different costumes such as a Nurse… with pigtails no less.

(Cynthia Pepper Collection)

Tommy Ivo, was a veteran child actor who had played many roles in the movies like *The Babe Ruth Story* and numerous TV shows such as *The Lone Ranger, Adventures of Wild Bill Hickok, Leave It To Beaver* and *The Donna Reed Show*. Tommy knew his way around a studio set. He was also a huge drag racer. Not just a fan but an actual tear an engine apart, put it back together blindfolded, get behind the wheel, take off the blindfold and drive it like you stole it, award winning drag racer.

Tommy was the total opposite of the klutzy Haywood Botts character that he played on our show. He was Clark Kent on our show but in real life he was *Superman*. On the race circuit, he was known as *TV Tommy* or *TV Tom* to his fans. Thanks to Tommy, he and I made the cover of the December 1961 edition of *Hot Rod Magazine*. It was a great picture of Tommy and me in our *Margie* character costumes, posing with his 32 cylinder *Roaring Showboat Hot Rod*. To this day, it's still one of the most memorable covers in *Hot Rod Magazine* history, but I digress.

Tommy reminded me of a particular joke that was pulled on me one work day in 1961. Our director Don Richardson, some crew members, and Tommy were all in on it.

We had been rehearsing a scene where I was to open a door, walk through it, and yell: "Haywood, where are you?" We were just about to shoot the scene when I was called away to hair and makeup. I had to leave the set and go back to the dressing area to get my hair, lips or something fixed up for the scene. I never asked a lot of questions in those days and just did what I was told to do. As soon as I left the set the crew came in and quickly nailed the door shut that I was about to walk through. When I got back to the set, I was not aware of what they had done. The director told us to take our places which we did and then he yelled "Action!"

I walked up to the door, grabbed the knob, gave it a turn and a pull and it wouldn't open. It was stuck solid. I quickly gave the knob a bigger turn and a harder pull, but it wouldn't budge. Not realizing yet that this was a prank, I grabbed the door knob with both hands and yanked on it as hard as I could, but it wouldn't move an inch. At this point, I heard a couple of giggles from the crew which made me even more determined to open and go through this stubborn door. I grabbed the door handle, put my foot up on the door frame for extra leverage, and yanked at it with all my might. As the crew and the cast were laughing their heads off I clued into the gag. I simply walked around the door frame of the stuck door, onto the set, and yelled: "Haywood, where the HELL are you?" which made everyone laugh even louder. "Wow, Margie can even walk through walls." At times, I could be a very resolute girl. I took it all as great fun as did everyone else. Thanks Tommy.

I made the cast and crew laugh out loud again when they surprised me, but this time I was totally embarrassed.

Our show was a family show and we appealed to a large demographic that included children. We ran a very clean ship on and off the set in those days. We were barely out of our teens, then, ourselves. Almost everyone smoked back in those days, including myself, but we never smoked on the set and we tried to keep it invisible from the public. These were the studio's unwritten rules and it just seemed like the right thing to do. The other thing that we avoided was cursing. Bad language was not allowed on the set. I never had a problem with this as I didn't curse, unless I was scared that is. I think profanity has become a way of life now for the younger generation, but back then it was not common place at all, and certainly not for a lady.

TV's Tommy Ivo. He preferred race car driving over acting. He was great at both.

(Cynthia Pepper Collection)

This particular working day was Monday, September 4th, 1961 and it was special to me as I was turning 21 years of age. However, it was work as usual that day. Normally we would have a read through on Mondays but this day the producer wanted me to do a TV promo. I was to walk down the stairs and say a few lines for the network promo shoot. While I was in the make-up room, unbeknownst to me, they set up a big birthday cake and had everyone gather around at the bottom the stairs. There were some studio people, folks from the press, and even some young fans that they had brought in to surprise me. I was lead to the top of the stairs from a different area so I didn't see the party setup. The director yelled action and I emerged at the top of the stairs for the shot. As I came half way down the stairs, I stumbled quickly but caught myself before I fell. The stumble scared me and I said: "Oh Shit!"

The set was silent. I couldn't see anyone because the lights were blinding me. All of a sudden people started to laugh as they yelled, "Happy Birthday!"

The lights were turned off of me and came up on the folks below. I saw a big beautiful cake, but I also saw some young girls that had been brought on the set to meet Margie... And Margie just swore right in front of them. I was mortified. I made a beeline down the stairs and straight over to the kids and apologized profusely.

This was just like the Cary Grant swearing incident all over again. I was shocked when he did it years before in front of me and I'm sure I just shocked these kids too. After some cake, I'm sure they forgot all about it... I hope.

Towards the end on 1961, I was given a wonderful surprise as it was announced that I would be representing 20th Century Fox Studios at the *9th Annual Deb Star Ball*. It was to take place in the New Year and be televised from the Hollywood Palladium. The Host for the TV show portion would be none other than Bob Hope. Mr. Hope was glad to see that Pepper's kid was doing so well.

The *Deb Star Ball* was a big industry event that was held each year in Hollywood with the proceeds going to the IATSE Local 706 welfare committee.

The *Deb Star Ball* included me, and 11 other girls representing the different studios and movie companies. (One girl was Darlene Thompkins who would also go on to work in an Elvis movie). It was a night of pure glamour. Even though I didn't think I was a princess of any sort, I was required to play the part and bring more good promotion for *Margie*. The Sunday News magazine ran pictures of us in our gowns and tiara's, holding large bouquets of red roses. The blurb below my picture stated:

"Cynthia Pepper wears peau de soie in modified princess style. Born in Los Angeles, Cynthia was a model, now plays the title role in the *Margie* TV series."

We did a lot of walking, posing, smiling and looking like something special. It was posh, posh indeed. My escort for the Ball was sex-symbol, Troy Donahue. He was a perfect gentleman and the perfect escort. For one full day, I got to feel like a Princess.

Cynthia Pepper wears peau de soie in modified princess style. Born in Los Angeles, Cynthia was a model, now plays the title role in the "Margie" TV series.

A newspaper clipping about The Deb Star Ball – 1961

(Cynthia Pepper Collection)

Chapter 15

Aloha

In 1950, the Special Service Officers and a Hollywood committee created a program called Operation Starlift. This program was designed to get movie stars of the day to entertain wounded soldiers that were brought back from the Korean War. Operation Starlift was so successful that in 1951, a movie, loosely built around this program, was produced by Warner Brothers. It was called *Starlift*. It starred Ron Hagerthy, Dick Wesson, Janice Rule and Ruth Roman. It also included Hollywood cameos by Doris Day and Gordon MacRae.

In 1961, Johnny Grant decided to put his own band of Hollywood TV stars together to entertain the troops. I had some time off from filming *Margie*, so when I was first asked to go I didn't hesitate to say yes. Then they told me that we'd be flying to Hawaii. I responded with an even louder YES! They asked me if my husband wanted to go, but Buck was already knee-deep in work at the studio, so he declined. He did say that he'd feel better if someone went with me. He suggested Patty, but she also declined. I thought of my good friend Diane Phillips. She would love a trip like this. I felt that the committee wouldn't just let a friend of mine come along so I told Diane she'd have to be my sister for a week. That was how I got my second sister, Diane Pepper. There was a newspaper article with a picture of our troupe in Hawaii. They listed all our names below the photo. Right beside Cynthia Pepper was her sister, Diane Pepper. I'll bet Mother and Daddy were surprised to see that article.

We visited and entertained all of the army, navy and air force bases that Hawaii had to offer, plus the Tripler Army Medical Center, (the big pink hospital). Along with Johnny Grant, we also had Julie Newmar, Ann B. Davis, George Arlen, Jane Wald, Charles Watts, France Nuyen, Irish McCalla, Ruta Lee, and Pat Moran. We were there just before Christmas and returned home before New Year's.

Pan American Airways Photo

STARS FOR THE MILITARY—A troupe of Hollywood and Los Angeles performers arrived via Pan American Airways this week to stage four shows for military personnel in Hawaii. They include television's Ann B. (Schultzy) Davis and Cynthia (Margie) Pepper and Diane Pepper; first row; George Arlen, Charles Watts and Irish McCalla, second row; and Pat Moran and disc jockey Johnny Grant, top. Arriving earlier in the week were starlets Julie Newmar, Jane Wald and Ruda Lee.

A newspaper clipping of our Starlift trip to Hawaii to entertain the troops.

(Cynthia Pepper Collection)

Every day was jam packed with a full schedule. We were entertaining the military but at times it felt like we were actually in the military. For my part of the show, I basically performed as Margie, except without the pigtails. I danced and sang some of the songs that I had performed on my TV show. At one point, I even did a little soft shoe routine with our troupe leader, Johnny Grant. He became a good friend of Daddy's when they worked together in the USO during WWII. Johnny must have known that I had inherited a little Vaudeville from Daddy. After the shows, we would sign autographs, and sometimes do a Question and Answer session with the audience. At one point, while signing autographs, I looked up to see that Diane was signing autographs too. She looked at me and shrugged her shoulders as if to say: "When in Rome..." She later told me that someone asked so she obliged to sign a few. If anyone out there has a Diane Pepper autograph, then you really have yourself a very rare and collectable piece of memorabilia.

It was a fantastic trip. Everyone was so friendly and kind to us. They made sure we were well taken care of. Diane and I were in our early 20's, and very naive at the time. Ann B. Davis protected us like a mother hen and we appreciated it.

When we had a little down time, we were given rooms at the fabulous Hawaiian Hilton Village. We were in our room on Christmas Eve when we received a phone call asking if we'd like to have dinner that night with Pamela Mason and Ann Landers. Now that was a request we couldn't say to. It promised to be a fun dinner with those two. Pamela Mason was a seasoned actress that could answer any acting questions that I may have had. Ann Landers, well she could answer every other question in the world. Pamela Mason's husband, James Mason, was not on this trip, but Ann Landers' husband was. His name was Julius Lederer. (Ann Landers real name was Esther Pauline Lederer. She had a twin sister named Pauline Esther and she wrote a column called *Dear Abby*.)

During the dinner, the conversation was stimulating and fun. I explained to Pamela that Buck and I were renting one of her properties. She had no idea that I was a tenant of hers, due to the fact that she had a property management company handle her buildings. At one point during dinner, I looked at Diane and she had an odd expression on her face. It wasn't quite panic or surprise, maybe more confusion. Later that night, she told me how embarrassed she was because Julius, Mr. Ann Landers, was playing footsie with her under the table during dinner. I often thought that we should have written a letter to Ann's sister *Dear Abby*, asking – "what should I do when Ann Landers' husband is fervently flirting with me under the dinner table, while his wife is sitting right beside him"... signed "Horrified in Honolulu".

We did have a scary incident that both Diane and I still talk about to this day. We had an evening show on the other side of O'ahu Island. It was a fair distance away. The sun was setting and it was pouring rain. The only way to reach our destination was to travel across Hawaii Route 61 also known as the Pali Highway or Pali Pass. We had actress France Nuyen with us on this trip. She had played the part of Liat in the hit movie musical, *South Pacific*. Later on she would be better known for playing Elaan in the original *Star Trek* television series. France was in Hawaii for the premiere of her latest movie called *Satan Never Sleeps* with William Holden and Clifton Webb.

The Pali Highway was not a very smooth road, and it had a lot of turns and twists as it wound through the mountains and valleys. Diane, France and I were sitting in the back of the jeep, with France sitting in the middle. Our driver was motoring at a pretty fast speed so that we could make our show in time. Diane and I were getting very worried that our drive was not going to end well. We both had a good grip on the leather seats, but no one worried about seat belts back then. As a matter of fact, there weren't any in the jeep at all.

As I was imagining us missing one of the corners and tumbling down the mountain side, I saw that France was sound asleep. I pointed this out to Diane. We both thought this was crazy. Here we were, on a possible death-drive, driving in a jeep during a horrible tropical rain storm, over the dark highway roads, and France was sleeping. She would occasionally open her eyes then fall back to the safety of her nap. I had no idea how she could have slept through that drive. Diane and I were hanging on for dear life while France was oblivious to our peril and possible doom. When we finally reached our destination, Diane and I were finishing up our prayers and thanking God for not dashing us down the mountain. France woke up, gave a little stretch and said: "That didn't take long." That's when I really understood the saying: "Ignorance is Bliss."

During our tour of Hawaii, we were having so much fun that we let our guard down a little too much. Johnny Grant got wise to my new sister. Diane and I were relaxing in the lounge, with Johnny and some of the Navy Brass. Diane was engrossed in a conversation with one of the officers. He was telling her about his life in the Navy when Diane started telling him about her brother that was also in the Navy. Johnny Grant overheard their conversation. Johnny said: "I didn't know that Jack had a son." We both froze. Diane then did some very fast back peddling and said: "Oh, well, our brother is from another marriage." When Johnny looked at me I just smiled and waited for the other shoe to drop. He just gave a knowing nod and the conversation went on. From that point on, I think he knew that Diane wasn't my sister, but he didn't say a word. He was very diplomatic which is probably why he was considered the honorary Mayor of Hollywood for so many years.

Diane always called me her "Little Sis". I have to admit, it was a lot easier for me to make a good friend my sister, than to make my sister a good friend.

We had such a great time touring around by Officer Captain Turner and his staff. The crowds cheered and applauded at all of our shows. Diane and I were wined, dined and treated like princesses. She was the perfect traveling companion. There was only one incident that happened between us. I'm still not sure why it happened. It took place in our hotel room. Diane and I were getting ready to go out for a night of mingling and entertainment. I had done my hair and was finishing up my make-up. I never wore a lot of make-up so it didn't take long. Diane came out of the bathroom and announced that she was ready to go. I looked at her and saw that we both had the same hair style. Her hair looked just like mine. Maybe I was out of sorts because it was Christmas time, and I was missing my family or I was just having a bad day. I guess she could see some disappointment in my face. She asked: "Is everything ok?" I sarcastically answered: "Sure, fine." I then gave her the silent treatment and sulked. I was tired and feeling insecure, and took it out on Diane. She took it, but she didn't deserve it. Within an hour, all the pettiness was forgotten. I realized I was being foolish and I guess she did too. It was the only time we ever had a falling-out in our long, sisterly friendship. She's such an understanding friend and I love her dearly.

Chapter 16

Margie Gets Direction
New York with Patty
TV Guide

We never played to a live studio audience when we filmed *Margie*. It was always a one-camera shoot that was shot in black and white on 35 mm film. They would add the laugh track later in post-production. When we filmed our show it was always great to hear some nice words from the director after the scene or, even better, to have the crew laugh or applaud at the end of something they thought was good. Most actors need that kind of support from the director and others, not because they are insecure individuals, but because it's like a barometer for the job they are doing. You need that guidance to affirm that you're going down the right path. A live audience could immediately tell you what they did or didn't like, but we didn't have that luxury. I needed to know that I was doing something right; otherwise it was easy for me to second guess what I was doing in a scene and for the rest of the day.

I was very young at the time and starring in my own TV show, so as you can imagine it was a lot of weight for a young girl to carry on her shoulders. Anyone in my situation was bound to have some insecurity issues with all that pressure. I credit my Mother and Father for grounding me with the reality of what show business was and more importantly what it wasn't.

An incident of my insecurity came up one day with one of our directors, Don Richardson. Don directed the majority of the *Margie* episodes. I think he did about sixteen of them. He was a very good director and had done several TV shows before *Margie*. He would also go on to direct episodes of *The Virginian, Get Smart, Lost In Space* and *Bonanza*. It took me a few scenes to get comfortable working with his style of directing.

On one particular rough day of filming we finished a scene and he yelled; "Cut! We're moving on." He then turned away without a word to me or my fellow actors. This had happened a lot in the last couple of days. At first I thought that he didn't like me at all. There was never anything said to me directly, just a feeling that I had. We finished a scene that was a tough one for me to do. When it was done, I felt it went quite well. I then waited for Don to say: "Good Job." or "... That was awful let's do it again."

Instead, he said: "Let's go to the next scene."

There was no feedback at all from him so I started to cry. I just couldn't help myself. I'm not a great one for confrontation but maybe things just boiled over inside of me and I realized that I had to ask him what I was doing wrong. I approached him and through a salty waterfall on my face I asked him: "Mr. Richardson did you like the scene?"

He replied: "Yes. Why?"

Choking back the tears, I said: "You didn't say if you liked it or not and I didn't know if you liked how the scene was played and I don't know if..."

As my words and tears dribbled off my lips he just looked at me with a smile, albeit a little smile, and as his face softened a bit he said: "You silly girl, If I didn't like the scene I certainly would have said so and we would have done another take, but if I say 'Next' we move on because the scene was just fine."

I stared at him for a moment and then I said: "Ok."

I got it and we moved on.

I was a 21 year old girl, so can you blame me for feeling a bit insecure? Once I understood how he worked, things were fine.

I liked working with director Gene Reynolds and found him to be a fun and interesting leader. He gave us a lot of feedback on how we were doing. He directed three episodes of *Margie.* As a successful actor and writer, Gene came at the job from a different angle than most directors. He was a little more sympathetic towards the actors and what they had to go through to get things to work in front of the camera. He must have been good at his job as he went on to direct many successful TV shows that included *My Three Sons, Hogan's Heroes, Lou Grant, M*A*S*H* and he even picked up six Emmy Awards along the way.

How does a guy who started out in show business as a dancer for the *Ziegfeld Follies* end up as a director of movies and television? Jack Donohue knew the answer to that question because that's just what he did. He directed a few episodes of Margie and I just loved him. Hey, I've always had a thing for great dancers. One of his tap dance students was Eleanor Powell, so now you know he was good. When he blocked a traditional scene, without dancing, his style was very fluid and choreographed. He had an eye for movement and flow. He went on to direct many episodes for *The Lucy Show, The Brady Bunch, The Odd Couple,* and *Chico and the Man.* I loved working with all our directors and crew. I wish that it could have gone on forever.

My Recording Career (*Have you got a Nanosecond?*)

Shortly after signing on to play Margie, I was booked to appear on *Dick Clark's American Band Stand* TV show. I didn't have a hit record and wasn't really in the music business, but I guess it was a cross promotion idea that ABC had since we were both on the same Network. I dressed in my *Margie* outfit, painful pigtails and all, for the show. Dick interviewed me for a while and I then sang a song that I had done on an episode of my show. Actually I lip-synched a song on *American Band Stand.* Most of the acts on his show did that at the time because it was easier for their production people and it always sounded great. Dick was all business, but polite, to me. He seemed to be in charge of every little detail that was going on around us, in the studio and beyond. Our off camera chitchat was limited to about five minutes of pleasantries before we filmed. I thought I might meet some of the big hit makers of the day, but it was just me, Mr. Clark and the crew. I hit my mark, answered his questions, hit another mark, sang my song and said goodbye. Shortest career in music you say? Well, wait there's more to come.

In 1961, as *Margie* was climbing the TV chart's, I was approached by the studio and my business manager to make a record. They wanted to get something climbing up the music charts too. I guess they thought if they can turn singers into actors, they could easily turn an actor into a singer.

My appearance on Dick Clark's, American Bandstand, complete with pigtails.

(Cynthia Pepper Collection)

Singers like Sinatra, Dean Martin, Pat Boone, Bobby Darin, and Elvis had all become actors so the reverse must be possible too, or so they thought. It had worked for the likes of Ricky Nelson, Fabian, James Darren, and Frankie Avalon, so why not me. Remember this was someone else's hypothesis, not mine. I did what I was told no matter how much I felt out of my element. Nothing ventured, nothing gained, right?

If you want to get the heart pumping just get yourself into a recording studio for an hour or two.

It was an amazing and scary experience to be in a huge recording studio with an eighteen piece orchestra comprised of some of the best L.A. studio musicians' that money could rent. They were placed all around me and played as I sang. Wow, did I feel like a lone note on a music sheet. I felt like I was in way over my head, but I just kept treading water. They hired the musical director from our show, Lionel Newman, to orchestrate and conduct the session.

As we recorded each song I could feel my nerves firing off like a nasty, electrical, spring storm in Florida. If that doesn't bring on the sweats, I don't know what does.

I recorded six songs at this session. They chose two songs to be released to the public. One was called *A First Time Love* and the other was *Baby Blues*. They were released as a 45 record on the Felsted label with *A First Time Love* being the "A" side. Now back then, if you had sold 500,000 units *(records)* they awarded you with a Gold Record. Apparently my sales were a little below that mark. My record didn't make Gold or Silver or even Bronze... I think it went Plaid.

I never knew what the end unit sales were or where the songs placed in any of the music charts. Oh, and true to form for a person that didn't take care of the business side of her career, I didn't receive a penny for my efforts. I was given a few boxes full of the released 45's that sat in my basement. I kept them there just so I could take one out and show it to someone and say: "This record is my Million Seller... that's right, I've got a Million in my Cellar." *(rim shot)*

As part of my contractual obligations, I would have to do lots of radio, TV, and print interviews to help promote the show. I would also have to travel and make public appearances. All my expenses were paid for on these junkets, but I never received any extra pay for my time and effort. Some of these trips required a lot from me as I was taken away from my home and family. However one trip in particular was worth the endeavor and very satisfying for me.

The studio approached me to make an appearance in New York to help promote our new show. I asked if my sister Patty could accompany me and they said yes. I was all of twenty-two and Patty was twenty-six. All of our expenses were paid and it was top drawer all the way. I think Patty really loved and appreciated such nice treatment, and I know that I sure did. Our trip was only a week long, but it was what we both needed. She laughed and smiled a lot on this tour and it was so good to see her have such a good time. I couldn't believe that after all this time we seemed to be bonding as sisters should. At the time, I felt we really got close on this trip.

We flew first class from Hollywood and were put up at the luxurious St Regis Hotel. I would have been content just to sleep in the opulent lobby of the St Regis, but the suite they gave us was a much better idea. Patty and I couldn't believe how big this suite was.

Patty quipped: "This room is bigger than my whole apartment."

As we walked through the suite, we came to the luxurious bedroom. The bedroom contained two queen size beds. I couldn't believe it. Even on a first-class trip, I was still sharing a bedroom with Patty.

I was excited about all the work I had to do during this trip. I had to give interviews, (I made Walter Winchell's column that week), attend photo shoots for magazines and make an appearance at the American International Toy Fair.

The reason I was at the Toy Fair was because 20th Century Fox, in conjunction with a number of different companies including *Milton Bradley* and *Dell Comic Books*, had come up with a whole line of *Margie* merchandise to unleash upon the public. Merchandise from a TV show was a relatively new way to capitalize on its popularity. Thus, the creation of the *Margie* Comic Books, *Margie* the Board Game, *Margie* Lunch Boxes, *Margie* Hat and Cosmetic cases, *Margie* Paper Doll Cut Outs, and a few other items that I can't recall. All of this merchandise had my picture or likeness on it and to this day, I have never received a single penny for any of it. Why didn't I get anything for merchandise sales you ask? Let's just put it down to creative accounting at the studio end of things.

I was excited about my down time because now we could paint the town red. Patty and I had lunches and dinners at places like Sardi's, The 21 Club and Delmonico's.

The one thing I loved, other than my private time with Patty, was that we got to attend a couple of Broadway shows. Oh, sure I'd played Broadway when I was a little girl, but I wanted to see what had changed since the 40's. Well, a lot had changed, and we got to see some of it.

Flying to New York on a Margie junket with my sister Patty.

(Cynthia Pepper Collection)

We saw *Carnival* at the Imperial Theater on 45th Street. It starred Anna Maria Alberghetti as Lili with cast members James Mitchell, and Kaye Ballard. Making his Broadway debut was the wonderful Jerry Orbach. (The *Law & Order* fans know who I'm talking about.) This musical produced the beautiful hit song *Love Makes The World Go Round*. We were so fortunate to be there to see this original production and nothing could top it... That is until the following night when we saw *The Unsinkable Molly Brown*. Wow. It was at the Winter Garden Theater at 50th and Broadway. You don't get much more Broadway than that. As we sat in our seats waiting for the curtain to go up, Patty and I speculated on what it must have been like when Daddy performed there. How he must have felt working a room of this size. When the curtain finally went up we were spellbound by the amazing performances of Tammy Grimes, Harve Presnell and Jack Harold. The entire cast was fantastic. Ms. Grimes won a Tony for her performance as Molly. Just a couple of years later Hollywood and MGM turned it into a film by the same name which starred Debbie Reynolds as Molly. (Shirley MacLaine was supposed to do the part but had to bow out as she was under contract to Hal Wallis and he said no.)

When Patty and I weren't hobnobbing with New York's high society, I was working. While I worked, Patty visited friends that she had in New York so she was never alone and we both had a perfect week. We both fell in love with New York during that trip. I guess Patty fell in love with it even more than I did as she moved there about five years later. This trip had been wonderful for both of us. We talked and shared and laughed a lot, but unfortunately this bonding between sisters would be all too short lived.

When I returned home from my New York junket, I got back into the busy Hollywood swing of things. Buck and I were working and socializing so much that neither one of us had the time for house work. We hired a housekeeper to come in once every couple of weeks to help keep our place clean. She was a lovely lady named Louise Oliver. You must remember that Buck, like most men of that era, was above housework and I was so busy with my TV career that I really needed and appreciated the help. Louise was our saving grace. We would also hire Louise to work anytime that we had a dinner party so that we could socialize and have as much fun as possible with our guests.

We had such a good rapport with Louise that one day she even invited us to her daughter's wedding. That was a memorable day. We drove to the other side of L.A. and when we arrived for the wedding we quickly found out that we were the only white couple there. I initially felt out of place and soon realized what it felt like to be a minority in this world. When I say, "this world" I mean 1961. Just a year before, outgoing President Eisenhower had severed diplomatic relations with Cuba, John F Kennedy was the incoming President and we were right in the middle of the African-American Civil Rights Movement. However, within minutes of arriving at the wedding we were made to feel welcomed by everyone. We had the best time at both the wedding and the reception. I wish that a few of the uptight people I knew in Hollywood could have been at this wedding. Can the world really change or is it our own perceptions that need to change?

In November of 1961, I was asked to do a photo shoot for *TV Guide.* It was to go with an article they were doing on me and my show *Margie.* I thought of it as an honor to be included in a magazine that covered all of North America. These days, *TV Guide* is not what it used to be. Back when TV was still relatively new *TV Guide* was the best source of finding out what was on TV, and when it was on, for the week. There was no such thing as the recording of shows to watch later. You had to watch the program when it was aired or you missed it. Most households in America, with a television set, had a copy of *TV Guide* sitting near their favorite chair in the living room. It had all the TV listings, but it also featured celebrity interviews, television-related news, gossip, and film reviews, If you got tired of looking at your TV, there was even a crossword and horoscopes located on the back pages.

The photo that *TV Guide* used from our photo shoot was a clever New Year's theme. It was of me, dressed as Margie, rearranging the numbers of the New Year. I was taking the numbers, 1962 and changing them to now say 1926, the year and era that our show was based in. I thought this photo would be used inside the magazine with an article, but they decided to use it for the cover. I was going to be on the cover of *TV Guide*? How cool was that? The producers and the PR department of 20th Century Fox, were thrilled to hear that news. This could only mean good things for the show.

They released the magazine on the last week of December. That meant that it would be on the stands for the next week and into January. As I said it, was a thrill to have it happening, and then within a week it was all said and done. We gained some more viewers and everyone was happy.

A month later I received a *Western Union* telegram, (Google that one kids), from *TV Guide's* Publisher, James T. Quirk. (To all the *Star Trek* fans and to my friends that performed in a *Star Trek* episode… I swear I'm not making that name up.)

It was to inform me that the issue of *TV Guide,* with me on the cover, had set a circulation record. It had sold over eight million copies. WOW, all that in one week? Set your phasers on stun. Back then *TV Guide* sold for fifteen cents a copy. That would be approximately

$1,200.000 worth of sales. I'm not taking credit for why it sold so many copies, but *TV Guide* seemed to think I needed to be congratulated. Here's what the telegram said:

Western Union Telegraph

Miss Cynthia Pepper

10975 Bluffside Dr Apt 7 North Hollywood Calif

We know you will be pleased to learn that the DEC 30 issue of TV guide, which featured your picture on the cover, has set an all-time circulation record. Figures just received show that our New Year's issue crossed the big eight-million mark with an estimated sale of 8,073,608 copies. Congratulations and Best Wishes from the entire staff of TV Guide.

James T. Quirk Publisher.

What an honor it was to appear on the cover of TV Guide. They sold over 8,000,000 copies. Inside was an article with me and Daddy.

(TV Guide Magazine cover courtesy of TV Guide Magazine, LLC © 1962)

You don't get paid to be on the cover of *TV Guide,* but I wonder what they would have said at the time if I had asked for just a penny from each sale. What could a penny hurt? That would only be $80,000... Yes, I agree, I think the answer would be no.

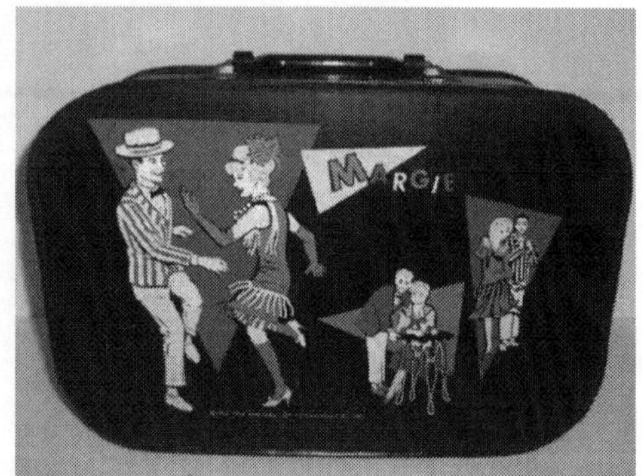

There were board games, Cut-Out doll books, Comic books, and even Margie lunch boxes. Unfortunately, I never saw a penny from the sale of any of these items.

(Susan Hanson Collection)

Chapter 17

How Do You Do '62

Halfway through the *Margie* season Buck and I had decided to move again. We needed a bigger apartment so we decided to really treat ourselves. We moved to a very fancy place at 8495 Fountain Ave, Apartment D3. The building was owned by actress Pamela Mason.

It was an amazingly spacious apartment with very high ceilings and a second floor. The apartment was incredibly decorated, and was a place where we could be proud to host gatherings with our friends. People's priorities change all the time. Having a nice place to live, and entertain, was one of ours. We were paying $221 a month for rent. Sounds like a deal, but once again that was in 1961 which translates to about $1,600 a month in today's world.

People have asked me "Why didn't you and Buck buy a house in Hollywood, as opposed to renting?" Good question and I don't have a good answer. I do believe that in the 1960's, the hip, working Hollywood people were into the apartment mindset. We were always free to move, keeping that free-spirit alive inside us, in case something better came along or at least that's how I remember it. In reality, Buck probably said we're moving to a new apartment and I just went along with it. I had to put so much focus into the show and career that I wasn't too worried about where we were living at that point in time.

My pay had gone up since I started working on *Margie*. I was bringing home about $600 a week now, so the expensive apartment made sense to me at the time. I was still a contract actor with 20th Century Fox, which meant that I didn't bring in really big money from these projects. However, I got paid every week whether I worked or not, and that was dependable. Since Daddy and Mother were going through some tough financial times, I would send them money anonymously. Why did I do it anonymously? I'm not really sure. I guess I didn't want them to know where it came from because they might refuse it or that their pride was so great that they'd have to say no. I made sure that I sent my parents cash every week. How did I send them cash you ask? Hold on to your hats kids, I sent it to them in a mailed envelope. I told you I wasn't good with money. Yes, they always got the envelope. It was a different time then and a lot of people sent cash in the mail. We also didn't lock our front doors or our cars. It seemed to be a more trusting time. Sure, there was some crime but I think people just strove to be better in those years.

All throughout Hollywood Daddy had friends in high places. He just wasn't out to use them. They were his friends for many years, and you don't abuse your friends. Bing Crosby wrote about Daddy in his autobiography, *Call Me Lucky: Bing Crosby's Own Story*. Referring to their Vaudeville days, he said that Daddy could "sing like a bird". He also went on to say that Daddy was more interested in jolly times, as opposed to a good paycheck. He summed up Daddy's love of the horse races by saying: "I have known him, (Jack), to turn down cushy Vaudeville routes so he could be present for the racing inaugural at Saratoga in August." Bing knew Daddy very well.

At the end of 1961 Bing Crosby had been taken to the hospital for an undisclosed alignment around the time my *TV Guide* cover came out. Since Daddy was very well known in Hollywood, he was also featured in the article with me. Daddy sent a humorous note and a copy of the *TV Guide* to Bing when he was in the hospital. Daddy was proud of his little girl but also concerned about his friend. He found a way to make Bing smile and to show his pride in me at the same time. Bing sent back a lovely telegram that I had kept all these years.

Bing Crosby Hollywood

January 26, 1962

Dear Jack:

Thanks for your note and you're good wishes when I was hospitalized.

Very amusing, the clipping about you and your daughter.

Hope you're getting some action in the local area, and I hope, too, to run into you soon so we can exchange a few yarns -

Always your pal,

Bing Crosby

Mr. Jack Pepper

5144 De Longpre

Hollywood 27, California

Daddy visiting and serenading me on the set of Margie.

(Cynthia Pepper Collection)

When you become a TV personality, the job is never really left behind at the studio. Even though I said that we had Saturday and Sunday off from shooting, we would rarely have those days to ourselves. Weekends were usually filled with other studio obligations. There would be public events, interviews, broadcasting conventions anything that would help put the show in the minds of the viewers. These requests came from both the studio and the sponsor. It was wise not to say no and I rarely did. Some of these appearances were fun to do and others could be heart wrenching. One such heartbreaker of an appearance happened with my co-stars Tommy Ivo and Dick Gering.

I was told that we had a huge fan in Burbank that wanted to meet the cast of her favorite show, *Margie*. We were told that she was ill and this would really pick up her spirits. What I didn't find out until we were on route to Burbank was that she was just 7 years old and that she was ill with cancer. This was a dying wish from a little girl. Why would she want to see us? What could we do for this poor young soul? I had no idea that our show was something people looked forward to every week or how much we affected people in a positive fashion until that very moment. When our car pulled up in front of the little girl's house, I knew that I really had to dig deep to make this work. She didn't want to see the cast of her favorite TV show sitting around her bed crying. Before we went into the house to meet her, I had to take a big breath and become Margie for the next couple of hours. That was the only way I could get through it.

We went in and met a wonderful little girl lying in her bed. She was very frail and weak, but she managed the most beautiful and appreciative smile you could imagine. Her face just lit up. We had brought her some gifts from the show and she loved them all. We played and talked with her for a long time. Her parents said that this was the best they had seen her look in the last six months. After a while, I could see that she was losing a lot of energy but she kept trying to play and keep up with us. Her mother suggested that it was time for us to go. I felt that if we could just stay with her she'd be ok and that she could beat this hideous disease. Others had recovered from it in the past. She was a good and innocent soul that had yet to experience much of life. She deserved a better deal than this and it just wasn't fair. God would fix this. I just knew he would.

I had convinced myself that she'd be fine, but once we were in the car and back on the road I started to cry. I just couldn't keep the sadness in anymore. By the time I got home, I was all cried out. I didn't have a single tear left. However a week later I did find more tears when I was told that the wonderful little girl had passed away. It's still not fair.

In February of 1962, I was asked to do a TV show on NBC called *Here's Hollywood*. It was to help promote *Margie* so I was happy to do it. I asked what kind of show it was, and I was told it was a daily talk show that a lot of celebrities like Edward G Robinson, Bette Davis, and Judy Garland had appeared on. "Well, if it was good enough for Garland it was good enough for me."

The interviewer was singer, turned TV personality Helen O'Connell. In the 1940's, she had huge success with the songs *Green Eyes* and *Tangerine*. She was a very well-spoken lady, and when she smiled her dimples went on for miles. Buck was quite taken with her. What they didn't tell me initially was that the interview would take place in our home.

Buck didn't mind having a camera crew come in and take over, but our cat Pepe had a thing or two to say. She was named after the lead character in the 1960 movie called *Pepe*. The great comedic actor Cantinflas played the part of Pepe in the movie. It was brilliantly directed by George Sidney. I adored this movie. It was all about the bond between a young Mexican guy named Pepe and his horse. I was always a fan of a good "animal reunited with loving person" movie, especially if it's a comedy. There were so many cameos in this movie. Bing Crosby, Bobby Darin, Kim Novak, Sammy Davis Jr., Jimmy Durante, Joey Bishop, Donna Reed, Debbie Reynolds, Frank Sinatra and that's only half of the star cameos. The movie is a nice snapshot of Hollywood and its stars of the early 1960's.

Our Pepe, was a beautiful black and white cat that came to live with us in a very unusual way. A neighbor asked us if we would look after their cat. They were going on vacation for a week and had no one else to turn to. Being an animal lover, of course, I said we would. She warned me that the cat would likely bolt through any open door if it had the chance. I told her not to worry and to enjoy her holiday.

A few days later we had a delivery at our front door, and sure enough, the cat made a mad dash out the entrance. It ran straight down the driveway and onto the road just in time to get hit by a passing car. Oh God, I had just killed the neighbor's cat. Ok, maybe not directly but I was still devastated. A beautiful animal had died in a terrible accident, and I still had the unenviable task of telling our neighbors the horrific news. "I hope you had a marvelous vacation. The weather here has been good since you were gone. Here's your mail that I saved up for you, and let's see… Oh yes, I killed your cat." I cried all the rest of the day.

The only way I thought that I could even attempt to make it right would be to replace the cat. I got Buck to drive me to the local pet shop where we bought a beautiful black and white kitten. When our neighbor came home, I gave them the horrible news. She was extremely upset that her cat had been killed, but she didn't blame us. I then offered her the new kitten. She thanked us but declined the offer. She felt she was too distraught to have a new pet so soon. I wasn't taking this little fellow back to the store so we named him Pepe, and that's how we adopted him. A few days later we found out that Pepe was a girl. Oh well, too late the name had stuck.

When the production crew from, *Here's Hollywood* arrived, they set-up quickly. Before the crew arrived, I envisioned twenty or more strangers in my home making a complete mess. As it turned out there were only twelve production people and they were very good at getting in and out without disturbing much of anything at all. While they setup camera and lights, Pepe was being very quiet, and not in the way at all. However, it was a whole different story when the cameras were turned on. Buck and I were placed on the couch where they wanted us for the interview. As soon as the TV cameras were turned on, and Helen began her questions, Pepe decided this was the time to make her debut. She first jumped up on the couch, and walked across my lap in a very animated manner to show the world how beautiful she was. She then jumped up on to the back of the couch to show off her athleticism. As she walked by my head, on the back of the couch, she began to talk. "Meow, meow, meow…" You would have thought it was her interview. I loved it, and so did the production people. With Pepe, I knew that we had a good segment for the show. After it was all done, Buck said: "I don't know how well we did, but Pepe got lots of airtime."

I'm not sure what the neighbors thought of the huge video remote trucks that took over the streets for the day, but I did get a couple of odd looks from a few of them for the rest of the week. My interview ran on the same show as actor Ray Milland's segment. Between Pepe and Mr. Milland, I was finding myself in very good company.

On the cover of "TV Star Parade" with our cat Pepe. She was the real star.

(Cynthia Pepper Collection)

When you are in the middle of working on a show like *Margie*, you are so busy memorizing lines, getting made up or spending time getting your costume just right that you don't always take the time to notice and appreciate your surroundings and all those you're working with. I certainly appreciate and miss them all now more than ever.

We had some amazing character actors come through our TV show in a number of different episodes. Some of these fine actors were on their way up the ladder to fame and fortune. A few others had already built their fame from days gone by. I miss them all.

I want to share with you a list of some of these performers that had been on our show. I think you might recognize a lot of them. I will title this section:

"Oops, I Dropped a Name."

Raymond Bailey

You will remember him as the banker Milburn Drysdale on The Beverly Hillbillies. Well, he was our banker first. He did four episodes as Mr. Yates on Margie. As an actor, he was straightforward and very professional to work with.

Jack Albertson

He was Grandpa Joe in the movie *Willy Wonka & The Chocolate Factory*. From there he went on to a very popular TV show in 1974 with his co-star Freddie Prinze called *Chico and the Man*. He played Ed Brown, The Man. (He was also a very good friend of Daddy's from the Vaudeville days.)

Eddie Foy Jr.

Another Vaudeville friend of Daddy's was in our show and his name was Eddie Foy Jr. He was from one of Vaudeville's famous family teams called Eddie Foy & The Seven Little Foys. They were so popular in Vaudeville that they ended up portraying the family story in the 1955 film called *The Seven Little Foys* starring Bob Hope and James Cagney. Daddy played the theater manager in this movie. Eddie Foy Jr. was a riot on our show. He was in an episode called *The Jazz Band*. I can still picture Eddie Jr. doing his crazy rubber man dance on our show. How I kept from laughing, I'll never know. He was something else.

James Brolin

Believe it or not, James Brolin did a *Margie* episode. He played Freddie Coates in our 1962 episode called *Madame President*. Is that the same James Brolin from *Marcus Welby M.D*, the movie *Capricorn One*, the TV show *Hotel* and the guy that married Barbara (Babs) Streisand? Yes, that's the guy. In a scene that we did together he was riding a bike and I was sitting on the handlebars. I'm proud to say that he has great balance and we never fell over once.

Sterling Holloway

Sterling played Bettenhouse in a *Margie* episode called *False Alarm*. What's that? You've never heard of Sterling Holloway? Well, he did a lot of movies in the 30's and 40's and if you can't picture his face, I'll bet you can remember his voice. Sterling is the original voice of that cute little bear known to the world as *Winnie the Pooh*?

Kathleen Freeman

In an episode called *Flaming Youth*, Kathleen Freeman played the part of Mrs. Botts. Kathleen was a comedic actress that you would recognize instantly. She worked with everyone from Gene Kelly to Jerry Lewis to John Belushi. She's been in movies as diverse as *Singing In The Rain* and *North To Alaska* to *The Nutty Professor*. The role you may remember best was Sister Mary Stigmata (The Penguin) in *The Blues Brothers*. She had a very long career in show business. Her parents were in Vaudeville, which is why she graced the Vaudeville stage at the ripe old age of two years old.

Garry Walberg

Garry Walberg was a very productive television actor, best known as Lt. Frank Monahan in *Quincy M.E.* and as Speed, Oscar's good buddy on the TV version of *The Odd Couple*. He started out doing a lot of Westerns, but later moved into the tough cop roles. Most of his TV characters were gruff and crusty but in person he was a doll. In 1962, he did an episode of *Margie* called *The Wolf Of Wall Street*.

Howard McNear

Howard McNear was an actor with one of the most identifiable voices and line deliveries in the business. It was great to work with him. You'll remember him as Floyd the Barber on the *Andy Griffith Show*. He was such a shy, yet delightful, guy. He did our show in 1962 as a character named Selkirk in the episode *Margie, The Gossip Columnist*.

Margie - The Vamp strikes again.

(Cynthia Pepper Collection)

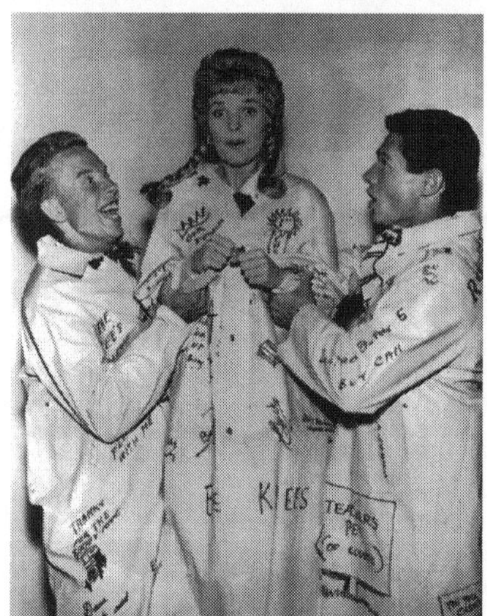

Tommy Ivo and Dick Gering are giving me a lift… what were we wearing?

(Cynthia Pepper Collection)

Chapter 18

The Death of Margie - Or - "Gee, I Didn't See That Coming"

It was 1962 and life had been rolling along at a very busy pace for me. I was up to my neck in the Hollywood river of work. I was so busy treading water and focusing on the daily survival of my career, I lost sight of the things that were going on around me. Like the day we all arrived at work and were told that this week we'd be creating our 26th, and possibly our last, episode. There had been talk that ABC was going to drop us. I didn't really pay much attention to it as I thought it was just a nasty rumor. My agent assured me that all was good. I later found out that, that's what agents say to clients, even in the face of disaster. He explained that if that did happen, another network could still pick us up for the next year, and the show would continue. He assured me that it was a solid show, and the TV audience loved it.

We finished our 26th episode of *Margie*. It was called *The Professional Man*. I was looking forward to our hiatus from the show to recharge my batteries for the next season.

As we finished the last scene, the cast and crew were told to gather around for a meeting. Within a few minutes our producers, Hal Goodman and Larry Klein were on the set, and they were not smiling. By the expressions on their faces, I thought maybe someone had died. I was close. It wasn't someone that died, but it was something. They didn't beat around the bush as they said that ABC had decided not to pick up the option on the show for next year. In effect the actors, directors, and many crew members were instantly unemployed. I was in complete shock. I didn't see it coming. I had my head down doing my job, and ignored the rumors. I figured they'd just go away. Even when people told me that these rumors had some very reliable sources. I choose to stand in a large river in Egypt... Yes, I was in de-Nile.

So what happened? I've had a few years to think about it, and I'll just offer up a hypothesis or two, and how I've justified this loss through the years.

I was told that our show had a 20% share which was considered a good percentage. Let me explain what a share is. A share is a term they use to rate your show. It's part of a statistic that was put together by the *Nielsen Media Research Company* and is a measurement of audience viewership on any one particular show. How they do it is still a mystery to me, but back then the Hollywood studios lived and died by these ratings. They still do.

You are now asking me, "Cynthia, is a 20% share a good thing?"

Well to put our 20% share of the *Margie* show into perspective look at these highly successful shows; *Seinfeld, ER, 60 Minutes,* and *Cheers.* They all had an average show life score at around the 20% share mark. Other hit shows such as *Survivor, American Idol, CSI, Friends,* and *Who Wants To Be A Millionaire* had show life scores ranging lower than 20%. They scored between a 14 to an 18% share. Heck, even *Sunday Night Football,* sits around a 13 share. So what happened to *Margie?*

I can't say directly what happened and most others I've talked with can't either. No one could tell me then and no one can tell me now for sure. However I can don my *CSI* sitcom cap and speculate a little.

Looking back upon it, I believe that a number of factors contributed to Margie's demise. TV westerns like *Gunsmoke, Wagon Train, Bonanza,* and *Rawhide* were becoming more and more popular. The demand for 1920's themed shows like *The Untouchables* and *The Roaring 20s* was declining. Despite this I think that Hollywood politics and high finance were the biggest reasons for our shows' demise.

You see, in 1960, the studio that was producing our show, 20th Century Fox, had started production on a huge epic drama film called *Cleopatra*. It was directed by Joseph L Mankiewicz and starred Elizabeth Taylor, Richard Burton, Rex Harrison, and Rowdy McDowall. In the beginning, this film was to cost $2 million dollars and be completed within a year. Production on this movie involved detailed location shoots, complicated and elaborate sets, and thousands of props and costumes that had to be constructed for two different locations, London and Rome. It took three years to finish at a cost of $44 million dollars.

The amount of money required to make *Cleopatra* was unheard of back in the 60's. (In today's financial terms that would be over $320 million dollars.) 20th Century Fox almost went bankrupt because of this. Elizabeth Taylor's record setting contract would net her a cool one million dollars, but due to numerous production delays, her pay ballooned to seven million dollars. She got all that money and a new love affair. (Nice job Liz) This was the film where she and Richard Burton first met and as they say; "...the rest is history."

Cleopatra was still in production when our show was cancelled in 1962. It was obvious that the studio was slashing and burning to cut costs. They had a fire-sale and *Margie* was the show that someone in the accounting department decided they could chop to save money.

I have come to believe that the other factor that caused The *Margie* termination was sponsor related. Today a TV show has many companies, or sponsors, that buy commercial ads which in turn pays for the expenses of producing the show. In the early days of television, one sponsor would foot the bill for the entire production. The sponsors held a lot of weight around the studios and had input on what was being produced. If they didn't like something in the show, a meeting would be held and things would be changed. Our sponsor was *Proctor & Gamble*. They made all kinds of different cleaning products and still do to this day. One of the perks of doing this show was that P&G made sure that the cast was given boxes and boxes of their products to take home. I had more Ivory soap, Tide detergent, Prell shampoo and Crest toothpaste than I had skin, clothes, hair, and teeth to clean. In fact, I had so much of it in my house that I started giving it away to friends, relatives and even strangers. (The way things turned out, I wish I'd kept a box or two for myself.)

I think that *Proctor & Gamble* decided that their interests would be better served by backing some daytime TV soap operas instead of an evening family show. They had been backing "soaps" since they first started on radio back in the 1930's.

P&G also got behind a great little show that aired the same year we did. It was called *Hazel.* This comedy show starred Broadway star Shirley Booth as a maid that worked for an upscale modern family. Everybody loved Hazel. So I'm sure *Proctor & Gamble* saw more potential in having *Hazel* sell their cleaning products. She was a maid, for gosh sakes, and a maid knows what's better for the household than a teenager in pigtails from the 1920's.

Let's face it. A quality television show with a decent 20% share, but without a sponsor, is like DiCaprio without a life vest in *Titanic*... You look good, but you're going down.

I was certainly devastated at the time. I took it personally and thought I didn't do a good enough job or that people didn't like me. However, if that was true why was I getting all those pieces of fan mail from people, telling me how much they loved *Margie*? It was confusing and upsetting at the time, but it was out of my control so I had to just accept it.

Tommy Ivo had a different take and reaction to the shows' cancellation. You remember my good friend Tommy the actor / drag racer? He loved racing. It was his passion and he was very successful at it. During the production of the show, the producers of *Margie* were very nervous that Tommy would have an accident racing and that it would mess up production. To protect their interests, they refused to let Tommy race while he was under contract to the show. Since he was making a lot more money at the time from the TV show he reluctantly agreed not to race. Money speaks volumes in Hollywood.

After Tommy had been told that the show was no more, he went quietly to his dressing room, and instead of being depressed or crying like the rest of us, he shrieked for joy. He was so happy to be out of the contract that handcuffed his racing career. He could now do drag racing as much as he wanted. "Free At Last, Free At Last." Well at least one of us was happy.

Life After Margie

They shopped *Margie* around after we lost our sponsor, but there were no takers so that was that. The river of work was instantly down to my ankles... Not good. My agent told me not to worry, and that I was still a viable commodity and he would have something for me soon. Within a week, he called and told me of an interesting project that was part of a TV series called *The United States Steel Hour.*

Presented by the Theater Guild, the *US Steel Hour* was an anthology series, which meant a different story and different cast were presented for every show. It was sponsored by the United States Steel Corporation, thus the name.

It first got its start on radio in the 40's and migrated into a TV series in the 50's. It would air a new show every two weeks. The delivery of this show had changed through the years, but one important and scary fact remained the same... It was performed live and delivered straight to your TV set, instantly.

The episode that I was hired to co-star in was called *The Inner Panic.* It starred Tommy Sands, Glenda Farrell, Simon Oakland, Teri Keane, and two new, young upstarts. Now let's see, what were their names again? Oh yes, Martin Sheen and George Segal. (I wonder what ever happened to those two guys.) It was a great acting experience and everything was first class.

A summary of the episode I did is as follows:

A young man, with a speech impediment and having a hard time landing his first job, gets hired in the mailroom of a big company through his mother's intervention. He quickly gains confidence, loses his stutter, and finds love with a young woman who works at the same company. Tommy Sands was the young man with a stutter, and I was playing his girlfriend.

Tommy Sands was quite a talent. He had a great regional Rockabilly singing career, which eventually led to an even better acting career. He became nationally famous after performing in Kraft Theatre's *The Singin' Idol* in 1957. His hit single, *Teenage Crush* came out of that performance. The song made it all the way to #2 on the Billboard charts. He was also in the movies *Babes in Toyland, Sing Boy Sing,* and *The*

Longest Day. Tommy had both a singing career and acting career and was balancing both pretty well by the time that we worked together.

This show was going to be anything but easy as it was a live show and live show meant just that... LIVE!

The actors had just the time it took for the 60 second commercial to begin and end, to get from one set to the next, and make it look like we hadn't run a full mile to get there. The cameras were already in their places so when we arrived the floor manager gave us a sign and we started the next scene. If you weren't there in time, it was too bad as the others would be starting without you. I thought; "If I can do this and not mess up, I can do anything."

One week before the telecast I arrived in New York for rehearsals. Every morning Tommy's limousine, with him and his wife, would come to my hotel, pick me up, and take me to the studio. Since I had only ever done one live drama TV show before, I was very nervous about getting it right. The initial ride to the studio was also a bit nerve racking when I met his wife. The first day I got into the limo and sat down beside a woman who stuck out her hand and said: "Hello Cynthia, I'm Tommy's wife, Nancy."

I hesitated for a second and said: "Hi Nancy, it's so nice to meet you."

Why did I hesitate? Well, it's not every day you meet Nancy Sinatra now is it. It was a strange and awkward drive to the studio that morning as I didn't really know what to say. I'm in a car with Tommy Sands and Nancy Sinatra... what do you talk about? "So Nancy... How's your Dad?" I was really feeling out of place. Every morning, during the rehearsal week, I felt the same strange feeling. Tommy was great, but I found Nancy to be quite reserved, polite and nice to me, but not very warm. We made small talk as we sat in the back seat of the Limo, but we never did get to know each other very well. Hey it was only a week together so what more could I expect.

I do remember spending a lot of time with George Segal and, especially, Simon Oakland. Somehow, we just clicked. When we had a little down time during rehearsal, you would find Simon and me talking. We were just two friends talking in the corner of the studio and enjoying each other's company. You know how you just connect with people as soon as you meet them. Well, this was the way it was for Simon and me.

One night, after a day's rehearsal, George, Simon and I decided that we would go to the movies. That night we went to see a rerun of the movie *Sabrina* at a local theater. This was the original, directed by Billy Wilder and starring Humphrey Bogart, William Holden and Audrey Hepburn. It's such a great film. Afterwards, we went to a small café and had a bite to eat and discussed the film for hours. It was so nice to share, listen and be heard on the profession that the three of us loved to be working in.

George Segal was a very interesting guy. He would go on to become a famous movie and TV star. He had very few lines on this particular project, as he was just starting out.

Simon Oakland was a sweetheart. He always seemed to be typecast as "the heavy". He plays the persona of a tough guy, usually a thug or mobster. When he wasn't cast as a villain, he would play a tough cop. However, these roles did not define him in his personal life. He was such a dear sweet man. Of course, I only knew him a short time but he left such a lasting impression on me. I do miss him, but at least we can still see him in his many, many roles on TV and in films. Just bear in mind that if you see him in a rerun of *Psycho, Murder, Inc, Sand Pebbles* or in *West Side Story* as the tough, racist cop, you are seeing a great actor because he was anything but the bad guy that he portrayed in his roles.

The Elvis Connection #4 - 1961 / 1962

(Look out gang, it's a lot.)

In the *My Three Sons* episode called *Mike In A Rush* an actress named Christian Kay played a character named Suzy Carter. She also performed in Elvis's 1961 film *Blue Hawaii*, playing the part of Beverly Martin.

I had mentioned earlier that Darlene Thompkins was part of the 9th Annual Deb Ball. In 1961 she played Patsy Simon in Elvis' *Blue Hawaii*. Later in 1963 she played Miss Stevers in *Fun in Acapulco*.

In 1966, Dave Willock, who played Margie's father, also played the role of a bartender in Elvis' MGM movie *Frankie and Johnny*.

Jack Albertson. I first worked with him in an early *Margie* episode where he played a town official. He then joined the (movie) army and became Capt Robert Salbo in a film by MGM, that I'm very fond of called *Kissin' Cousins*. Shortly after that he joined the carnival by playing the character Lou in Elvis' 1964 Paramount movie *Roustabout*.

Bud Lewis was a fine character actor and was in the *Margie* episode called *Matchmaker*. He also ended up in *Roustabout* with Elvis.

George Sidney who directed and produced the movie that our cat was named after, Pepe, also directed and produced one of Elvis' most remembered films, *Viva Las Vegas*.

Here's a two for one deal. George Cisar and Claude Stroud were both in the *Margie* episode called *The Jazz Band*. In 1968, they both appeared in Elvis' film *Speedway*.

This one will amaze you... (Well, it does me.) My friend Charlotte Stewart, who was married to Tim Considine, is best known as the schoolteacher Miss Beadle on the TV show *Little House On The Prairie*. She was in a *My Three Sons* episode with me called *Deadline*, and she was in a *Margie* episode called *Hail The Conquered Hero*, both in 1961. Here's the kicker. In 1968, she was also in Elvis' movie *Speedway*. Brother that schoolmarm got around.

I spoke of Garry Walberg earlier. He was best known for playing Lt. Frank Monahan in *Quincy M.E.* Well, in 1969, he strapped on the cowboy boots as Martin Tilford in the Elvis film *Charro*.

In 1961, a young actress named Suzie Kaye was in a *Margie* episode called *The New Dress*. In 1967, she played Sally in Elvis' movie (all about seafood) called *Clambake*.

Gigi Verone was also in the *The New Dress* episode on *Margie* but no clams for her. She decided Hawaii was the place to be so in 1966 she played Peggy in Paramount's *Paradise, Hawaiian Style* with Elvis.

Cliff Norton was a character actor on *Margie* in 1962, in an episode called *Lady Of The House*, and also in Elvis' *Frankie & Johnny* in 1966.

Howard McNear was in the *Margie* episode called *Margie, the Gossip Columnist*. He was Floyd the Barber from the *Andy Griffith Show*. In

1961, he performed with Elvis in *Blue Hawaii* and in 1962's *Follow That Dream*. Then, in 1963, he was Elvis' doctor in the movie *Fun in Acapulco*. No, I don't think he gave Elvis a haircut in any of those films, but you may want to watch them again just to be sure.

Frank Puglia played a number of different ethnic roles in over 150 movies. He was in an episode of *Margie* called *The Wolf of Wall Street*. He was also in Paramount's Elvis production of *Girls! Girls! Girls!*

As I have mentioned earlier Raymond Bailey was the banker Milburn Drysdale on *The Beverly Hillbillies* and was in four episodes of *Margie*, Well in 1958 he also played Mr. Evans the school Principal in Elvis' favorite Elvis film *King Creole*.

Jimmy Hawkins started out as a child actor and he started pretty big at just five years old in Frank Capra's *It's a Wonderful Life* with Jimmy Stewart and Donna Reed. He played George Bailey's son, Tommy. Jimmy was in an episode of *Margie* called *The Initiation aka Sheik*. He continued on to perform in two Elvis vehicles, *Girl Happy* in 1965 and *Spinout* in 1966.

My good friend Simon Oakland played a mob boss, with great comedic skill, in Elvis' *Follow That Dream* in 1962.

Tommy Sands wife, Nancy Sinatra, co-starred with Elvis in MGM's 1968 release, *Speedway*. She also performed a couple of songs in her father's 1960 TV special called *Frank Sinatra's Welcome Home Party for Elvis Presley*. This show marked Elvis' return to show business after he was released from the army.

Here I am in a scene with Tommy Sands from the US Steel Hour's episode called The Inner Panic. When doing live TV like this show, inner panic is not just a title but a way of life.

(Cynthia Pepper Collection)

Margie was finished... But what would the future bring?

(Cynthia Pepper Collection)

Chapter 19

Sally & Sam
Take Her, She's Mine
Wagon Train

Even though I had lost my show *Margie* just a year earlier, I still had high hopes that I might be able to have another show on TV. That hope was pushed into action at the beginning of 1963. That was when I went to work on a new TV pilot. It was called *Sally and Sam*.

I played Sally Marten and Sam Cody was played by Gary Lockwood. It was a sitcom about a couple of newlyweds trying to make a go of life in the big city. It was shot in New York. We used Manhattan and Central Park as part of our backdrop. I really felt like this pilot would sell. We seemed to have all the right ingredients. At that time, Gary had been working in the industry for about four or five years, and was just starting to hit his stride as an actor in the industry. He had been in the movies, *Wild In The Country* and *Splendor In The Grass*. He would later make a huge mark in the Sci-Fi world playing Lt. Cmdr. Gary Mitchell in the popular *Star Trek* TV episode called *Where No Man Has Gone Before*. In 1968, he got an even bigger taste of space by being cast as Dr. Frank Poole in *2001: A Space Odyssey*.

Gary and I had a great working relationship, both on and off the set. We worked very hard for a week, shooting scenes in various locations around New York. When we finished our final scene together for the pilot Gary offered to walk me back to my hotel room. I said yes. I thought to myself: "What a nice gentleman Gary is."

When we arrived at my hotel room, I thanked him for walking me and said: "It was great working with you Gary. I really hope this show sells so we can continue working together."

He leaned on the door frame and lingered for a while. After a long, uncomfortable pause I said: "Well, good night."

He backed away slowly, and turned to leave. As he was walking down the hall, he turned back to me, smiled and said: "When you get home, you better make sure you swing with your husband."

What the hell did that mean? I didn't get upset about the comment because I think I was more confused than anything about what he just said. I laughed to myself as I entered my room. I closed the door behind me, and went to bed alone.

In spite of what I perceived as a come on, Gary and I remain friends.

I thought that *Sally and Sam* had a good shot of being bought by a network. The writing was good, and I thought Gary and I had a good rapport together on camera. The other ingredients that were working for the show's success included the other cast members. We had a strong supporting cast such as character actor, John Qualen. John had been in more Hollywood movies than the spoken line: "Let's go!"

Bernie Kopell was another great actor we had on our side. He went on to do some amazing comedy roles on shows like *Get Smart, That Girl*, and *Bewitched*. Of course, you remember him as Dr. Adam Bricker that sailed the oceans blue on TV's long running *Love Boat*.

The other two great elements to make this show work was our director Vincent Sherman, and the shows writer Hal Kanter. Mr. Sherman was a very good director, and I got along with him famously. When we first met he told me: "You know that I directed a movie that was based on your old man, when he was married to Ginger Rogers."

"You did?" I said.

"Yes I did. It was in called *The Hard Way*. It was loosely based on their marriage, and what Ginger had to go through with her mother trying to get her into showbiz in the old days. Instead of a mother we had an older sister as the antagonist."

We talked a bit more about Daddy and what life must have been like for him in the Vaudeville days. Mr. Sherman was a dream to work with.

Hal Kanter was the other element to make this show a success. He was our writer. He had worked with Daddy years ago on some of Bob Hope's movies. He had written for Ed Wynn, George Gobel, Danny Kaye, and Martin & Lewis so he knew comedy.

I figured that this was a sure fire recipe for success. You combine all that talent into a big cooking pot, add a few cups of water from the Hollywood river of work, bring to a boil and this pilot couldn't lose. Guess what, it lost. I guess the pot boiled over. They shopped it around for a long time, but there were no takers. *Sally and Sam* was eventually released as a TV special and aired in 1965.

When I returned home from New York, I was worried that my last job may actually have been my "last job". I was still a contract player with 20th Century Fox, but you just never knew what the executives at the head office were going to do.

After some time had passed, I wondered if the river of work was drying up. Then I got a call for a movie part that would be starting in March. They decided that the 1961 Broadway comedy, *Take Her, She's Mine*, needed to become a movie.

The play was written by Phoebe and Henry Ephron, and was based on the letters they received from their daughter Nora when she was away at college. Nora Ephron would become a big deal in Hollywood later in life by writing *Silkwood, When Harry Met Sally*, and *Sleepless in Seattle.*

The Ephron's wrote the play, *Take Her, She's Mine,* but Nunnally Johnson wrote the screenplay. Mr. Johnson had also written the screenplays for *The Grapes of Wrath, How to Marry a Millionaire* and later *The Dirty Dozen*.

The basic story for *Take Her, She's Mine* is about a father who is overprotective towards his teenage daughter, especially when she leaves home to attend college in Paris. It stars Jimmy Stewart as Frank

Michaelson, the father, Audrey Meadows as Anne Michaelson the mother and Sandra Dee as Mollie Michaelson the teenage daughter. I had landed the role of Adele, one of Mollie's college roommates. The third roommate, Sarah, was played by Jenny Maxwell.

I think this was one of the first generation gap comedy movies to be made. Even though he had a small part, this also marked James Brolin's movie debut. Bob Denver and Jim Nabors are also in the film. I always felt bad for Jim Nabors as his voice ended up being cut out and dubbed in by another actor. Maybe he should have sung his lines with that beautiful baritone singing voice of his.

Sandra Dee, me and Jenny Maxwell in "Take Her, She's Mine"

(Victor Hanson Collection)

Our director was Henry Koster. He already had about 46 movies under his belt before *Take Her, She's Mine*, including *Mr. Hobbs Takes a Vacation* and *Harvey*. Mr. Koster was also the person that discovered the comedy team of *Abbott and Costello* working at a nightclub in New York. He convinced Universal in Hollywood to hire them and the rest, as they say, was history.

Most of the scenes I had in *Take Her, She's Mine* were with Jenny and Sandra. The studio told me that since Sandra and Jenny were both blondes, I would have my hair colored and be the brunette gal pal of the movie. I didn't argue because as a contract player you did what the studio told you to do.

It was a fun movie to work on, but I didn't really get to know Sandra Dee all that well. She seemed very pensive and preoccupied between takes. I know that she had a lot of demons inside her. She had married Bobby Darin three years earlier in 1960. Their well-publicized dysfunctional relationship was in full swing by 1963. They would end up divorcing in 1967.

I found Sandra to be very professional, pleasant and yet a careful person. I never got to know her between takes as she always had something else to do. Reporters, photographers, and magazine people, among others, just kept hounding her relentlessly for her time. I realized then that maybe it's not a good thing for a person to aspire to be famous. We had a small birthday party for her on the set. It should have been a big, fun celebration for her as she was turning 21 years old, but she didn't have much fun at all. She had such an adorable face, but even on her Birthday you could see there was something troubling her.

Sandra and I didn't spend a lot of time together, but when I did see her between takes I was amazed to observe that she was a very nervous chain smoker. She was one of the worst I had ever seen. As soon as her cigarette was out she lit another. I felt so badly for her and what she seemed to be going through, but it wasn't my place to do anything.

Jenny Maxwell was a fun person to work with. We became closer than I ever could with Sandra. Jenny had been a guest player on numerous television shows throughout the 1960's and was just a great person to know. As things tend to happen in that Hollywood river of work you move on to other projects and as the years go by you lose that close connection with people. In 1981, I was so saddened to hear that both Jenny and her husband, Irvin Roeder, were gunned down during a robbery in the lobby of their Beverly Hills Condo. She was only 39 years old. She deserved better.

The two people that I got chummier with were Charla Doherty, who played Sandra's younger sister Liz Michaelson, and Monica Moran, who played Linda Lehman in the film. I stayed in touch with both of them after the film wrapped.

Monica is the daughter of actress Thelma Ritter and Joseph Moran. Monica didn't do a lot of work after this film, but she was lucky enough to get to sing a couple of songs in it. She was so much fun and a great person.

Charla Doherty was the kind of person you just gravitated to instantly. She was fun and outgoing most of the time. After filming *Take Her, She's Mine* she did a number of TV guest spots on numerous shows but her longest recurring role was in the early years of the soap opera *Days of Our Lives* where she originated the part of Julie Olson.

Charla passed away at age forty-one of pancreatitis, due to chronic alcoholism. She was far too young when she left us.

The crew made the set a fun and pleasant place to work. Then there was Jimmy Stewart. I don't mean to cast any disparaging remarks towards anyone, let alone Hollywood's favorite male actor, but Mr. Stewart really surprised me on the set. We were shooting a scene and he became very upset. I was standing behind a closed door, waiting for my cue. The studios were very sound proof in those days so I couldn't hear what was being said behind the thick closed door. To combat this problem, there was a red light set to the side of the door. When the cue line was delivered a crew member would turn the light on, and I was to enter the scene.

We rehearsed a couple of times and were now ready to film the scene. I stood behind the door waiting for the light to turn on, but it never did. Then I heard Jimmy Stewart yell: "Where the hell's that God Damn actress!"

I was mortified. The sweetest actor in Hollywood just lost it and was yelling at me! I opened the door and said apologetically: "I'm sorry Mr. Stewart, but the light didn't go on."

Then he turned his attention to the crew: "Well then where the hell's the God Damn electrician!?" I just stood there. I'm sure this was an isolated incident, but I was silently mortified. The crew finally got the technical side of things worked out. We shot the scene a few more times and moved on to other business, but I must say, was still a little rattled.

Wagon Train.

Directly after *Take Her, She's Mine* I was told that I'd be a guest star in an episode of ABC's hit TV show, *Wagon Train.* I was very excited to get this role but also a little worried as I had never appeared in a Western before.

The TV show was about the adventures of a wagon train that left Missouri to head to California. The show was on the air from 1957 to 1965. After 8 seasons and over 280 episodes I'm still not sure if the wagon train ever made it to the Golden State.

Once again, I was the interloper among an established cast on a hit show. I didn't need to worry as I was welcomed with open arms and had a great time during the shoot. Since the show was a period piece, taking place in the late 1800's, I got to wear some great dresses from that era. However, I also had to wear all the things that a lady had to wear with these dresses, like billowing petticoats and full body bloomers. I gained a whole new respect and empathy for what women had to wear all the time back in those days. When I went to wardrobe it was 1963 but after I put on my costume and left wardrobe it was 1870. I felt as if I were transported back in time to the Wild West.

The episode was called *The Sandra Cummings Story*. My character's name was Paula Cummings.

Rhonda Fleming portrayed my character's mother, Sandra Cummings. Rhonda had a lot of experience in the Western genre and was well prepared for her role. She got her big movie break in 1945 with her work in Alfred Hitchcock's thriller *Spellbound* with Gregory Peck and Ingrid Bergman. She would go on to work with other great Hollywood stars.

In the script Paula Cummings mother is trying to control her life especially when it looks like young Paula is falling in love with the wagon train's scout Cooper "Coop" Smith played by the dashing Robert Fuller and to be honest what women wouldn't? Miss Flemings' character gets what she wants from the men in her life by seducing them with her feminine charms. When she sees that her daughter is falling for Coop, she tries to intervene by getting him to fall in love with her instead.

There was a dramatic scene where Miss Fleming and I were having a heated argument over why her character had Cooper beaten up. During this argument, she had to slap me across the face. During the rehearsal, she went easy on the slap which I appreciated, however; I knew it wasn't going to look realistic in the finished product. I asked her to hit me a little harder when we actually filmed the scene so that my reaction would appear to be real. She promised that she would.

It was a wonderful little scene that was written for us by Norman Jolley. The scene took place in a covered wagon. Our director, Virgil Vogel, yelled action and before I knew it we were into the moment. The scene went like this.

Mother: *"Darling don't you understand? I just can't let you get involved with a man that doesn't love you."*

Paula: (angry) *"How do you know he doesn't? Just what makes you such an expert? You're always telling me that I should trust your judgement, you've had more experience... Well, I'm beginning to wonder just what that kind of experience was!"*

Mother: *"Paula!"*

Paula: *"Is that why you have so little faith in other people? Because you judge them by yourself?"*

Mother: *"Stop that!"*

Paula: *"Is that could be what really killed Daddy...? A Broken Heart?"*

(Mother slaps Paula)

Paula: *"Thank you Mother. It makes it a lot easier. I'm meeting Coop tonight... And I want to marry him. I pray that he'll ask me."*

The scene was progressing nicely, and then came the slap. Miss Fleming kept her promise as she hauled off and really let me have it. I remember seeing stars for a second, and I don't mean Hollywood stars! I kept it together without breaking character and delivered my last lines and exited the scene. I think there was some applause from the crew at how well it went, but I couldn't say for sure as my ears were still ringing from the slap.

"Wagon Train" with Robert Fuller. Yes ladies, he was that dreamy in person too.

(Cynthia Pepper Collection)

After hearing the director yell cut, Miss Fleming followed me and apologized for slapping me so hard. She was really quite sweet. She said that I should be happy that we got the reaction that the director was looking for. I told her that I was just happy that we got it in one take.

The episode was kind of a mini musical as it contained three musical numbers. Two were performed by Miss Fleming, and I had the third song. Miss Fleming was a great singer so I knew that I had to step my game up vocally. I rehearsed the song a lot until I got it to where I thought it was going to work.

The song was called *Where Is Love,* written by Sidney Fine. It was a simple, but heartfelt, song with just voice and guitar. I don't play guitar, but they wanted me to pretend to play it while I sang. After watching Daddy play the ukulele all those years, I could fake guitar playing quite well. The director, Mr. Vogel, felt the guitar blocked my body too much, so I was asked to lay it flat on my lap and play it. It is virtually impossible to play one that way, but I aim to please so that's what I did.

I'd like to add that the cast and crew couldn't have been nicer. They made me feel welcome while making this episode, especially the series regulars, Denny Miller and Robert Fuller.

You'll remember Robert Fuller not only as Cooper Smith in *Wagon Train* but as Jess Harper on the TV show *Laramie* and as the iconic Dr. Kelly Brackett in the hit TV series *Emergency*.

Denny Miller was a big, athletic actor that played Duke Shannon on *Wagon Train*. You'll know him from a lot of other great performances including his role as *Tarzan* in the 1959 movie *Tarzan, the Ape Man*. My favorite performance of his has to be from the movie *The Party* starring Peter Sellers. Denny played "Wyoming Bill" Kelso. When this giant cowboy actor and Peter Sellers' character intertwined, it is just too funny.

The Elvis Connection #5 - 1963

The writer of *Sally and Sam*, Hal Kanter is very connected to Elvis Presley. In 1957, Mr. Kanter co-wrote the screenplay for Elvis' second film *Loving You* with Herbert Baker, AND Mr. Kanter also directed it. Things went so well with that project that in 1961, he co-wrote *Blue Hawaii* with Allan Weiss.

Gary Lockwood played Danny Burke in Elvis' 1963 movie *It Happened At The World's Fair*. The other fascinating fact here is a little bit of a stretch but still strikes me as interesting and valid. Gary starred in the film *2001: A Space Odyssey*. In the soundtrack of that film, there was a very powerful song that launched the film as no other song could. It was written in 1896 by Richard Strauss and is called *Thus Spoke Zarathustra*. A lot of people now refer to it as the Theme from 2001. When Elvis started to perform concerts live again in the 1970's, he used this iconic piece of music to open his shows.

Nunnally Johnson, who wrote the screenplay for the movie *Take Her, She's Mine*, also wrote the screenplay for Elvis' movie *Flaming Star* in 1960.

Jenny Maxwell played Sandra Dee's other roommate Sarah in *Take Her, She's Mine* and she was lucky enough to get to play Ellie Corbett in *Blue Hawaii* opposite Elvis.

The great cowboy actor John McIntire, who played Chris Hale on *Wagon Train*, also played Sam 'Pa' Burton in *Flaming Star* with Elvis. (The more indirect Elvis connection is that he was also in a movie called *Sing Boy Sing* with Tommy Sands. That movie was loosely based on Elvis' rise to fame.)

John Archer played Jonathan Lott in the *Wagon Train* episode that I was in. He also played Jack Kelman in *Blue Hawaii* with Elvis.

A fellow by the name of K.L. Smith played a sentry on the *Wagon Train* episode. Well, he did even better with the King of Rock & Roll as he worked his way up to the role of Sheriff in *Roustabout* with Elvis.

Another actor that played the part of a sentry from my *Wagon Train* episode was Paul Baxley. He was an actor, but better known as a Hollywood stuntman. He has worked in over 140 movies and TV shows *including Star Trek* as William Shatner's stunt double. Later on he was the stunt coordinator for *The Dukes of Hazard* TV show. He took his stuntman expertise and applied it to team Elvis by performing in *Viva Las Vegas*, and *Harum Scarum.* You didn't really think that Ann-Margret pushed Elvis off the diving board into the Flamingo's pool now did you? It was Paul that got wet that day.

Wagon Train's set decorator, John McCarthy, decided that Elvis needed a "Change of Decorator" for his film *Change of Habit*, which turned out to be Elvis' last scripted movie.

The music supervisor on my *Wagon Train* stint was Stanley Wilson. He later supervised the music for Elvis in *Change of Habit.*

Chapter 20

Kissin' Cousins - My Elvis Story

It was a normal, nothing special Friday in the month of October, 1963, when I had gone shopping for groceries. When I got back home, our housekeeper Louise said that she had taken a call while I was out. It was from my agent, Sam, and that I should call him back right away.

Wondering what was so urgent; I picked up the phone and called him back: "Hello Sam. Louise said you called, so what's the emergency?"

He asked me: "What are you doing right now?"

I said: "I'm just putting away groceries and then I'll start making some dinner for Buck... Why?"

He said: "Well I just got a call from MGM, and they want you for a movie part that they thought you'd be perfect for."

I said: "That sounds great. When is the audition?"

He said: "Well that's the thing. They want to see you right now."

I said: "Right now? I'm not ready to audition right now. I need some time to prepare."

He said: "Well there is no audition. They said that if you can be in Culver City in the next thirty minutes and fit into the costume, the part is yours."

I said: "Gee, it's such short notice and Buck will be home in the next couple of hours. What's the name of this movie?"

He said: "It's called *Kissin' Cousins* and it stars Elvis Presley so if you are the right size for the costume…"

Before he could finish his sentence, I said: "A movie with Elvis? Sam, I'll be any size they want me to be. Why are they offering this part to me out of the blue?"

He said: "Well I was told that Elvis saw you on a TV show and said: 'who's that girl? I think she'd be right for the part of Midge. I want her in the film.' So one of his guys jumped into action to find out the name of 'that girl' and contacted 'that girl's' agent… But if you don't want it?"

I yelled: "I do! I do!"

I said goodbye to Sam as I threw the phone back on the hook. I grabbed my car keys and asked Louise if she'd finish putting the groceries away for me. She looked at me in shock as I ran to the front door. To put her mind at ease, I looked back and said with a big smile: "I'm going to be in an Elvis movie."

When I arrived at the studio, I went straight to wardrobe. They brought out a WAC uniform for me to try on, which I did, and I thought it fit like a glove. The wardrobe lady wasn't so sure. She looked me up and down and from back to front. When she got to the front, she had a frown on her face. I thought: oh no, am I going to lose this part because it does not fit the way she'd like?

She turned away, grabbed a few tissues and started to stuff my bra with the tissues. When she was done she stood back and said: "There, that's better."

Any other time I would have been insulted, but those magic words clinched the role for me.

After I changed into my regular clothes, she sent me to the Production Office where I was given a production schedule and my call time. My call was for early Sunday morning at the studio. We would then be transported to the film location at Cedar Lake, just west of Big Bear Lake. Usually things move slowly in Hollywood, but this was going crazy fast. I couldn't help but wonder why, but by the same token I was going to be the last person to ask why. I was too thrilled about co-starring in a movie with Elvis to start asking too many questions.

Over the weekend, I talked to Buck about what I'd be doing for the next few weeks and he was fine with it all. As I started to pack for a week-long trip to Cedar Lake, I pondered my good fortune. Is this for real? Am I about to do a movie with Elvis, the guy that lived at *Heartbreak Hotel*? If I'm dreaming, please don't pinch me.

As I looked over the production schedule, I realized that the entire movie was slated to be shot in about two and half weeks. This included location and studio time.

I thought: "Only two and a half weeks? That's crazy. Can that be done with a professional production?"

Most studio movies take anywhere from two months to a full year to complete. Remember the 3 years it took to finish the movie *Cleopatra*?

When I arrived at the studio, I was shown to the trailer/dressing room I would use when we got back from location at Cedar Lake. As I was shown to my quarters, I saw a big beautiful bouquet of red roses sitting on the table. I went over to see them and I noticed an envelope nestled amongst the flowers. I opened it up and the card read: 'To Cynthia. Love E.P.'

A wild thought ran through my mind: "Oh My Gosh, he has a crush on me. We'd never even met and he's got a crush on me."

I later found out that he was just being a gentleman and gave all his leading ladies flowers at the beginning of a movie. What a classy guy.

Later that morning there was a knock at my trailer door. I opened the door and a young man who was a personal assistant said: "Miss Pepper, I'd like to introduce you to..."

As he continued to speak, his voice seemed to disappear into a foggy mist as I looked past him towards the bottom of the stairs of my trailer door. There stood the most beautiful man that I had ever laid eyes upon. I know that beautiful is not a word that usually gets used to describe a man, but he was beautiful. He was painfully good looking with his big smile and full head of dark black hair. The personal assistant announced my guest's name, but he didn't have to. No woman on the planet would have mistaken this guy for anyone else. Elvis Aaron Presley stood at the bottom of my stairs and looked up at me with those piercing blue eyes. He was wearing a simple white collared shirt, and a pair of blue jeans that fit him oh so right. He had the most amazing aura around him.

As I walked down the stairs I extended my hand and said: "Hello Elvis"

He looked at me for a half second and said: "Don't give me that hand. Give me a big ole hug." He then proceeded to give me the biggest hug a girl could have ever wanted. For the ladies out there that are asking, yes he smelled good too.

I thanked him for the beautiful flowers and he said: "I'm glad you like them. I have some things to do before we leave but I just wanted to come by and say hello. I look forward to working with ya. We'll see you up at the lake later."

As he walked away I still thought that I might be dreaming but if I was, that was ok as it was one of the best dreams I'd had in a long while.

Before the day was done I was handed a script and quickly loaded into a car with two other cast members, Yvonne Craig and Pam Austin. Yvonne had been on *Margie* a couple of years ago so we kind of knew each other but this was my first time meeting and working with Pam. For the next eighty plus mile drive to Cedar Lake, the three of us laughed and bonded. It was also at this time that I was able to glance at the script. Yes, this was the first time that I saw the script. I guess they figured I'd have a good eighty miles or so to work on it.

The screenplay was written by Gerald Drayson Adams and Gene Nelson. Mr. Nelson was also our director. The writer and the director are hardly ever the same person so I thought he must have a very clear image of what he's looking for. I was a big fan of Gene Nelson, and so was Elvis.

I once had a big crush on Gene Nelson from watching him on the big screen years earlier. He was a song and dance man from days gone by. He had starred in numerous musicals from the early 1950's including *Lullaby of Broadway* with Doris Day, *She's Working Her Way Through College* with Virginia Mayo, and *Oklahoma* with Shirley Jones. He was a very athletic dancer, similar to Gene Kelly. When I was 11 years old, I watched Gene Nelson and Doris Day in *Warner's Tea for Two.* As I watched the movie, I wished that I could morph into Doris Day and be on that screen with him. I was really looking forward to working with him. I don't mind saying that there may have been a little lingering crush there too.

The long drive to the film location was a pleasant drive with my head in and out of the script. Most of the time I was trying to figure out what this film was all about. Yvonne and Pam were already up to speed with the story and helped me out a little. It was somewhere between West Covina and Pomona when I learned that my character was PFC Midge Reilly of the United States Army, serial number W2349687. I was a WAC that eventually falls in love with a hillbilly named Jodie. That hillbilly was played by Elvis and he had blonde hair. Huh?

As I read on I realized that I'd be doing most of my scenes with Elvis as I was, after all, one of his love interests in the film. Yahoo! Then I read that there would be two of him in the film. What?

As I read the script further it slowly made more and more sense but I just couldn't picture Elvis with blonde hair.

If you've yet to see *Kissin' Cousins* a quick synopsis of the film is as follows:

An Army officer named Josh Morgan returns to the Smoky Mountains where he's originally from and tries to convince his kinfolk to allow the Army to build a missile site there. Once he gets up into the mountains, he realizes that he's got a lookalike hillbilly cousin named Jodie Tatum that lives there. The big difference is that the cousin Jodie has blonde hair not black. Pa Tatum doesn't want to give up his still and will put up a fight to keep it. Oh yes, and there are also some mountain women known as, the Kittyhawks. They are man-crazy, and they keep attacking the soldiers. They attack them with their love making.

As we drove on I realized that there was a lot of work for me to do in such a short period of time with dialogue, big dance numbers and songs that I had to catch up on. I could have been upset that I was the last one to get a script and the last to know what I was in for, but it's a movie with Elvis for gosh sakes. If the script said that I'd be dressed as a giant avocado for the entire shoot, I'd still have said yes. In this world, there are jobs and then there are jobs. I couldn't believe my good fortune with this one.

Finally, we arrived at Cedar Lake. We were each given our own rooms at The Cedar Lake Lodge to live in for the week. It wasn't exactly home sweet home, but I had hot and cold running water, a shower and the freshest mountain air that my lungs had tasted in a long time.

I had no idea that Elvis had been coloring his hair since the early part of his career. He was originally blonde but dyed it black for the movies. In the 1950's, the majority of the leading men in films had dark black hair. Elvis thought it played better for the camera and I had to agree. He wanted the hair color that Tony Curtis and Dean Martin had. Since Elvis was playing two characters in *Kissin' Cousins*, they had to do something to easily differentiate the two characters for the audience and that was to make one of them blonde. The irony of this has never been lost on me through the years.

In order for Elvis to be two people in the same scene, they had a wonderful actor named Lance LeGault play whichever character Elvis wasn't playing at the time. The plan was that you'd only ever see the back of Lance's head in the movie. Due to some editing oversights he got his face on the screen a couple of times. You may remember Lance much later as Colonel Roderick Decker on *The A-Team* TV show. He played a great bad guy throughout his career but on the set of *Kissin' Cousins* he was always a gentleman with me.

To achieve the blonde look for the character Jodie, Elvis was given a wig to wear. He confided in me one day how much he hated wearing it. He said it didn't feel natural. I told him of the wig and pigtails that I had to wear on *Margie*. He knew that I could relate. One particular day of shooting he was getting very annoyed with his wig as it had shifted a couple of times. Between shots he expressed to me how much he wished he'd never agreed to wear it: "Man, I hate this stupid thing. It really makes my head itchy and I look stupid."

I said: "Oh Elvis you look fine. Besides you've got it easy."

He looked at me with an annoyed look: "What do you mean?"

I said: "You have to wear that thing for a couple of weeks and you're done. I had to wear my pigtails for over two years and I'm still itchy."

He started to laugh saying: "You're all right Speckled Pup." Speckled Pup was a nickname that he gave me. It caught on too. Our director / writer Gene Nelson overheard him calling me that, and liked it so much that it made it into the script. This is as to how Jodie playfully referred to Midge.

PFC Midge Reilly – Elvis called me his Speckled Pup

(Cynthia Pepper Collection)

Elvis had his gang of guys with him on the set. I think he may have been the first to invent the fulltime Hollywood entourage. Some of these guys had actual parts in the movie, like Joe Esposito and Charlie Hodge, who played soldiers. Elvis' entourage was usually close by to take care of any of his needs. He fed off them as they did off of him. It seemed odd at the time, but it was a relationship that worked for all parties involved.

This was Elvis' fourteenth film. After doing that many movies, an actor realizes that there's always a lot of waiting around between scenes. As they say in the business, "hurry up and wait". A release valve is often needed for actors. Elvis loved pulling practical jokes on the set to get a reaction from people. It helped him pass the endless hours of down time. After you completed a scene, it could take hours to setup the next scene. While you waited you could read a book, go over your lines, learn another language, write letters or post cards OR you could put firecrackers under someone's chair, hit them with a water balloon or shoot them with a water pistol. Elvis chose the fun route.

I was not immune to Elvis' jokes. The scariest one he ever did to me had me both nervous and worried. There's a scene in the movie where Jodie is getting fresh with Midge. He defies her to get past him and back to her jeep. She turns the tables on him by cozying up real close and without warning, she flips him over her shoulder with a hard Judo throw to the ground.

Elvis said we should rehearse it so that it looks real on film. I agreed. He walked us over to a secluded area, laid a crash mat on the ground and we proceeded to do our lines and practice the throw. We had gone through the scene with the Judo throw three or four times, with him landing perfectly on the mat each time. He said he wanted to try it once more just so it would be perfect. I was always looking to please, so again I agreed. Bear in mind that there was just the two of us and no one else was nearby.

He said: "Now remember this has to look good so give me a good ole toss."

I said: "Not to worry, it will be a good one."

He said: "Ok, don't hold back now."

I said: "I won't" We then did our dialogue that lead up to the throw.

Jodie (trying to kiss Midge) "Hello there you pretty little Speckled Pup."

Midge: "Let me go!"

Jodie: "What's the matter?"

Midge: "You let me by. I'm on an important mission for Capt Salbo."

Jodie: "You know, I knew that the first time I laid eyes on you that you was meant for me."

Midge (angry): "Well you're not for me buster, and I'm coming through."

Jodie: "Hey, no need to try and fight me. I'm champion wrestler of this whole mountain mam. Now how about it?"

Midge (softening): "Well maybe you're right." (moving towards him smiling) "You poor moonstruck ape."

I then pretended to hug him, but instead I grabbed him and flipped him over my shoulder to the ground just the way he wanted me to, hard.

Elvis hit the mark as he had in the past, but this time his head landed high and off the mat. It looked as though he may have hit his head on the ground. He laid there perfectly still.

I said: "Elvis get up now."

There was no response. I said: "Elvis, are you all right, please get up."

He didn't say a word and he didn't move a muscle. Now I started to get a little panicky. Did I hurt one of the world's greatest singers? Did I just damage the man that is beloved by the entire planet? Loved so much that they all know him by his first name alone? Did I just kill Elvis Presley? I was really scared. I might have to go into the witness protection program. What am I saying, that's just for witnesses. I'm a murderer! After ninety seconds, which seemed like an eternity, Elvis opened his eyes and with a smug smile on his face said: "Gotcha!"

I was at once relieved, and then livid. I gave him the same angry look that I give Jodie in the movie. I was fuming that he did this to me. I was very mad that he had taken advantage of my good nature and he knew it. I was about to get my Irish up and tell him what a rotten trick it was but then he grinned, then I grinned, and the incident was over. How can you stay mad at that smiling face?

Dancing with Elvis in MGM's Kissin' Cousins… how could I not smile.

(Courtesy of Alamy Limited)

I did get to hold one thing over Elvis in a fun away. During one of our breaks, Elvis and I were making small talk, and he started to laugh his infectious laugh that he had. He started to reminisce about tricking me the day before when we were rehearsing the shoulder throw.

He said (laughing): "Oh man, Speckled Pup I got you good yesterday. The look on your face was fantastic."

I said: "Elvis you sure did." I tried to think of something that I could do to get back at him. I know that he didn't like jokes pulled on him, so I was trying to come up with a different angle of attack. Then it came to me.

I realized that I had something that he didn't have. It was an experience. He had never had this particular experience, and it was one that he never could have. My prank on Elvis would be a combination gift for him, and a 'gotcha'.

I knew that one of his all-time favorite actors was James Dean so that's where I steered the conversation.

I started by asking a question that I already knew the answer to: "Elvis did you ever see much of James Dean's work?"

He answered: "Just everything he ever did, and more than once. *East of Eden, Rebel Without a Cause.* I wanted to learn his acting style, and be as good as he was. I was on the road a lot with my band in the early days, but when I could I'd go to a Dean film. He wasn't afraid to open himself up to the camera. You know they wrote the movie *King Creole* for him? I mean without the singing. Danny Fisher was supposed to be a boxer, but they changed that character into a singer for me. When we were making it, I tried to play it the way I thought Dean would play it."

I asked: "Did you ever get to talk to him?"

He said: "James Dean? Ha, hell no. That would have been something. He died before I got the chance."

I said: "I did."

Elvis said: "You did what?"

I said: "I talked to James Dean."

Laughing at me, he said: "No you didn't."

I said: "I did so."

Leaning in towards me, he said: "You're pullin' my leg. When would you have talked to Dean?"

I said: "My Daddy was visiting a movie set that James Dean was working on. It was my fifteenth Birthday, and Daddy called me from the set. He then gave the phone to James Dean, who was working on the set, and we talked. He wished me a Happy Birthday and everything."

Elvis had a shocked yet smiling look on his face: "Honest?"

"Honest." I said.

When Elvis spoke to you, he gave you all of his attention. Now he was giving me all of that, and even more. I went on to explain that my Daddy had been in Vaudeville, and he knew a lot of people in the business, which is why he was on the set that day. Elvis didn't really care about Vaudeville, or what Daddy had done in the past, he wanted to know all about James Dean.

Kissin' Cousins with Elvis

(Cynthia Pepper Collection)

He was still a bit skeptical. He asked: "So you talked to Dean? What movie was he working on?"

I quickly shot back: "Giant. My Daddy is friends with Chill Wills."

He said: "Oh yea right, Giant. So what did he sound like? What did he say? How did he say it...?"

Elvis had a hundred questions about my short encounter with James Dean. I did my best to answer all of them, but I kept reminding him that it was just a phone conversation. He didn't care if it was a phone conversation or radio call from Mars. He was so impressed and fascinated with my story. I could see the envy in his eyes.

At that point in his life, there wasn't much that Elvis could want for, but he didn't have this experience. I was thrilled to be able to share my story with my friend. He may have hooked a little fish with a prank the day before, but now I had landed a big fish with nothing more than a shared experience.

After telling Elvis that my Birthday was in September, he said: "You know, Dean died not long after talking to you on your Birthday."

I said: "I know. That's always been kind of eerie to me."

He said: "Yes that is and he was just 24 years old when he died. Man, you talked to James Dean. That's something."

We both agreed that James Dean died way too young, and then we went back to the task of making our movie.

I'm not into numerology by any means, but I've always found it curious that James Dean died at age twenty-four, and Elvis passed away at age forty-two. Those numbers reverse perfectly. I think Elvis too would have found that statistic oddly fascinating.

As we continued on with the task of finishing the film, I had another scene that worried me. It was a scene where I had to drive the army jeep and stop it on the mark. The driving of the jeep didn't worry as I had a ton of practice with the standard shift transmission of Buck's little MG. The thing that worried me was the mark I had to hit. It was a spot about three feet away from Jodie who would be lying on the ground in the direct path of the vehicle. I had to stop the jeep, put it in neutral, put on the emergency brake, turn off the lights, turn off the engine, jump out of the jeep and run over to Jodie who's lying on the country road. We practiced it a few times for the camera with Elvis' double, actor Lance LeGault.

The character, Jodie, wanted to get Midge to stop her jeep as she drives through the mountain roads. He decided that the best way to do this was to lie down on the road and pretend to be injured. She would stop the jeep and then he could profess his undying love for her.

The camera angle was set low so that Jodie's body would be in the scene as Midge drives up quickly. She would see him at the last minute, hit the brakes, and stop the jeep on the mark that is a mere three feet away from Jodie's seemingly lifeless body.

It was now time to shoot the scene. I jumped into the jeep as Elvis, in full costume as Jodie, laid down where Lance had been.

Before I started up the jeep, I thought: "Why is Elvis lying there? Shouldn't it be a stuntman? Where is Lance? Oh my gosh, this is my second opportunity to accidentally kill Elvis. Why is this happening to me? Why would the director let this happen? No insurance in world would cover this accident."

Once again I asked no questions. With a shaky hand but a steely determination to make this work I started up the engine. As I waited for the director to give the signal I just kept thinking, all I have to do is hit the brakes with the same timing as I did with Lance, and all will be fine. What's the worst that could happen? Maybe I miss the mark and park the jeep on top of Elvis. Maybe the brakes give out, and I run right over Elvis and take out half of the crew while I'm at it. That would certainly make the following day's newspapers. I could see the headlines… "MARGIE KILLS THE KING OF ROCK AND ROLL" or "PRESLEY PUMMULED BY PEPPER"

I quickly purged these negative thoughts from my mind and focused on the task at hand. The director yelled: "Action" and I slammed the jeep into gear and off I went. As I approached my mark, I hit the brakes as the jeep stopped just three feet away from Elvis. I then shifted into neutral, put on the emergency brake, turned off the lights, turned off the engine, jumped out of the jeep and ran over to Elvis, who's lying on the country road. The director yelled: "Cut!" and the crew applauded my work as I exhaled with total relief. Elvis jumped up from the ground and gave me a big hug. Then I heard the director yell: "Ok people, reset and let's do it again." Elvis laughed. We then proceeded to repeat the scene two more times successfully before the director was satisfied. I was a wreck afterwards, but thanks to a strong focus and great driving skills that day, no one died on the set.

I think the reason Elvis decided to lay on the road and wait for me and the jeep is because he was somewhat of a thrill-seeker. If you watch that scene in the movie, you will see Elvis' breathing getting heavier as the vehicle gets closer. Don't get me wrong, I'm not saying he had a death wish, but he may have just wanted something to bust up the boredom of the day. Why they let him do it, is still beyond me. Then again, if Elvis wanted something from you, he could charm you into it and have you thinking it was all your idea in the first place.

I was told by our director, Gene Nelson to keep eye contact with Elvis in this scene. Let's be honest, did I really need to be told that?

(Courtesy of Alamy Limited)

When making a musical film, all the music tracks are recorded long before the filming begins. Then they use a big playback system so that the music can be heard as the actors lip-synch to the songs they recorded in the studio. There were a number of songs in *Kissin' Cousins* and I was lucky enough to be in the center of two of them.

One song that I was involved with was one of the *Kissin' Cousins* songs. I say one of them as there were two different versions of the title song. The first version is a jazzy edition that is played over the opening credits. The second version is the one that was used in the final number at the end of the movie. This version was later released as a single and went to #12 on the Billboard Charts with the song *It Hurts Me* on the B-side. It's a shame that *It Hurts Me* never made it into the film.

The *Kissin' Cousins* finale dance number was a great experience. I danced with both Elvis and Lance at separate times based on whether our backs were to the camera or not. In 1964, they didn't have all the special effects that exist in today's movies. No blue screen, no computer animation tricks and no CGI. If you wanted two of the same person in the same shot you either did a split screen, which was a tricky thing to get right, or you got two guys that shared costumes and wigs. They did both those things in *Kissin' Cousins* with marginal success.

The finale was a big dance sequence with a ton of action from the entire cast. The cast had some very good, athletic dancers in it. It's still a fun scene to watch. If you look closely, you may see a very young dancer named Teri Garr (*Tootsie, Young Frankenstein, Dumb & Dumber*). You may also spot a young Kent McCord (*Adam-12*) as a background artist, and Maureen Reagan as one of the Kittyhawks. Maureen is the daughter of Ronald Reagan and Jane Wyman.

The second number I was involved with was filmed outdoors on location near Cedar Lake and it is my favorite by far.

After I flipped Jodie (Elvis) over my shoulder, he gets up and expresses his love for Midge (me) in a song. The song was *Tender Feelings*. This was a difficult number for me to get through. Was it because I had a lot of tough choreography to learn? No. Was it because of all the close-ups I had? No. Then what? This scene went against all my instincts. Gene Nelson had directed me to keep moving away from Elvis as he sang to me. I wanted to walk forward to be closer, but that's not what the script called for. Can you imagine, backing away from Elvis when he is singing to you and professing his love?

As he sang the song to me I was directed to back up, but at the same time never lose eye contact with Elvis. That was tough. I was also directed to look puzzled and hypnotized by his song. It was a fascinating scene of foreplay for these two characters and it turned out great in the final cut.

While we were filming the *Tender Feelings* scene, the weather decided not to cooperate with us. It started to drizzle a bit, so Elvis and I sat down in our chairs under a tarp and talked while we waited for the drizzle to subside. It was a sweet warm rain that was coming down. It was the kind of rain that pulls a lot of lovely scents from the top of the trees down to where you can really appreciate them. A warm, safe drizzle that can make a person reflect on a number of things in life. The rain and the song that he had been singing to me had put him in a melancholy mood. I'll never forget what Elvis said to me at this particular time.

He said "Cynthia, I don't know what I'm doing here making these films. I should be back home driving a truck"

I couldn't quite believe what I was hearing. This was the Elvis I knew. Not some abstract figure, but a real person with frailties. He's one of the world's biggest movie stars with a load of hit songs under his belt and oozing natural talent from here to next Sunday, and he's telling me he thinks he should still be driving a truck? I honestly didn't know how to respond to that.

I put my arms around him and said: "Oh Elvis I think you're wrong. You are very wrong to feel that way. You have fans all over the world that appreciate everything that you do. They don't want you to go back to driving a truck."

He said: "I suppose so, but do you think anyone will remember me? Like, when it all ends, will people still remember me?"

I leaned into him, gave him a big hug and whispered: "Of course they will."

I could see that he was searching for something more out of life. He had everything almost anyone could want, but he seemed to be looking for a meaning or a goal.

To me, Elvis was a very playful person, almost like a young boy at times but a young boy with an old soul.

The people that knew and worked with Elvis always felt that he was a very generous person. Others can tell you about his generosity as a friend, but I'll tell you about his generosity in regards to his acting, and being an all-round professional.

Through the years, I've heard some people say that Elvis didn't like making most of his movies. If that's true, it must have come out later in his life. I never saw any evidence of that when we were working together on Kissin' Cousins.

First of all when Elvis the actor came to the set he always knew his lines, your lines, and what catering was serving for lunch that day. In other words, he was prepared. He was on time and up for anything the director would throw at him.

His generosity was evident because he was always there for the other actors. Generally speaking, the star of the film does his or her close-up scenes then heads back to the dressing room. The supporting cast would then do their close-ups with an off camera script person, or someone else. (In Fred MacMurray's case, a mop) As an actor on camera, you have to play your part with all the emotion that is required but you are generally being fed lines from a person giving you an emotionless read.

Elvis always stayed. He did his principal shots, and then he stayed and fed you his lines with feeling, and that helped you do a better job. What is better: trading lines of love with a person that has their head stuck in a script, or trading the same lines with Elvis while looking deeply into his eyes that are locked onto yours? When you see the close-ups of me in this movie, you can be sure that Elvis was standing beside the camera giving me my cue lines. That is pure generosity from a fellow actor, and in this case, a movie star.

Dancing to the theme song Kissin' Cousins. When acting with Elvis he knew all his lines, AND all your lines so you had to be on top of your game.

(Courtesy of Alamy Limited)

The one question I'm asked more than any other is: "What was it like to kiss Elvis?"

When people, mostly women, ask me that question I always answer: "It was wonderful."

Elvis didn't disappoint in the kissing department. His lips were very soft, as if someone had combined silk and velvet into one fabric then turned it into his lips. He knew how to kiss a woman, and I enjoyed kissing him back. So much so that I think I must have messed up our kissing scenes about five or six times. Well, I wanted to get it right, of course, and I must tell you that Elvis didn't seem to mind either. I didn't want to get fired, but I knew how far I could go with that little trick before the director would have steam coming out of his ears. Let me ask you, wouldn't most women do the same?

With his fun, childlike antics, it was hard not to follow along with Elvis when he was being playful. An example of this was a scene that we did on the MGM soundstage in the back of a buckboard wagon full of straw. The scene was to have Jodie and Midge hiding out of sight in the back of the buckboard until Ma Tatum (Glenda Farrell) calls for him. His head would then pop up and then my head would pop up revealing the make out session that was going on in the back of the wagon. This scene lasts about fifteen seconds in the final cut, however; it took a lot longer to shoot.

When Elvis and I loaded ourselves into the back of the buckboard and ducked down out of site he smiled at me, and I saw the mischief in his eyes. Our director, Gene yelled: "Action!" This was Elvis' cue to pop up for the camera, but he didn't move. As a matter of fact, we didn't move at all as we were laying in each other's arms getting... well let's call it motivated. A few seconds went by, and the director yelled: "Action!" Again Elvis didn't move away from me. I whispered: "That's your cue."

He said: "I know, I'm just havin' some fun with Gene."

I smiled and said: "Ok" signaling that I was now in cahoots with him.

The director then said: "Elvis that's your cue to come up."

Elvis yelled back: "Sorry sir we're just tryin' to get comfortable back here."

Upon saying that he grabbed handfuls of straw and began throwing it straight up from the back of the buckboard, and I did the same. It must have looked like one hell of a make out session to the camera. The cast and crew were laughing hysterically, and so was Elvis. Hopefully, Gene was laughing too. After a couple of fun false starts, we finally got the scene finished.

The Producer of *Kissin' Cousins*, Sam Katzman was a real character, literally. If you were to stereotype a Hollywood movie producer by describing him as a short, fat, loud, balding man, who is constantly chomping on a cheap fat cigar that hangs between his lips, you would be describing Mr. Katzman.

He was the King of producing cheap Hollywood movies quickly, and always turned a profit. He could identify a fad and turn out a movie about that fad before it faded away, thus selling lots of tickets and filling his bank account. When The Twist was all the rage, he made a film called *Twist Around the Clock* for $250,000. Six months after its release, it grossed $6,000,000.

Yvonne Craig with her dark haired Elvis and me with light haired Elvis. "Two Elvi, No Waiting."

(Courtesy of Alamy Limited)

One famous Katzman story goes that he had heard one of his movies was going over time and, therefore, going over budget. He marched down to the set of the film to see the director.

He asked the director: "How many pages of script do you have to shoot today?"

The director responded: "Ten"

Katzman asked: "How many scenes have you shot already?"

Director answered: "Five."

Katzman then took the director's script and ripped out five pages and said: "There. You're done for the day."

Mr. Katzman did one particular thing to me that I didn't find amusing at all. One morning on the set in front of everyone he said to me, in a loud enough voice for all to hear: "Cynthia, why didn't you wake me up when the alarm went off this morning?"

I couldn't believe what he just said. He was trying to be funny by implying that we had spent the night together. I was so embarrassed. A few people gave a small laugh, and I said to anyone who would listen to me: "He's joking. We weren't together last night!"

I was mortified for the rest of the day. Well, if that wasn't enough the next day he proceeded to repeat the same declaration as the day before. Once again my face turned beet red, and I was embarrassed. A few people giggled again. They knew that he was a kidder and didn't take Mr. Katzman seriously but he was the guy paying the bills, so they laughed.

Elvis, bless his heart, quickly took Mr. Katzman aside and quietly told him: "Knock it off. You're embarrassing her."

Needless to say, the incident never occurred again. Thank you Elvis, for coming to my rescue. I know now that I overreacted to his comments, but I was young and didn't know how to handle the situation. If it were to happen today, I would just go along with the joke, humor Mr. Katzman and give the blarney right back to him. I realize now that no one took him seriously that day, and I shouldn't have either. I guess youth really is wasted on the young.

The actors and crew were all living in cabins not too far from the film location at Big Bear. My cabin was very close to the wooded area. One day I noticed a skinny little, calico colored kitten, lurking around the cabins. She was wandering here, there and everywhere. The day before, I had noticed a dead adult cat on the side of the road. I figured that could have been her mother. The kitten looked lost and hungry so I left some food out for her. She wouldn't come near the food when I was watching, so I hid, but kept an eye out for her. She finally did come to eat. I watched as she gobbled up the food quickly. She was such a thin and sad looking little stray. With no mother cat in sight, I decided to rescue her.

As I slowly approached, she got scared and bolted into the nearby forest. I now feared for her life as there was a road on the other side of the forest that she could wander out to. I started into the forest while calling out to her. Elvis and a couple of his guys were walking nearby and heard me calling into the woods. Elvis came over and said: "Hey Speckled Pup! What are you up to?"

While frantically searching I said: "There's a lost little kitten in here with no mother. I want to help her."

Elvis smiled and motioned to the other two guys to come over. He then looked at me and said: "Don't worry; I'll help you find her."

So for the next twenty minutes I was trekking through the forest with an international superstar trying to save a cat.

Jodie with blond hair and Josh with black. Oh how he hated that blond wig.

(Courtesy of Alamy Limited)

This was the Elvis I knew. He was just a regular guy that would rather do a good deed for a friend then worry about it being beneath him. The fact that it meant something to me made it mean something to him.

We finally found the little kitten hiding under a fern near a tree. She was scared and breathing hard. Elvis gently picked her up and held her to his chest. He spoke to her gently as he slowly rubbed the kitten's head. He said: "There you go. Don't be scared. You're gonna be fine. I hear you lost your Momma. I sure know what that feels like." As he handed me the kitten, he said: "Well we got a brand new Momma here for you now." As Elvis walked me and the newest member of my family back to my cabin. I thanked him. He said that he was happy to do it and that he was needed back on the set. As he started to walk away, he turned and gave a little laugh. I asked: "What's so funny?"

He smiled and said: "Nothin'... Just that I'd never seen a kitten that had a Speckled Pup for a Momma before."

I ended up taking that kitten home, and she had a nice long and loving life with me. I named her Callie. When I tell this story to people, they always ask why I didn't name the kitten Elvis or Presley. My answer is twofold. Firstly, the cat was female and secondly, there was only one Elvis Presley.

This next story was not something I was a part of, but it relates to the whole movie shoot. It's about another incident that could have left us without Elvis even sooner.

When location shooting finished, it was time to head back to the MGM studios. It was November 6th when we all piled into different vehicles to drive back to the studio. Elvis had decided that he would drive the big bus that had brought people up to the location. Elvis enjoyed being behind the wheel. Many times he would be the one to drive the tour bus or motor home, when going from Memphis to Hollywood, because he enjoyed it. If he had to do any other job than what he was doing, I think he would still have been a truck driver. He loved it.

He and his entourage, including Joe Esposito and Charlie Hodge, got into the big bus and settled in for a long ride back to MGM. We had left before Elvis, so I wasn't around to see this but we heard about it afterwards.

As Elvis put the big bus into gear and headed down the steep hills of Cedar Lake road, he was shocked to find that the bus had no brakes. As he pushed on the brake pedal they just gave out. There was a car ahead with some crew on board, and the bus was rapidly picking up speed. Seeing that there was no room to pass the car and with a sheer drop on one side of the road Elvis used all his truck driving skills and tried to slow the bus by gearing down until they got to the bottom of the hill. They eventually made it down safely and just let the bus run until it rolled to a stop. Good thing Elvis was such a proficient driver or both musical and movie history would have been quite different today.

When we arrived back at the MGM studios, they had made a beautiful set that looked so much like the Cedar Lake setting, right down to the old mill house that they used as Ma and Pa's cabin. The magic they could do in the studios always intrigued me. When I wasn't in front of the camera, I was always watching the crew build, change and create amazing sets. They were an amazing artistic team.

The one thing that amazed me were the amount of friends that I had come visit me on the studio lot. When a couple of girlfriends found out that I was doing a movie with Elvis, they asked if I could get them on the set. I said sure. When they arrived at the gate, I got a call from security telling me that all twelve of my guests had arrived. Twelve guests? How did my two girlfriends turn into so many? Elvis just had that effect on women. Yes, they all got in, and yes they all met Elvis. I was quite popular with my friends that day.

I enjoyed watching my friend Yvonne Craig work. No one did "sexy" better than Yvonne. She played Azalea Tatum, who would eventually beat out Selena (Pam Austin), for the love of Josh. Yvonne had such an expressive face and amazing stature as an actress. She had once been a ballet dancer, so classic form and body movement was second nature to her. We had a lot more time together and got to know each other better on *Kissin' Cousins* than we ever did on *Margie.*

It was great to be working with Glenda Farrell again. She played Tommy Sands mother in the live broadcast we did for *The United States Steel Hour*. She started out as a Warner Brothers contract actress in the early 1930's and was one of the original flappers. She ramped up her career as Edward G. Robinson's girlfriend in the 1931 movie classic, *Little Caesar*. A great trivia question for Elvis fans would be; "Who, other than Elvis sings, a song all by themselves in the movie *Kissin' Cousins*?" Well, that would be Glenda. As Ma Tatum she got to sing a bluesy number called *Pappy, Won't you Please Come Home* and Elvis was nowhere in sight. How Colonel Tom allowed that to happen, I'll never know.

Glenda did have an unfortunate accident on the set and had to work through part of the movie in a great deal of pain.

When the location shoot finished at Cedar Lake we still had a week's worth of work at MGM Studios to finish the film. Glenda had a scene where she was stepping off the porch of the Tatum cabin. I think she was carrying a big plate of corn on the cob or something else that was very heavy. She miscalculated the last two steps down to the ground, slipped, and fell down hard. She threw her back out and had to do the rest of her scenes wearing a back brace. Once again, with the magic of Hollywood and her acting skills, no one was ever the wiser.

Glenda's son, Tommy Farrell, was also in the movie. He played Master Sgt. William George Bailey. Tommy was known as the Hollywood B-Western sidekick from the golden era of westerns.

Through the years, a few people have asked me to comment on *Kissin' Cousins*. Even though I worked on the film, I don't feel the need to defend it as a piece of art. However, I think it's great as a piece of entertainment.

Judging a movie is a very subjective thing. Over the years, some reviewers were harsh, and yet others have praised *Kissin' Cousins*. The fan's opinions carry the most weight with me. Many fans have told me that it's their favorite Elvis film. Since it is a subjective thing, I urge you to watch the movie and makeup your own mind.

I can tell you that there were numerous factors that contributed to the finished product.

Colonel Tom was very upset with *Viva Las Vegas* going over budget. He was looking to make up the financial losses by doing his next film quickly and cheaply. The next film was *Kissin' Cousins*. Its budget was approximately $800,000 which was almost half of what it cost to make *Viva Las Vegas*. When *Kissin' Cousins* was released, it grossed about $2.8 million. Not a bad return for a movie made in a fast paced eighteen days. The majority of the songs for the movie were recorded in two days.

The Colonel hired Sam Katzman to produce *Kissin' Cousins* because Sam had a reputation for cranking out films in a short time frame, and coming in on, or below, budget. He was also hired later to produce *Harum Scarum*.

Very few people remember this, but the screenplay for *Kissin' Cousins* was nominated in the category of best written American musical by the *Writers Guild of America*. The film reached #11 on the Variety national box office chart and finished at #26 on the year end list of the top-grossing movies of 1964. The title single from the soundtrack reached #12 on the Billboard Hot 100 and was certified Gold by the RIAA.

I will always have fond memories of the film because I got to work up close and personal with Elvis Presley, and, as a result, we became good friends. I always felt very comfortable around Elvis, as he did around me. During the filming we had quite a few private talks, some that I've shared and others that I will keep to myself.

Obviously, my thoughts and memories of Elvis come from working together as colleagues and knowing him as a friend. Other people that have worked with him, or befriended him have their own stories to tell. We all agree that Elvis Presley was a wonderful, kind, and generous person. He also had a fantastic sense of humor. He loved to laugh, and he loved to hear others laugh.

Some fans tend to see Elvis Presley as an icon, not as a human being. It's understandable because most fans have never met the man, yet they have been inundated through the years with the legend of

Elvis. People get so wrapped up in all the hype surrounding Elvis that they begin to see him as a godlike figure. In my opinion, there is only one God and it's not Elvis. He wasn't perfect, but then again none of us are.

Elvis was a humble man searching for the reasons behind our existence. He certainly had a bigger impact on the entertainment world than most of us ever will, but he never forgot his humble beginnings.

When Elvis was with a group of guys, the conversation would be about things like favorite sports teams, or the latest in cool, fast cars. If he was with a group of women, which happened to him a lot, and for good reason, Elvis would flirt with all the ladies, while making each and every one of them feel special. He was just an ordinary guy with extraordinary talents.

Working with Elvis was a dream come true.

(Cynthia Pepper Collection)

Through the years we kept in touch, mostly with phone calls. In the 70's, he asked me if I would come to Las Vegas and see him and his show. I would tell him I would love to, and that I would try to make it happen. Unfortunately, I was never able to get to Vegas. Life and work get in the way when you try to meet up with old friends. I always thought that we could have a drink afterwards and how great it would be for the two of us to pick up on some unfinished conversations from the past. All my well intentioned thoughts turned into regrets on Tuesday, August 16th, 1977.

Elvis was 42 years old when he died, and that was far too young for him to leave this earth. He died about 18 days before my birthday. Oddly enough, that was about the same number of days we spent making the movie together.

I've been asked if I regret that I didn't get to see Elvis perform live in concert. Yes, of course I do. Then again I realize that I did pretty well as an Elvis fan. I had him lock his eyes with mine and sing a song of love directly to me numerous times in one day. I also got to dance and trade lines with him. I got my own special Elvis concert. I will always miss him and cherish the time that we shared together.

The Elvis Connection #6 - *Kissin' Cousins*

It's obvious that I have an Elvis connection with the entire cast and crew of *Kissin' Cousins*. Here are a few people that have had more connections than just *Kissin' Cousins*.

Yvonne Craig better known as TV's iconic character *Batgirl* had been in two of Elvis' movies. The first was *It Happened at the World's Fair* where she played Dorothy Johnson and later in *Kissin' Cousins* as Azalea Tatum. That's right; Elvis made out with *Batgirl*.

Arthur O'Connell played Pappy Tatum in *Kissin' Cousins*. His role was trying to be a father figure to Elvis' character. He played one of the best comedic drunk characters in this film. Arthur seemed destined to teach Elvis' characters right from wrong in the movies. In 1962 Arthur was Pop Kwimper trying to show his son Toby Kwimper, played by Elvis, how to make a go of things in *Follow That Dream*.

Jack Albertson, whom I already mentioned was a guest actor on my show *Margie*. He would also co-star with Elvis in 1964's *Roustabout*.

One of Pamela Austin's first professional movie parts was in Elvis' 1961 film *Blue Hawaii*.

Beverly Powers can also be found in *Viva Las Vegas* and as Miss Beverly Hills in *Speedway*.

Dallas Johann was a Hillbilly Dancer in *Kissin' Cousins* and was able to dance himself all the way over to *Viva Las Vegas* before he was through.

Teri Garr had such a huge career in Hollywood, but it started out small. She started out being in a number of Elvis movies as a backup dancer or unaccredited as an extra. She was in *Fun in Acapulco, Viva Las Vegas, Kissin' Cousins, Roustabout, Girl Happy,* and *Clambake*. Her parents were very good friends with Mother and Daddy. As a matter of fact, they had similar careers. Her father Eddie Garr was an actor comedian in Vaudeville, and her mother Phyllis was a dancer with the Rockettes.

Lance LeGault had been Elvis' stand-in, stunt double, and body double. When it came to early Elvis films, Lance had done a lot. He was in *Girls, Girls, Girls, Kissin' Cousins, Viva Las Vegas,* and *Roustabout*. He can even be found playing the tambourine on a little TV special called *Elvis*. It would later be better known to the world as *The '68 Come Back Special*.

Joan Staley played Jonesy in *Kissin' Cousins* and would later play Marge in *Roustabout*. She was also a Deb Star with me at the *9th Annual Deb Star Ball*.

Kent McCord, who would later reach stardom as Officer Jim Reed in TV's popular series, *Adam-12* was an extra in *Kissin' Cousins*. He was just starting out in the business at the time, but would go on to work in more uncredited roles in *Viva Las Vegas, Roustabout,* and *Girl Happy*.

Sailor Vincent was in over 150 movies with a little more than 30 as a stuntman. The rest of the time he was a background actor. He'd either be a barfly, henchman, bystander, rancher, gang member, or in any scene that just needed a warm body. He was in a number of films my father was in too, including *Cat Ballou* billed as "Townsman with Hairpiece". He was also in Elvis' film *Roustabout*.

Fred Karger was musical supervisor on *Kissin' Cousins* and would also be conducting the musical sound track for Elvis' movies *Harum*

Scarum and *Frankie and Johnny*. I went to Hollywood High with his daughter Teri.

Gene Nelson & Sam Katzman would go on to produce and direct one more Elvis' film *Harum Scarum*.

However, I think the Elvis connection winner has to go to a behind the scenes fellow named William Tuttle. Bill was billed as makeup artist or makeup supervisor for over 360 films including - *Jailhouse Rock, It Happened at the World's Fair, Viva Las Vegas, Kissin' Cousins, Girl Happy, Harum Scarum, Spinout, Double Trouble, Stay Away, Joe, Speedway, Live a Little, Love a Little,* and *The Trouble with Girls*.

Kissing Elvis - His lips were very soft. It was as if someone had found a way to combine silk and velvet into one substance, from that they created his lips.

(Cynthia Pepper Collection)

Chapter 21

The Times They Are A Changin' Bittersweet

I was on an actor's high. I had just completed my first co-starring role in an MGM musical and with Elvis Presley no less. When we parted he gave me a big hug and kiss goodbye, and said that he'd like to stay in touch. I told him that would be great and that we'd see each other again soon. It never occurred to me that this was the last time that I'd see him face to face. I was still in a spin over how quickly we had made the film. I was now home in my comfy apartment. It had been just 18 days earlier that I got the part. I was walking on air, and I felt that the sky was the limit for what might come next. What came next was a punch to the gut for all of America.

It had been eight days after the filming of *Kissin' Cousins* had wrapped. I was now at home relaxing with a little bit of quiet, alone time. Buck was working, and Louise had the day off. I had just finished eating lunch and turned on the TV to watch my favorite soap, *As the World Turns*. This was one of my guilty pleasures. I loved to escape into the fictional town of Oakdale, Illinois and all of its interesting, and sometimes outrageous, characters. I was watching the daily episode, Nancy Hughes, played by actress Helen Wagner, was in the middle of a scene with actor Santos Ortega, who played Grandpa Will Hughes, when without warning the screen went black, and the audio was gone. Then a banner appeared across the screen that read "CBS News Bulletin". Then, the voice that all of America recognized began to speak. It was Walter Cronkite. He said: "Here is a bulletin from CBS News. In Dallas, Texas, three shots were fired at President Kennedy's motorcade in downtown Dallas. The first reports say that President Kennedy has been seriously wounded by this shooting."

I couldn't believe what I was hearing from the voice of the most trusted man in the TV news world. Could this be a prank?

He continued: "More details just arrived. These details are about the same as previously...President Kennedy shot today just as his motorcade left downtown Dallas. Mrs. Kennedy jumped up and grabbed Mr. Kennedy; she called "Oh no!" the motorcade sped on. United Press says that the wounds for President Kennedy perhaps could be fatal. Repeating, a bulletin from CBS News: President Kennedy has been shot by a would-be assassin in Dallas, Texas. Stay tuned to CBS News for further details."

I was in shock. How could this be? Who would want to shoot the President? Why in Dallas? I kept thinking, hoping and praying that he would be ok. I thought of past Presidents that had been assassinated, Lincoln, Garfield, and McKinley, but these things happened decades ago. This shouldn't be happening in today's modern society. It's 1963 for God's sake.

The report went on to say that the President was taken to Parkland Memorial Hospital, just outside of Dallas. Patty and I had been to that hospital as little girls for various injuries. Eventually, Mr. Cronkite threw the television feed back to the regularly scheduled program. I watched as the actors were now in an entirely different part of the episode. It was live TV, and they just kept going to meet their time commitment. I don't think they were even aware of what was going on in the outside world.

The presidential assassination was all everyone was talking about. So much had gone on in two days. They captured a guy named Lee Harvey Oswald whom they figured had pulled the trigger. Within two days, some guy shot and killed Oswald. It was like the world had gone mad in an instant, and it all seem to be originating from Dallas. I didn't remember Dallas being so insane. It was so personal to me as I listened to all the details discussed on the news. The fact that he was shot while driving on route through Dealey Plaza blew me away. I used to get on a bus that took me through Dealey Plaza every day on my way to and from school. I could picture the entire place where it happened, and it left me unnerved.

I decided to visit Mother and Daddy just to see how they were faring. Daddy had never been a supporter of Kennedy but as he said: "You don't shoot the President of The United States, no matter how much you hate the guy."

That seemed to be the view of most Americans at the time. The shooting bonded the American people together. This was the only positive thing to come out of such a heinous crime.

While I visited my parents that day, we had the radio on in the background, just in case there were any more updates.

Mother said: "Listen to this."

As she turned up the radio, the news reported that the man who had shot Oswald was a guy named Jack Ruby from Dallas, Texas.

"Ruby?" Daddy yelled. "I know him."

Oh great, now Daddy was losing it too. I asked: "What do you mean, you know him? Is he a friend of yours?"

Daddy said: "No, he's no friend. He's a guy that came into the club a few times in Dallas. He was from Chicago originally. He ran another club on the other side of Dallas. He would drop in from time to time to see me. He was a bit off... sort of a weird guy. I never trusted him. I always knew that he'd do something stupid one day."

The one thing that was obvious to Patty and me as we grew up was the fact that Daddy knew a lot of people, but this was crazy. I suggested that it could be another Jack Ruby, but the next day Daddy saw Mr. Ruby's picture in the paper and exclaimed: "Yep, that's the bum." My father knew movie stars, producers, directors, corporate giants, famous politicians, and now killers.

The "Camelot Administration" had been a nickname for President Kennedy's time in office. *Camelot* was the president's favorite Broadway musical. A lot of idealistic hope and expectation was wrapped around his presidency.

To me November 22nd, 1963 was the day the US changed. It could have been because I was personally transitioning from an age of innocence to grownup reality, but I felt that America was too. The Camelot era was now over, and there were more and more serious issues that seemed to surround us. The Cold War, Cuba, civil rights, and nuclear weapons, were just a few of the serious concerns for all Americans at this time. Life didn't feel as optimistic as it did just a few months ago. My time of playing the young, innocent, and ingénue roles was quickly passing too.

Who Poked A Hole In The River?

By 1963, my parents still had their problems and I continued to send cash to help them stay afloat. Mother was still working at the Broadway Hollywood, and Daddy was searching for work in the entertainment field. It was all he knew how to do. He just didn't know how to go out and get it. It was like he kept waiting for work to find him.

Daddy featured with his pal Jack, on The Jack Benny Program.

(Cynthia Pepper Collection)

Daddy ended up with a lot of unaccredited roles, because he didn't push to get credit for the movies and TV shows that he worked in.

His agent was now more focused on other clients and he allowed Daddy to slip through the cracks.

From 1959 to 1964 Daddy had found work in *The Five Pennies* with Danny Kaye, *Bachelor in Paradise* with Bob Hope and Lana Turner, *Papa's Delicate Condition* with Jackie Gleason, *Critics Choice* with Bob Hope and Lucille Ball, and a Perry Mason episode with Raymond Burr. He had small parts in these productions and no credit for doing them. Most of these parts came from his buddies, like Hope and Gleason. They would throw him a bone whenever they could. The fact that Daddy had the love and admiration of his friends seemed to be enough for him, but it was hardly paying the bills.

In the spring of '64, Daddy got a call from another friend Jack Benny. He wanted Daddy to do an appearance on his TV show *The Jack Benny Program.* Daddy did one episode in 1964 and another two in 1965. One episode was called *Jack's Navy Buddy Returns.* Daddy played Jack's Navy buddy named Stub Walker and he and Jack were fantastic together. There were a lot of laughs provided by these song and dance men from the days of Vaudeville. I was very proud of Daddy in that role.

In 1964, Patty moved to New York City to live. Maybe she wanted more independence and had had enough of living across the way from her, sometimes, volatile parents. Perhaps Patty had been missing New York since she was a child, when we lived there years ago. I do know that when she visited New York with me in 1961 she was smiling from ear to ear for most of that trip. Long before the "I Love New York" song or logo came about, Patty loved New York. I guess her roommate Carol did too because she moved with her.

I didn't have a lot of contact with Patty for the next few years since she moved so far away, and the fact that we really didn't have anything to talk about. The reality was that we had a lot to talk about and try to fix, but we didn't. I offered an olive branch to her on numerous occasions just to have it slapped to the ground. I wished her the best on the East Coast.

I thought that the work would really start to flow in after my movie with Elvis, but that wasn't exactly the case.

I was no longer a contract player with a studio so I had to get out there and make it happen. I pounded the pavement and did a lot of auditions.

I eventually scored a job for an episode of the *Perry Mason* TV series. It was called *The Case of the Drifting Dropout.* I played Annalee Fisher, the secretary of the guy that got murdered and the girlfriend of the guy that was accused of my boss's murder. My boyfriend was the drifting dropout. It was a mess of finger pointing but if anyone could figure it all out it was Perry Mason.

Working with Raymond Burr was very easy. He was all business, as was the entire crew, but he was also a very warm man. His character Perry Mason, and later in life *Ironsides,* were that of tough guys. However when the cameras were off, he was a very caring and generous person.

William Hopper played P.I. Paul Drake. He was a very large and tall man with an intimidating look on camera, but he was really a pussy cat of a guy. He was the only child born to comic stage actor and singer DeWolf Hopper and gossip columnist Hedda Hopper. I enjoyed doing scenes with him, but I did end up with a sore neck from hours of looking up an extra two feet just to make eye contact with him. In 1943, he played the hotel clerk in the movie *The Hard Way* which was loosely based on Daddy and Ginger Rogers' relationship. Once again it is a small world.

I didn't have any scenes with Barbara Hale, but her character Della Street was just as famous as Perry was. Later in life I found it funny that in certain episodes they would try to create some light sexual tension between Perry and Della. They would get all flirty and then nothing would ever come from it. I would think 'well how could it? He's gay.' It was such a well-guarded Hollywood secret that no one knew. Working with Mr. Burr at the time I didn't know either but I found out a few years later. He remained in the closet his entire life. Think of how difficult that must have been for him.

Speaking of sexual tension and the professional side of doing a scene, let me tell you of my first day on the *Perry Mason* set. TV production companies always shoot scenes out of sequence for cost savings reasons. That way if they have several scenes that take place in the kitchen or living room, for example, they can set it up and light it just once and do all the different scenes on the same day.

Shooting out of sequence really keeps an actor on his or her toes. Think about this, you could be filming a scene in the morning about making up with your boyfriend. Later in the afternoon, but on the same day, you could be filming the big breakup scene that precedes the makeup scene. Thank goodness for editors. They will even film the end scenes of a movie or TV show first so that they are assured of having the star in the final scene just in case the lead actor was to get ill and or die along the way.

When I first arrived on set, I was to do a scene with my TV boyfriend Barry Davis played by a wonderful actor named Carl Reindel. This scene will be edited into the middle of the TV episode. I had never met Carl before and didn't know a lot of his past efforts in the business, but that didn't matter as it was now time to get to work. I was lead over to the inside of the truck cab where Carl was already sitting behind the wheel. The director Arthur Marks introduced us to each other as we shook hands and shared a cordial "Hello, nice to meet you."

Mr. Marks then moved out of the shot as someone yelled: "Quiet please, Quiet!" A man with a clapper board reached in between us and the camera getting ready to slate the scene. Holding up the clapper, he said: "The Drifting Dropout. Two Ten, take one."

He then clapped down the clapper as he jumped out of the scene. Mr. Marks said: "Roll camera." He then called for quiet and followed that with: "...and Action!"

Carl and I then threw our arms around each other locked lips for a long 10 second kiss of pure passion. I ran my fingers along the back of his neck as his strong arms embraced me even closer to his body. I was deep in the throes of a romantic on screen kiss, with both of us giving it all we got. We then pulled away from each other as he delivered his line to me, and I responded with my line. As we sat there looking into each other's eyes, I heard the director yell: "Cut! Did we get it Howie?" The cameraman confirmed that everything was good.

Walking towards us, Mr. Marks said: "Great job kids." Then to the crew: "Ok we are moving on!"

I shook Carl's hand, got out of the truck, and we went to our separate trailers. Sometimes that's how crazy fast things can happen when doing an intimate scene with another actor. To prepare you make sure you brush your teeth so that your breath is minty fresh and with any luck your acting partner did too.

Sorry, what was that? You're asking; how was the kiss? Well, Carl's breath was fresh sure enough but as far as the actual kiss goes... Well, let's just say he was no Elvis.

Buck and my personal manager looked at our finances and it was decided that we were spending way too much on rent. We moved from our expensive apartment to a much cheaper place, located about a block away on Hacienda Place. It was a ground floor apartment, not far from a restaurant called Barney's Beanery. We definitely took a step down in our housing. To make matters worse, we found out later, that we had a prostitute living in the apartment above us. Without fail, whenever she would entertain a "client" in her apartment, she would blare, Petula Clark's song, *Downtown* on her stereo. To this day I associate that song to the world's oldest profession.

The rest of 1964 was a bit sparse for me, work wise. I did a lot of auditions but things were not clicking like they had in the past. I missed out on one particular show that year. I auditioned for a sitcom pilot in the spring of '64. It was for a show created by Sherwood Schwartz. He had been a writer in Hollywood up until this time writing for a TV show called *I Married Joan* starring Joan Davis and Jim Backus. He was also a writer for *The Red Skelton Show* and a couple of Red's TV specials.

Now Sherwood had created something that he thought the public would really go for. It was a TV show about seven castaways marooned on an island that no one can ever seem to rescue them from. Does it sound familiar? *Gilligan's Island* seemed like a pretty strange concept to me but as time would prove there are worse things in Hollywood than being stranded on a deserted isle all day. I was auditioning for the part of Mary Ann Summers.

Wholesome, innocent, perky, bubbly and virginal was what they were looking for from the character. Well, I figured I could give them four out of five of what they were looking for. It finally came down to me and another actress from Reno, Nevada by the name of Dawn Wells. I knew that the competition was going to be tight as Dawn had won the Miss Nevada pageant title just five years earlier, and I still had piano legs.

We both did a screen test for the part and they hired Dawn. I was later told that since the character Ginger was a red head and the character of Mrs. Howell was blonde they would be going with a three color hair contrast. I was blonde at that time and Dawn was a brunette. If only I had gone in with my real hair color of brunette, I might have won the part. Well at least I didn't lose it because of the piano legs.

After *Gilligan's Island* aired I realized that they made the right choice with Dawn. She was fantastic as Mary Ann.

There wasn't a lot of TV work happening for me in the summer of '64. Buck and I hosted and attended a number of parties. We were just having a good time. We didn't give a lot of forethought towards our financial future. I was still the bigger money maker in our relationship but Buck didn't mind. He was still bringing in his regular paycheck, but it was my money that was used to pay all the bills. His earnings got put away for a rainy day.

In retrospect, I should have been a little more business minded but I was a very trusting person. I wasn't worried about the financial side of our lives. Acting parts always seemed to come my way just as they did in the fall of '64.

As the fall approached, I was cast for a guest appearance in a new TV pilot called *Many Happy Returns*. It starred John McGiver, Elinor Donahue, Mickey Manners and Mark Goddard. My friend Christopher Riordan would be added to the cast later as Ronnie. It was about a fictitious Department Store called Krockmeyer's in L.A. The show followed the strange and funny goings on between the employees that worked there and the people that shopped there.

I played Susan Jones in the pilot episode. She was a young bride that was left at the altar. Since she was jilted, she was in a rage as she brought all of her wedding gifts back to the store to return them. They were all still wrapped in beautiful boxes and Susan was still wearing her wedding dress. It was a very bizarre and fun role to play and I got to wear a wedding dress all day. What girl doesn't like that?

The one memory that stands out in my mind was having lunch in the MGM commissary with John McGiver. John played the manager of the complaint's department. When he spoke, he had such a precise and firm command of the English language. He almost sounded like he had an English accent when he spoke, but he didn't. He always sounded so intelligent and in control when he spoke even off camera. At first I was intimidated by his formality but as I got to know him better I realized that he was just a big cuddly bear of a guy.

As we were eating our lunch, we made small talk. He asked me: "My dear, have you yet to enter into the holy state of matrimony?"

Getting ready to shoot a scene for "Many Happy Returns".

(Rick Goeren Collection)

I said: "Yes. My husband's name is Buck and we've been married for four years now. Are you married?"

He answered: "Oh yes indeed. I am very blessed to have found the one woman that could put up with me and all my eccentricities for the past seventeen years. Her name is Ruth. May I be so bold as to ask, do you have any children?"

I said: "No we don't have any children yet but maybe later on we will have a small family together. Do you have any children?"

He said: "Oh yes, we have been abundantly blessed with ten children.

"Ten Children?" The milk I had just put into my mouth had almost come gushing out of my nose. I was in shock. I didn't know anyone who had ten children. I didn't even think that was possible. His wife Ruth obviously didn't have a lot of time to herself in the last seventeen years. How did she do it? Why did she do it? I was only twenty three years old at that time and he was an old looking fifty one. That seemed ancient to me. The fact that he wasn't the most handsome fellow in the world made me wonder why anyone would even have sex with him let alone ten times. Gosh to think that I was ever that young and shallow amazes me.

The TV pilot was picked up by CBS and ran for a year. I was just a guest player in the pilot so I didn't get any more work from it, but I was glad to help. I was just happy that John's ten kids would be provided for.

Bittersweet

In, 1964 I was asked to come back to *My Three Sons* but just as a guest. I had visited them all on the Desilu set many times since 1961. I loved the cast and it had always felt like family to me. They were now in season five and wanted to pull on some heart strings with the Mike Douglas and Jean Pearson characters. Playing Jean again was like putting on a pair of old, yet comfortable shoes. I found things were different in so much as everyone was three years older since I left and William (Bill) Frawley's drinking was catching up to him. Bub wasn't functioning as well as he used to.

Stan Livingston has a funny story of keeping Bill in the game. It was getting to the point that if you gave Bill too many lines he would just forget them, but, on the other hand, if he didn't have enough dialogue he would fall asleep in a scene. To help fix this if Stan wasn't in a scene with Bill they would have him sneak under the table to tickle Bill's feet to keep him awake. Stan has the best *My Three Sons* stories.

The episode I was asked back to do was called *Goodbye Again*. Since I had left the show abruptly to do my own show *Margie*, they had written Jean out by saying that she had gone off to college. For this episode, Jean had come back to Bryant Park with the thoughts of reconnecting with Mike. Unknown to Jean at this time Mike was already engaged to Sally Ann Morrison, who was played by Meredith MacRae.

As Mike and Jean reminisce, Mike begins to have a reawakening of his feelings for her and can't bring himself to tell her that he's now engaged to Sally. Robbie is the one that inadvertently spills the beans about the engagement. Jean then bows out of Mike's life so that he can be happy and she disappears brokenhearted.

I always thought that was unfair to Jean. Many fans have said the same to me through the years. They thought it was unfair to just have Jean thrown aside when they preferred that Jean and Mike reunite. It was a bittersweet episode to do. It was great to see everyone, but I knew that I wouldn't be seeing them again for a long time.

The cult classic gallows humor TV show, *The Addams Family* needed a girl next door so they called me. I was more of the young woman next door as I was married in this role. We were cast as the new neighbors next door to the Addams family. My husband was played by actor Peter Brooks. He had also had a reoccurring role in *My Three Sons* as Robbie Douglas's pal Hank Ferguson.

On *The Addams Family*, we played Hubert and Amanda Peterson. The Peterson's were newlyweds and had leased a lovely home for a year. Unfortunately for them the house they leased was right next door to the Addams family home. They go through all kinds of strange and humorous encounters with Gomez, Morticia, Uncle Fester, Lurch and Grandmama Addams. They try to get out of their lease only to find out that the lease is with Gomez Addams himself.

Even though the show is now a classic TV program back then it was brand new. The episode I was in was called *The New Neighbors Meet The Addams Family*. Even though it was only their 9th episode the cast seem to have their characters down to a tee.

When you're hired to do a TV, show you are generally on the set for one day. You don't get too close to people in one day. The eccentric character of Gomez Addams was played by John Astin. I found him professional and a real gentleman.

The beautiful and macabre character of Morticia Gomez was played by the beautiful and mysterious Carolyn Jones. Both John and Carolyn had such great chemistry together.

Ted Cassidy played the part of the Addams family's faithful butler Lurch. Ted had a lot of odd roles in his career but when you are six foot and nine inches tall what do you expect? As Lurch, I believe that the only line that he had on the shows entire run was "You rang?" The other part he played on the show was the character Thing. This character was just a hand that would appear where you least expected it. In one scene, my character Amanda and her husband were playing Bridge at the Addams home with Gomez and Morticia. Amanda has to discard a card but can't make up her mind. Just then a cigarette box sitting on the card table pops open and Thing pops up, takes a card out of my hand and plays it. Thing then goes back down into the box closing the lid along the way. Of course, Amanda freaks out at this event. How Ted got his whole six foot, nine inch frame under that table I'll never know. I do know that while he was under the table waiting for his cue he would tickle my toes for a laugh. He was a true gentle giant.

Another great experience I had on *The Addams Family* set was working with Jackie Coogan. He was a huge child star back in the days of Hollywood's silent film era. His biggest claim to fame was playing the kid in Charlie Chaplain's movie *The Kid* in 1921. With all the movies and the merchandising, child star Jackie had made as much as \$3.5 million which would be about \$55 million today. Unfortunately, his mother and stepfather spent it all before Jackie could see any of it. In 1938, he sued his parents for the money but there was very little of it left. The court battle did bring about some new laws for child actors. They included protection of the child's earnings, school time, and how much work time they have to do. It's commonly known as the Coogan Law.

Daddy was a good friend of Jackie's. Playing Uncle Fester was one of the longer roles he had since being a child star so I'm sure it gave him a little more financial stability.

Uncle Fester was always blowing something up with an experiment gone wrong. In this episode, he had dug a tunnel from the Addams' house to our house. As Uncle Fester comes up out of the living room floor of the Peterson's house, my character is terrified and clobbers him on the head with a huge frying pan.

When we were shooting this scene, the director had us run through the sequence of events. I was using a big prop frying pan made out of rubber, but it sure looked real. After the first take, I hit Jackie with the pan and he barely reacted to it. Before the director could say, anything Jackie looked at me and said: "Is that it? Girly, you're going to have to hit me a lot harder than that if this is going to work. Now put some muscle into it."

This got my Irish up!

On the second take, I let him have it so hard that I knocked him right back down to the bottom of the hole if not all the way to China. After the director yelled cut I heard Jackie's voice coming up from the bottom of the hole: "Now that's how ya do it sister!"

Elvis Connection #7 - 1964

Perry Mason

Episode: *The Case of the Drifting Dropout*.

Carl Reindel played Barry in this episode. He would go on to play roles in some well-known films such as *Bullitt* with Steve McQueen, *Tora! Tora! Tora!* and *The Andromeda Strain*. In 1968, he played the part of Mike with Elvis and Nancy Sinatra in MGM's *Speedway*.

Vaughn Taylor played Sanford Harper in my *Perry Mason* episode. He was a character actor whose face and pencil thin mustache you'll remember from hundreds of TV shows and movies. One of those films was Elvis' *Jailhouse Rock* where he played the part of Mr. Shores.

Many Happy Returns

Richard Collier played Harry Price in the TV series *Many Happy Returns*. He was in hundreds of movies and television shows. 1962 found him as a hotel clerk in Elvis' *Girls! Girls! Girls!*

Doris Packer played the part of Cornelia in my *Many Happy Returns* episode. In 1966, she played Mrs. Barrington in Elvis' movie *Paradise, Hawaiian Style*.

As I had mentioned earlier, Christopher Riordan wasn't in the *Many Happy Returns* pilot episode with me, but he was brought in a little later as a regular cast member named Ronnie. - He would go on to perform in not one, not two, but six Elvis films. *Viva Las Vegas, Roustabout, Tickle Me, Spinout, Double Trouble, Clambake*, and Elvis' 1968 TV show called *Elvis*. Now better known as *The '68 Comeback Special*.

The Addams Family

Carolyn Jones, who played Morticia Adams, had a role in *King Creole*. She played the sexy bad girl named Ronnie. This movie was Elvis' favorite out of all the roles that he played.

Peter Brook, who played my husband in *The New Neighbors Meet The Addams Family*, played Brentwood Von Durgenfeld in Elvis' 1965 film *Girl Happy*.

Eddie Marr had a bit part in *The Addams Family* episode that I worked on. He had been working in Hollywood for years. He worked mostly as a background artist in B grade movies. You can find him as a carnival barker in Elvis' film *Roustabout*.

Jackie Coogan, also known as the Kid in Charlie Chaplin's classic silent film *The Kid*, was the guy I hit over the head with a frying pan on *The Addams Family*. Jackie was great to work with. His career never did as well as it had when he was a child actor, but he ended up doing ok. He had a part as a police officer, Sgt Benson, in *Girl Happy* with Elvis.

Chapter 22

My Boy, My Boy
Three Coins In The Fountain

In November of 1964, I missed my cycle. I thought that my body had been stressed out from all the work I had been doing, so I went to see my doctor. After a quick test, he looked at me asked: "Have you had any morning sickness?"

I said: "No. Why?"

He then said: "That's unusual, most pregnant women do." As he smiled at me, I realized that I was pregnant. Initially I was thrilled, but later overwhelmed at the idea of being an expectant mother. I had never been around a lot of babies. Even as a young girl I never babysat for anyone. I didn't know the first thing about changing a diaper; let alone what foods a baby would eat. I felt that I was ill-equipped to be someone's mother. As an actress, I had been playing parts that were younger than my own age. I didn't feel that motherhood was a role that I was fit for. Throughout my life, I always felt like a "girl" and not a grown woman. The thought of having a little baby depending on me for everything was very daunting.

After mulling it over a little in the doctor's office, I reminded myself that I wouldn't be alone. Buck would be there for me and give me encouragement throughout the pregnancy. Buck and I also had two sets of Grandparents to help us out. My panic was slowing down a little. On the way home, I was thinking about Buck. I wasn't sure how he would react to the pregnancy. When I told him, he said he loved the idea of becoming a father. I began to feel better about bringing a new life into this world.

I will apologize now, to all the women out there that have given birth and are reading this section. My pregnancy was an easy one. I never had morning sickness, my hormones didn't make me moody, and I didn't gain too much weight during my pregnancy. I gained about twenty nine pounds at the most, and nine pounds of that belonged to the baby.

My son Michael

(Cynthia Pepper Collection)

The joy and ease I was experiencing with my pregnancy was not reflected by the state of the world. The TV news was broadcasting all the gloom and doom that there was to report. The Vietnam War was heating up. Earlier in the year Martin Luther King Jr. had been arrested in Selma, Alabama during demonstrations. Twenty days later Malcolm X had been shot to death at a rally in Harlem. Social and racial unrest was coming to a boil in the US, and then it boiled over. The Watts Riots erupted in L.A. I watched the news every day to see the death and destruction that was happening a mere 30 minutes away from our West Hollywood apartment. We could see the smoke rising in the air from the L.A. suburb of Watts. This didn't seem like the safest time to be bringing a child into the world. Then my water broke.

Michael and me at my second wedding.

(Cynthia Pepper Collection)

Michael Lloyd Edwards was born in August, 1965, at St Joseph's hospital in, as Johnny Carson used to say, "Beautiful downtown Burbank." It was an easy birth. In those days, if you wanted pain medication the doctors were very obliging. I opted to have a saddle block anesthesia. I don't think they even do that for childbirth anymore. I do remember waking up after the birth and being pushed on a gurney to my room by a nurse and my Doctor. My doctor was actress Joan Leslie's husband, Dr. William Caldwell. In my medicated stupor, I recall turning my head towards him and making a bold declaration: "I love you!" What was that about? I guess it just felt right at the time.

It was standard procedure at the time to stay in the hospital and recuperate for a few days. Michael and I got to know each other for three days in our hospital room. He ate, belched, slept, cried, filled his diapers and ate some more as the nurses taught me how to take care of him. By the time we left the hospital to go home, my extra twenty pounds of weight were gone. To this day I'm still not sure how I did that.

I fell in love with Michael, the new guy in my life. Looking back on my easy pregnancy and birth, I realized that it was a hint of things to come from this child.

Michael was such a happy baby and as he grew he gave me so much joy. I never had any problems with him. To this day he's still the light of my life.

Michael and me today.

(Cynthia Pepper Collection)

Three Coins

When I was pregnant with Michael, I thought: "I'm ok with this. What is nobler than being a Mom?" Besides, no one wanted a pregnant woman as a lead actress on a TV show. Lucille Ball was the only one to have done it and she was a big star when it happened. I was attempting to settle in as a stay-at-home mom by learning all I could about child rearing. Our household earnings would go down a little without any acting work, but we figured that Buck's pay would keep us afloat.

When my son finally arrived I thought, for a moment, that the Hollywood river of work might drain away. I was wrong. Michael was just two months old when I got a call from my agent about a part in a new TV comedy pilot. I was being called back to work. Someone was throwing me a life preserver and the river of work started flowing back in my direction.

The pilot was made for NBC and was called *Three Coins in the Fountain*. It was based on the movie of the same name. The movie was released in 1954. It starred Clifton Webb, Dorothy McGuire, Jean Peters and Louis Jourdan. Our version of Three Coins was led by the funny and multitalented Hal Kanter. He was the writer, director, and executive producer on the TV project. He knew me from our work together on *Sally and Sam* and insisted on me for the role. I didn't have to audition. I was to play the part of Maggie Walker. I was flattered that the character was written with me in mind, but it was still a tough decision to make as I now had Michael to take care of. To top it off it was to be shot on location in Rome, Italy for six weeks.

I would need some major family support to make this happen, and I got it. Buck, Mother and Daddy, and even my in-laws convinced me that they would all take turns taking good care of Michael while I was gone. Buck was very supportive of my career due to the steady flow of money and better life style that my job afforded us. Another reason to take this project was the fact that I was not under contract to 20th Century anymore. I had to take the work as it came to me. The studio was still reeling over the costs from the *Cleopatra* movie mess, so they let their entire stable of contract actors go. It was truly the end of an era. If the Three Coins pilot was a success and purchased by the network, it would become a TV series, and I did not want to miss out on being part of that.

Before leaving on this European adventure of a lifetime, Mr. Kanter still had to cast the other two coins, I mean ladies, for the pilot. When Hal asked me to help with the process, I immediately said yes. I read with quite a few actresses for the other two parts. Lee Meriwether and Paula Prentiss's sister Ann Prentiss were among the bevy of actresses that auditioned but were not to Hal's liking. In the end, he hired Joanna Moore to play Ruth and Yvonne Craig to play Dorothy. Yvonne and I hadn't worked together since *Kissin' Cousins*, and I was so happy to be working with her again. I had never met Joanna Moore before her audition. At that time, she was married to Ryan O'Neal. They had two young children at home, Tatum aged two and Griffin aged one. My first impression of Joanna was that she was very sweet and her beauty was stunning, but I thought that she had an air of being a ditzy southern belle. I had seen her work in the film *Last Angry Man* with Paul Muni and in *Walk on the Wild Side* with Jane Fonda. She was a very good actress. At that time she was probably best known for her TV work as Andy's girlfriend, Peggy "Peg" McMillan on *The Andy Griffith Show*. Now that we had our three coins cast it was time to see Rome.

The synopsis of the Three Coins TV pilot was that my character, Maggie Walker moves from America to Rome. She lives with her American girlfriends, Ruth and Dorothy, who already reside in Rome. Maggie is searching for a new life with a possible romance in mind. She meets a handsome Italian gentleman at the airport. This gentleman claims to be a Count, but he is not. She is very upset when she finds out that he lied to her. Along the way, a young Italian boy named Gino intercedes and tries to defend his lying friend. Eventually, all is made right and the three American women continue to live in Rome struggling with the language and cultural differences.

Did this comedy have enough going for it to become a full time show? I had no idea, but the thrill of going to Rome for six weeks was more than I could ask for. Plus, I was getting paid to be there. I had dreamt of going to Europe and now that dream was coming true. It was still very hard to think that I'd be gone from Michael all that time. I knew that I would miss him terribly. I justified my separation from him with the knowledge that he'd be fine with Buck and both sets of grandparents looking after him.

It was October 28th, 1965 when we landed at the Leonardo da Vinci - Fiumicino Airport. Even the airport sounded romantic. The weather was unseasonably warm for Rome that month. I flew first class with Yvonne & Joanna. The three of us were so excited about this project. We had a six week schedule for shooting and we were anxious to experience what this ancient and fascinating city had to offer us. Our heads were spinning. Anywhere my cast mates and I traveled, ate or slept on this trip was all done first class. Thank goodness the studio was picking up the tab. While in Rome, the actors and the executive crew stayed at the plush five star, Parco dei Principi Grand Hotel. It was located near the beautiful Villa Borghese Gardens. It was not a hardship to wake up in the early mornings and start your day in those surroundings.

"Three Coins in the Fountain" - Joanna Moore, Yvonne Craig and me.

(Cynthia Pepper Collection)

Our call to work was 5:00 a.m. depending on if you were in the first scene that was to be shot that morning. The make-up and hair team were all Italians and most had just finished working on Dino De Laurentiis's epic movie, *The Bible: In the Beginning*. John Huston was the director, narrator, and played the part of Noah and the voice of God. Most people in Hollywood at the time would have agreed with that casting decision. When we arrived for the day's work the language barrier between director, cast and crew made for some very interesting discussions on set.

We filmed at different locations around Rome, but the majority of the pilot was shot at one of Italy's most famous movie studios,

Cinecitta. (It's Italian for Cinema City). It was founded in 1937 by Benito Mussolini and his son Vittorio. The studio was initially used by Mussolini for prewar propaganda films. Later it was instrumental in making movies like *Helen of Troy* in 1956, *Ben-Hur* in 1959 and *Cleopatra* in 1963. (So this is where 20th Century sent all those big checks to Liz).

The actor who played my Italian boyfriend, Count Giorgio, was Nino Castelnuovo. In 1964, he had co-starred, along with the ever stunning Catherine Deneuve, in the film *The Umbrellas of Cherbourg*. He was quite charming, with a handsome, rugged look. He was a first-rate actor which I felt made me a better performer. We shot scenes in and around Rome's most historical locations. We found ourselves at The Roman Coliseum, the Roman Forum, and of course the Trevi Fountain, where we would make a wish and toss our three coins over our shoulders. What a thrill it was to be standing at these ancient sights. It was possible that Augustus, Tiberius, Caligula or Nero once stood here. It seemed everywhere we went, there was so much history! I would find myself touching the ancient walls; closing my eyes and imagining what it must have been like back then. It was at times overwhelming, yet seemed to make all my senses come alive.

The little boy who played Gino in the show was Antony Alda. He was so cute and had great acting skills even at the age of nine. He could jump back and forth between speaking Italian and English with such ease. Acting ran in his family. His father was actor Robert Alda, and his older, half-brother, was Alan Alda. Antony's mother was a lovely Italian actress named Flora Marino. She would bring him to the set but never interfered with what he was doing. Antony was a real cutie.

We had been working long hours every day for the first two weeks in Italy and I was exhausted. I had been calling home every other day to see how Michael was but eventually that wasn't enough. One morning before going to the set I mentioned to Joanna, how homesick I was. I explained to her how much I was missing my new baby. She had two young children at home so I knew that she'd understand. I told her how depressed and tired I was. Well, I hardly got the word, tired, out of my mouth when Joanna reached into her purse and produced a vial of pills. As she handed me a couple, I asked: "What are these for?"

She said: "Take one or two and it will make you feel better. It's ok. I got them from a doctor."

Without thinking too much about it, I said thanks, took one, and put it in my purse. Normally I would never have taken pills from someone other than a doctor, but I wasn't in my right mind at the time. Besides, I trusted Joanna so what could go wrong?

When I arrived at the studio, I was feeling even more stressed and depressed. I had quite a lot of dialogue in a scene with Nino later in the afternoon. To make matters even more interesting, when the assistant director calls for a lunch break that means that you take a couple of hours to eat and rest. It also means that you partake in a glass or two of wine. Its Italy after all and it would be rude to refuse. I had never been much of a drinker. I always joke and say I'm a cheap date, because a half a glass of wine gets me giddy. When I think of how alcohol had a hold of my mother and father, I always thanked God that the "need to drink" gene skipped over me. I was feeling so bad during lunch that I took the pill and washed it down with half a glass of wine.

When it came time to go back to work, I was a little drunk and spaced out. I was certainly not myself and just a tad out of control. Hal asked me quite a few times: "Cynthia, what's the matter with you? Are you feeling ok?"

What was I to say? I mumbled back: "Oh I'm fine Hal. I'm just a little tired. Give me a second and I'll be all right."

Hal said: "Cynthia, I think you're drunk!"

Without hesitation, I shot back: "I think you're drunk!"

Hal and the rest of the crew started to laugh, but at the time I wasn't quite sure why they were laughing. How embarrassing! I always strove to be professional when I worked and I was anything but professional that day. We finally did get the scene shot and the rest of the filming day was without incident. Never again did I take any sort of mood altering pill and I made sure not to drink during lunch on a working day ever again.

Chapter 23

When In Rome...
Europe on Five Dollars a Day?

When actors and crew go on location, there can be a few "liaisons" happening. How does this happen? Well, let me give you my recipe for Location Romances. You take a large serving of actors, actresses, directors, and move them away from home and their loved ones. Now force them to live in close proximity with each other and slowly add the local crew. Stir in a shared goal, like creating a successful film or TV show. Now let it bake in the warm weather of a romantic location for a couple of weeks. Once removed from the oven, sprinkle some shared chemistry over it and you have a Location Romance that will generally serve two. My point is that even with a solid relationship back home; things can get a little out of hand. My "out of hand" experience was the result of having a small crush on our make-up man, Umberto.

Umberto was Italian, gorgeous, sweet, and a true artist with a blush brush! Next to Elvis Presley, Umberto was the most handsome man I had ever seen. I was quite taken with him. Every morning, while applying my make-up, Umberto would be no more than a few inches from my face. He spoke and understood very little English and my grasp of the Italian language allowed me to say hello, goodbye, and to, maybe, order a cappuccino. I loved the way he would say my name. With his Italian accent, he couldn't say Cynthia. It always came out as (Chin'Chee-Ah). We smiled a lot at each other and constantly flirted. The language of love really is universal.

During my time, working in Rome, Umberto and I had two quiet, and what turned out to be romantic dinners together. At the end of one work day, Umberto took me on a drive out of Rome to a restaurant on the coast of the Tyrrhenian Sea. It was called Lido di Ostia. It was a very romantic location. Our dinner conversation, if you could call it that, consisted of pointing to the menu, and both of us trying a word or two in the other person's native language. What made our date work was the flirting. While driving back from dinner, Umberto stopped the car on the side of the road and proceeded to kiss me. At first I thought, this is too strange and uncomfortable, but I didn't really protest. I was able to justify the fact that it was just kissing. I had kissed a number of men on screen so what harm was this? I was feeling so lonely being away from my family and the kissing and hugging just felt right. The time with Umberto was magical. I was swept up in the adventure of it all. I knew nothing would or could ever come from it, but the temptation was there. A few days later we had another dinner together. Some flirting, some dinner and some kissing, but that was as far as it ever went with Umberto. He was my Italian romance that reminded me I was alive.

One day Hal Kanter told us that we were invited to have dinner at Anthony Quinn's villa located on one of the Seven Hills of Rome. Hal had received an invite from Robert and Flora Alda, who were very good friends of Mr. Quinn's. The thought of meeting Anthony Quinn was almost overwhelming for me. When I was in high school, I saw a movie that he had done and it haunted me at the time. The movie was Federico Fellini's, *La Strada*. Quinn's co-star was a remarkable actress who was also Fellini's wife, Giulietta Masina. To this day, *La Strada* is one of my all-time favorites.

I was so excited to discuss the film with Mr. Quinn. His characters motivation, Fellini's directing style, his incredible performance in general. An opportunity like this doesn't come around too often.

Anthony Quinn's villa was spectacular. Each room had very high ceilings and the walls were adorned with many gorgeous pieces of art. We were all welcomed by our gracious host with drinks and pleasant conversations. I was itching to discuss *La Strada*, Fellini, and the deep psyche of the brute that Mr. Quinn had played so well. I decided to hold off until a more appropriate time presented itself. Eventually we were all ushered into a huge dining room with an enormous dining table surrounded by a large number of high back chairs. The dinner we ate was fit for royalty. After dinner, we all sat back in our chairs getting ready for some spirited after dinner conversation. Our host lit up a cigar and was sipping from his glass of wine.

I couldn't wait any longer I had several questions that I was dying to ask. I said: "Mr. Quinn…"

He interrupted saying: "Cynthia, please call me Tony."

I corrected myself: "Ok, Tony. I really loved *La Strada* and particularly your part in it."

Before I could go on, he smiled at me and said: "Well, my dear, that's nice but I hated making every bit of it!"

That certainly wasn't a response that I had expected. I managed to squeak out a small: "Oh." He changed the subject and started talking with Robert Alda. Well, so much for my deep conversation with Anthony Quinn. I didn't think he was rude, but he obviously didn't want to discuss it. Now I had more questions than ever about *La Strada*. I was going to pursue it, but I thought that I'd let sleeping dogs lie. The lesson here is that the end product that enthralls the audience is not always created under the best conditions for the actor. Sir John Gielgud said: "Acting is half shame, half glory. Shame of exhibiting yourself, glory when you can forget yourself." Mr. Quinn, I mean, Tony is certainly the kind of actor that can lose himself within a character. Maybe he didn't like what he saw when he lost himself in *La Strada*.

As it happens with most productions, there is sadness when you have to split away from your newly found family of coworkers. Sometimes you stay in touch, but mostly you don't. I enjoyed being directed by Hal Kanter. He had a clever, sweet way of getting things done on the set. He was a very talented man with a great sense of comedic timing. I knew we'd be friends for a long time. Yvonne and I became even better friends during the production of Three Coins, and we still are to this day. Joanna, well she was another story. Even after six weeks of working and spending a lot of time together, I don't think I knew her much better than the first day we met. It was not for lack of trying on my part. Even if we had had sixty weeks together, I don't know if I would have ever understood what made her tick. She was living through a tough marriage and was turning to alcohol and other things to help her survive, but she wasn't letting it affect her work in Rome. We talked a lot about her kids and why things weren't working out with her husband Ryan. She was tormented by speculating on who he was sleeping with while she was away. I had a soft spot in my heart for her and felt so sorry for what she was going through.

We all worked very hard on the TV pilot of *Three Coins in the Fountain,* so it was a huge disappointment when it didn't sell. I thought that the characters all had good chemistry with each other, but the buyers in Hollywood thought otherwise. Then amazingly, in August, 1970, it aired as a made for TV movie. I thought it held up pretty well after sitting on NBC's shelf for five years. I guess making Three Coins was a good idea because someone decided to do it again twenty years later. In 1990, a made for TV movie was released with Loni Anderson, Stepfanie Kramer, Shanna Reed, and Anthony Newley. It was simply called *Coins in the Fountain*.

Europe on Five Dollars a Day?

The six weeks of filming Three Coins were finished and our time in Rome drew to a close. Yvonne and I decided that since we were already in Italy, one more week on our own would be a chance of a lifetime to see the rest of Europe.

We had talked to the Studio Executives back at 20th Century Fox, and told them our plan for remaining for another week and they kindly offered to pay for some of our incidentals. To keep our costs down, Yvonne had found a book by Arthur Frommer entitled *Europe on Five Dollars a Day*. Can you imagine? The book was written in 1957 so the book was eight years old by the time we got it. I was enjoying the first class treatment that we had in Rome, so five dollars a day was going to be a stretch to say the least.

The day before we left I found it difficult to say goodbye to Umberto. Through his broken English, he had promised me that he would come to the train station and say goodbye to us before we left. Knowing that I'd see him one more time got me through my last night in Rome. Yvonne and I packed up our belongings from the lush lifestyle that our 5-star hotel afforded us. We grabbed a cab to the Roma Termini railway station where we would take the train to Venice. We were both wearing our Sunday best for our European tour. I was wearing a lovely Italian designer outfit complete with white gloves. Even though I was now on a budget of five dollars a day, I was still going to look good. Umberto was nowhere to be found at the train station. As I reluctantly boarded the train I was still looking back to the crowd of people on the train platform, but Umberto was not there. The conductor was giving his last call to board the train. Yvonne and I made our way to the cabin that we had booked. I immediately threw open the window and hung out of it for one more look at the crowd. I looked up and down the long platform, but my Roman romance was nowhere to be found. I didn't really have the right to feel the way I was feeling, but I was extremely disappointed and sad. I was still half way out the window as the train started to slowly pull out of the station. I said to Yvonne: "Well, I guess this is it. So much for promises."

Yvonne said: "That's ok Hun. Don't lose any sleep over it."

As my heart sank, I answered: "No, Umberto was special."

I had taken my gloves off, and as I pulled my head back into the cabin I accidently dropped them onto the cabin floor. Yvonne quickly picked them up and handed them back to me, and said: "You know what that means?"

With tears in my eyes, I asked: "What?"

She explained: "When you drop your gloves, and someone else picks them up for you, it means that you are going to have a good surprise."

Just as she finished speaking, I looked out the cabin window, and there was Umberto, running alongside the train. He was waving and yelling: "Ciao! Chin-Chee- Ah! Ciao! Chin-Chee- Ah!" The whole time he was blowing me kisses and shouting my name. I couldn't believe what I was seeing. I hung back out the window, waving back and yelling: "Ciao Umberto!"

I still had the tears in my eyes as the train sped up, but now they were tears of joy. Umberto kept his promise! As the train left the station, I kept looking back and waving to Umberto until both he and the station were no longer visible. That's a moment I will never forget. Yvonne was so right about the gloves. I've often wondered what happened to Umberto. I hope he had a long and happy life. I guess I will never know.

As the train raced down the tracks towards Venice, Yvonne and I settled into our little compartment. For the next 350 miles, our private train window was like our own personal movie screen playing a travelogue of some of the most beautiful Italian countryside we had ever seen. We were heading north. Next stop, Venice.

Yvonne and I were both anxious to get home to our families. However, we reasoned, when would we be back to Europe? We put our homesickness aside and began our speedy, one week, two girl tours of three European cities plus swinging London. Since we only had one or two days per city to take in the local sights and sounds, we immediately started to plan our sightseeing assault.

When we arrived in Venice, the city was experiencing the worst rainy weather the city had seen in decades. For a city full of canals, I didn't think they needed the extra water. Yvonne and I got absolutely drenched going from the train to the water taxi. The taxi took us into town where we exited and began looking for a small pensione that we could lodge at for the night. The rain got even worse as we finally found an affordable place for the evening. We were so happy to be out of the rain, but we now looked like two drowned rats! Yvonne and I laughed so hard at each other because we looked so pathetic.

After we checked in I phoned back to the States to see how Michael and everyone was doing back home. My mother answered the phone. I was anxious to tell her about the deluge we had just gone through. I said: "Mother, you won't believe what Venice is like right now. It's a beautiful city, but all the streets are flooded." There was a small laugh on the other end of the phone as she said: "Of course, honey, the streets are always flooded, that's the way the city is built."

I paused for a second and then said: "Oh no, mother I mean the streets are really flooded because of the horrific storm that has hit Venice." As I explained our travel story and local weather she laughed even more but now she knew what I had meant. My mother and I had many laughs over that particular conversation through the years.

The following morning the rain had stopped. The sun peeked through the clouds and brought a sliver of blue sky with it. Yvonne and I were able to get around and see a few of the sights that this "city of water" had to offer. We took in churches and museums, all full of Renaissance art and incredible architecture. Since there had been so much flooding the day before we had to walk on small platforms that helped us get around the flooded areas. After getting lost walking through many of the small back alleys, we finally found the Piazza San Marco. It was worth the long walk. We fell in love with the entire atmosphere that the piazza had to share. We ended our day with a gondola ride that took us under the Bridge of Sighs. We had a great time in Venice and the Venetian people couldn't have been nicer. With little time to spare, we were now off to the airport to see what London, England had to show us.

It was December when we arrived in England and it was getting cold and our funds we depleting. We decided it was time to make full use of our *Europe on Five Dollars* a Day, book. We figured that we would save a ton of money by following the advice of the book. We read where we could get good accommodation for about five dollars a night. It suggested a hotel in the heart of London. The book was correct. We checked into our room for five dollars, and we got what we paid for.

It was a very small hotel in a seedy neighborhood. The room they gave us was a tiny plain room with two small twin beds. We weren't exceptionally tall women, and yet our feet still hung over the end of the beds. The bathroom was inconveniently located outside of our room at the other end of the hall. Since the temperature had dropped to about 48 degrees Fahrenheit, we had expected the radiator in our room to be working, but we were wrong. We were so cold that night we slept with our clothes on. We woke up bright and early to take in the sights and sounds of London. The fact that we were both frozen and had to get our blood moving played a large role in our early rise. As we checked out of the hotel, we tossed the five dollar a day book in the trash bin. I know that I said it already, but I just can't say it enough. "You Get What You Pay For!" After taking in the main sites, we gave jolly old London the Queen's wave, as it was time to see Paris.

Ah Paris. Très Magnifique. Our heads were spinning as we went from our "Dickens" style abode in London, England, to one of the fanciest hotels in all of Paris, France. We stayed at the Hotel George V. It was so plush. We were able to stay there because 20th Century Fox said they would pick up the tab. As a matter of fact, they were also paying for our transportation from country to country. Thank you 20th Century Fox. Hotel George V was located just off the Champs-Elysees and in the heart of the most fashionable part of Paris. It was not far from the Arc de Triomphe, and the Eiffel Tower, which made it the perfect location to experience the city. While we were in Paris, we went to the Folies Bergère, where the Can-Can dance reigns supreme. During the performance of the chorus line's high kicks into the air, Yvonne leaned over to me and said: "I can do that." I had no doubt. Before she got into acting, she had trained to be a ballet dancer. She was an excellent dancer. When the chorus line finished their high kicking, one by one, they fell to the floor ending up in the splits. I said to Yvonne: "How about that?" She just smiled a smile that said, yes. I just smiled back a smile that said, ouch.

Yvonne had some friends in Paris that invited us for a real French dinner at their home. We had a fabulous time with her friends even though the dinner conversation centered around our hosts body parts. It was nothing too rude, it was just weird. The talk in particular was about their kidneys. Why, I don't know. We never did figure out why the conversion went in that direction. Maybe it was a language issue. C'est La Vie! I really enjoyed the evening and their generosity. It was a fun way to wrap up our time in the City of Lights.

We boarded the train at the Gare de l'Est railway station in Paris and got settled in for our 760 mile journey to Vienna, Austria. My fascination with old world Europe kept me in good spirits on this long trip. This train ride would be largely at night. We didn't reserve a private compartment, so we rode in the public car that had regular seats. When we got tired and wanted to sleep, the only place to lie down was on the benches we were sitting on. We had fallen asleep late into the night.

Unbeknownst to Yvonne and me, while we slept the train had crossed the Austrian border. We were abruptly awakened by two border patrol officers. They were very large and intimidating men in uniform. With a very gruff voice, one of the officers said: "Zeigen Sie uns Ihre Passport!" We found out later that this was German for: "Show us your passport!" Yvonne and I were very startled by their presence. Neither one of us spoke German. To say we were alarmed at their invasion of our sleep would have been an understatement.

I was so nervous the only thing I could think of to say is a phrase that my dear Ivan taught me many years ago. I looked at the officer, and in a loud voice I said: "Ich Liebe Dich!" I thought to myself; "What the heck did I just say?" Yvonne was looking at me with a shocked look on her face. The two patrol officers looked at me strangely, for a second or two, and then I saw small smiles appear on both their faces. We found our passports and handed them to the officers. After they had our passports, their demeanor became stern again. Once they were satisfied that our passports were legit, they handed them back to us. Before they left, one them said, in broken English: "Sank you ladies, an gut evening."

After they left Yvonne asked me: "What did you say to them?"

I said: "I think I said I love you."

She asked: "Why did you say that?"

I said: "It's the only German I know."

Yvonne has since kidded me about those three little words that saved us from being hassled or worse, being detained in a foreign country.

We've laughed about this little incident through the years and I've always maintained that those border patrol officers probably thought I was just a little coo-coo, and didn't want to mess with those crazy Americans.

As we pulled into Austria, we realized that our long ride on the rails was going to be worth it. Since our travel time had been so long, we only had a short window to see it all. We had exactly one day, and night, to see the sights of Vienna, The City of Music.

We filled our time by visiting Palais Epstein, Schloss Schonbrunn Gardens, and Loos Haus. We even found a little time to catch our breath as we sat at a quaint sidewalk cafe. We pretended to be locals as we devoured a couple of wonderful pastries, and watched the people go by. Later that night, we went to a music concert at the Musikverein. The Concert Hall was a long room, with high ceilings but still had a feeling of intimacy to it. A string quartet was the offering for the night and it was glorious. I remembered all the classical music records that Mother would play for Patty and me when we were younger, but that didn't hold a candle to hearing it performed live.

How terrific was my life. Here I was in Vienna with my good friend Yvonne, eating pastries, seeing beautiful Palaces, and enjoying a wonderful concert. I felt at home in this beautiful city. Maybe I was a resident here in another life. I thought; "It doesn't get better than this."

What a wonderful experience I had in those few months. I would never have dreamt that I would be so lucky to have such an enjoyable career. I was meeting and working with terrific people, and seeing sights I had only imagined. However, I needed to get home. After Vienna, I got very homesick. I wanted desperately to see my family, and my sweet son Michael. I have to say that Yvonne was so much fun to travel with. I'm sorry that we never got a chance to do something like that again.

The Elvis Connection #8 - Three Coins

My friend Joanna Moore who played Ruth in the Three Coins pilot was also in Elvis' 1962 hit movie, *Follow That Dream*. She played Alisha Claypoole.

I have already mentioned Yvonne Craig's Elvis connections earlier, but I think they warrant mentioning again. The first was *It Happened at the World's Fair* in 1963 where she played Dorothy Johnson and later in 1964, *Kissin' Cousins* as Azalea Tatum. I had said earlier that Elvis made out with *Batgirl*. That's not quite true. Yvonne didn't bring the character of *Batgirl* to life until 1967. So really, Elvis made out with pre-*Batgirl*.

Hal Kanter the writer, director, and executive producer of Three Coins also wrote *Loving You* in 1957 and Elvis' very successful movie of 1961, *Blue Hawaii*.

Joanna Moore, me, and Yvonne Craig in Rome for Three Coins In The Fountain.

(Cynthia Pepper Collection)

Chapter 24

Home Again, Home Again, Jiggety-Jig-Jig

When I returned home from Europe, I decided to be a lot more of a stay-at-home mom and less of a working actress. I started to turn work down, much to the chagrin of my agent, business manager and personal manager. I wanted to be home for Michael.

My agent did convince me to go to one audition. He wouldn't take no for an answer. He said that the appointment was at the Beverly Hills Hotel. I was to meet with the writer, actor, and director. When I asked: "Who are they?"

He said: "They're all the same guy."

All the same guy? Who's interviewing me Charlie Chaplin? My agent said that the gentleman's name was Woody Allen. Woody? I use to think that Elvis was an odd first name. I had never heard of Woody Allen. I found out that he had done some writing for the *Sid Caesar Show* and *Candid Camera*. He was the screenwriter for the 1965 movie *What's New Pussy Cat*, starring Peter Sellers and Peter O'Toole. Apparently Woody wasn't happy with what Hollywood had done to his script. From that moment on he decided that the only way to get his movies done correctly was to have complete control of them. The film I was auditioning for was called *Take the Money and Run.* He was the writer, director, star, and since my audition was with him, I guess we could also add casting director. I was up for the part of Louise, who was his love interest in the movie. I was a little nervous about going to the meeting. I wasn't given a script ahead of time so there was very little time to try and do something great to impress Mr. Allen.

My appointment was for 1:00 pm, and I arrived at the hotel right on time. I always try to be on time for an audition or meeting. It's important to put your best foot forward when trying to get a job. Besides, I think it is very rude to keep people waiting.

As I made my way to the audition, I speculated on how many people would be in the room. Most auditions have a committee that make the decisions about who is in and who is out. I reached Mr. Allen's hotel door and quietly knocked on it. A small, rather unassuming, man with dark rimmed glasses, which seemed too big for his face, opened the door and said: "You must be Cynthia Pepper. I'm Woody Allen, come in." There was no committee in the room, only Mr. Allen and his assistant. He introduced me to his assistant and then we all sat down.

As we chatted, I looked around the room for a script. I was anxious to have a look at the scene that we'd be doing. There was no script in sight. He then said: "It's close to our lunch time, I was wondering if you would like to join us for a bite to eat."

I said: "Well Mr. Allen…"

He said: "Oh, please call me Woody." Then he handed me a room service menu.

What a strange audition this had become. I was given a menu to read, instead of a script. I said: "Thank you, but I'm not very hungry. I would like something to drink. A soda would be fine."

We chitchatted as we waited for room service to deliver their lunch. Woody asked me questions about my acting work and if I was available for filming on some particular dates. I quickly answered that I was available on those dates.

He seemed so timid and shy. I couldn't figure out how this guy would ever be able to direct a feature length film.

After room service had been delivered, Woody and his assistant ate their lunch while I drank my soda. We continued to talk, but it was all small talk. I couldn't wait to get a copy of the script. I wanted to look at some lines so that I could prepare something for him. The script was still hidden from me as they finished their lunch. I thought: "Great! Lunch is over. Now I can audition and show them what I had to offer."

Woody got up from the table, extended his hand towards me for a handshake and said: "Thank you very much for coming by Cynthia." He then followed with the proverbial words: "We will be in touch."

I said: "It was so nice to meet you both, and thank you for my drink." Then I left. Once I was in the hallway heading to the elevators I thought to myself: "What the hell was that all about?"

The part of Louise eventually went to Janet Margolin. She was terrific in the role. I'm not sure why I got an addition for this movie. Janet was brunette, not blonde like me. Casting directors usually had a hair color in mind for the character they'd cast.

My other connection to Woody Allen happened in 1985 when I went to see his film, *The Purple Rose of Cairo*. It was set in the depression era. In a scene at the beginning of the movie, Mia Farrow portrays a waitress in a diner. She's talking to another waitress while customers are yelling for their orders. The waitresses are discussing the latest films and the stars of the time. Within the dialogue, they talked about the fact that Lew Ayers had married Ginger Rogers. However, before she did she was married to Jack Culpepper. Wow, Woody really does his research. These were accurate facts that were in a section of the movie that contained throw away dialogue. Daddy lives on in a Woody Allen film. I think Daddy might have liked that.

We were now living on Buck's paycheck and whatever we had saved in the bank. I didn't even know how much we had in our account. Buck was always the go-between with the bank. He had a decent job, which I helped to get him a year earlier at 20th Century Fox. His job brought in about $100 a week. He said that we'd be okay financially, and I trusted him.

We still attended a lot of parties and hosted a number of them ourselves. People in the business knew me from all my work in Hollywood, but they gravitated towards Buck at the parties. I loved this about our relationship, as it allowed me to take a step back at these functions. I didn't have to be "on" as Buck was on for both of us.

I questioned some of his entertaining choices. He loved the dark side of humor, which I could never warm up to. Despite his sense of humor, he was always the life of the party.

In the mid 1960's, some Buddhist monks in Asia had set themselves on fire, as a political protest. Buck's dark sense of humor showed itself at a Halloween party we attended together. He dressed as a monk carrying a gas can. Everyone got the joke and most thought it was funny. I got the joke, but I never thought it was all that funny.

For the next couple of years, my relationship with Buck slipped away from a husband and wife relationship, into a good friend's relationship. It hadn't really been a romantic relationship for a couple of years now. At times, he could be insensitive towards my feelings. Such as the time we heard a loud noise outside of our apartment.

We had gone to bed for the evening, and at the time, I was about six months pregnant with Michael. I was very frightened. Buck said that he'd investigate. He got out of bed, put on a robe over his pajamas and went looking throughout the apartment. He eventually went out the front door to look around. I sat quietly in bed waiting for his safe return. Three minutes went by, then another 3 minutes. It was all very quiet. Ten minutes had now gone by and I was beyond scared. I sat in the bed worrying about Buck and my unborn son. After a total of fifteen minutes I summoned up all the courage that I had, and gingerly got out of bed, put on my robe and crept into our living room. It was dark, but I could see that our front door was ajar. Maybe something had happened at our neighbor's apartment across the way. It was rented by a Swedish blonde bombshell dancer, Gunilla Hutton. This was before she became famous for playing Billie Jo Bradley on *Petticoat Junction* and her long stint on *Hee Haw*. She was a dancer in Nat King Cole's show and was, at the time, having an affair with him. We had observed Nat going in and out of her place in the wee hours of the night but never said much about it.

I was so worried about Buck and where he had gone. I thought: "Maybe he's hurt or even worse, dead." I slowly opened the front door and looked across the way. What I saw left me empty.

Through the window, I could see into Gunilla's apartment. There was Buck, sitting on her couch, with a drink in his hand chatting away to Gunilla. Here I am petrified with fear and overcome with worry about my husband, and there he is, straight out of bed, and back to being the life of the party. I'm worrying about his life, and he's having drinks with a beautiful woman. I made my way to Gunilla's apartment and knocked loudly on the door. She opened the door and said hello, but I looked right past her to Buck, lounging on the couch.

He said: "Oh, hi honey I was…"

Before he could finish I stared at him and said: "You Son of a Bitch!"

I then turned and went back to bed. It wasn't that he was having a drink with a beautiful lady. It was that he was having a drink with a beautiful lady while I could have been in bed getting my head chopped off.

Beyond Buck's occasional insensitivity, our relationship had become mostly comfortable, easy, and somewhat dependable. He was there for Michael and supportive of my career. We were good friends and that seemed to be enough for us to function as a couple. However, things were about to change.

Buck decided that we should buy a house. He said it would be a great investment, and a much nicer place for Michael to grow up in. The "working girl" on the floor above us would have to play the song Downtown for someone else from now on. We bought a house on Shadyglade Avenue in Studio City. It was a great neighborhood, with lots of trees and beautiful homes with little white picket fences. I remember thinking: "This is just what we need to make things better for our family." I was worried that we wouldn't be able to afford a house, but Buck assured me that we had saved enough to make a purchase. Plus, his mother, Estelle, would help us out with financing. When it came time to sign the papers, Buck and Estelle did most of the signing. I was given a couple of different papers to sign. I didn't bother asking him what I was signing. I trusted that he knew what he was doing.

Buck had been working on a number of different projects for 20th Century Fox, and sometimes he would have to go on location. In the summer / fall of 1967, he had to travel across the country as a location manager for a couple of weeks. When he came home, he was different. He was still the same gregarious guy at the parties, but he seemed a little aloof towards me personally. If I tried to confront him with it, he'd say it was all in my mind. I tried not to feel suspicious of him, but I felt the trust we had was slipping away. There was very little intimacy between us. We were arguing more frequently, and I felt that I was losing him. He knew it too.

In the past, Buck and I would go to Vegas a couple of times a year for a short vacation. Daddy would, sometimes, be working in Vegas. He worked a lot with Phil Harris at the Desert Inn. Daddy would get us into all the best shows that Las Vegas had to offer. We had the pleasure of seeing the Rat Pack a couple of times. Seeing Frank, Dean, Sammy, and Joey perform live, is beyond description. They always seemed to have way more fun than anyone else in the room. Our visits to Vegas would usually leave us smiling.

We thought that a visit to Vegas might turn things around for us again, but when we got there we had a huge fight in our room. Buck stormed out without telling me where he was going. I decided to try to have a fun night in spite of things. I headed to the blackjack tables. One should never gamble angry, but I didn't care. I was so upset with Buck. I sat down at the first blackjack table I came to. I was so angry that I didn't care if I won or lost.

I found myself sitting beside a good looking man wearing a very stylish tuxedo. He smiled at me and said hello. I instantly recognized his face. It was Don Adams. He was best known as Maxwell Smart, (Agent 86) from the *Get Smart* television comedy. Within a short period of time, he had me laughing and feeling a little calmer. We played blackjack, and all the while flirting and playing footsie under the table. I had not had a lot of affection from my husband, so this felt good. At one point, Don suggested we go up to his room for drinks. I thanked him and told him I was married. That fact didn't seem to matter to him. I thanked him for the offer and for making me smile, but I told him that I didn't think my husband would appreciate it. The reality was that my husband no longer appreciated me.

In 1968, we decided that our marriage was hopeless. He lost what love he had for me, and I had lost love and trust in him. A lot of husbands and wives that didn't get along would convince themselves to stay together for the children. Buck and I both knew this was wrong. Children pick up on that kind of falseness. In the end, it's the children that suffer. Buck was afraid that I might try to keep Michael away from him, but that was never the case.

Buck's mother, Estelle, convinced me that Michael and I should stay with her for a while. I was naive, and distraught enough to think this was a good idea. Estelle didn't have a job so she could look after Michael whenever I went to an audition, or if I had to be away for any extended period of time. My parents were still working, and wouldn't always be home if I needed them to babysit.

It turned out that living with Estelle was not the best thing to do after all. It was good for Michaels' welfare and upbringing, which was important. However, living there wasn't healthy for me. At times, I would be so distraught about my separation from Buck that I would find myself crying from the stress and pain of it all. Michael and I lasted about two weeks at Estelle's house. In the beginning, she was very sympathetic with my heartache and sadness. As time went on, I found out that she was reporting everything back to Buck. As it's been said; Blood is always thicker than water.

Buck had moved out of our house, so Michael and I moved back in. This was the very first time in my life that I had lived alone. I did not relish living by myself in that big house. I never thought that I'd miss sharing a room with my sister Patty, but I sure was now. I didn't want to sleep in the bedroom so I slept on the pull out couch in the den. I could hear every part of the house from that vantage point. Michael was just three years old so I put his bed beside the couch. I was so frightened to be alone that I would leave the radio on all night listening to a talk radio station. KABC 790 AM was the station that got me through many a night. I would eventually get so tired that I would fall asleep, but I wouldn't be sleeping for long. Any little noise would bounce me back to life. My nerves were on end. I even took to sleeping with a knife under my pillow, just waiting for that unwanted prowler to arrive. I would've done anything to protect my son Michael.

This was my life for eight months. I thought things couldn't get any worse. My world was crumbling around me, and I didn't know what the future held. I was raw with emotion. My parents saw the mess that I was in, and convinced me that living with them was the best thing for Michael and me. I packed up and we moved in with my parents.

In the late 60's Mother and Daddy had changed their ways dramatically. Daddy had cut back on his drinking and smoking, and Mother had given up both vices completely. She just quit cold turkey. I really admired her for that. She would use a straw as a substitute for a cigarette. Eventually, she didn't even need the straw. There were fewer fights between my parents, and that was good for everyone. They'd always loved each other, but without the alcohol they seemed to focus on what was important, which improved their relationship.

Mother was now doing census work. She would go door to door asking people questions and take down their answers. She would ask about products and services, and report her findings back to the company. She really enjoyed her work. Daddy was still searching for work in the entertainment field. Performing was all he knew. But he didn't know exactly how to go out and get it, so he kept waiting for it to find him. Some work finally did find Daddy. The TV series *Petticoat Junction* starred Edgar Buchanan and Bea Benaderet. Daddy played Mr. Harrington in the episode, *Who's Afraid of the Big Bad Jinx*. He did a great job. A movie part came to Daddy with a Columbia Pictures film, *Cat Ballou*. This would turn out to be Daddy's last movie appearance.

Cat Ballou starred Jane Fonda, and Lee Marvin. Nat King Cole and Stubby Kaye had supporting roles. Once again, Daddy's part was unaccredited. He was a banjo player in the bar. Daddy was not a big fan of Jane Fonda. He found her very loud and hated her politics. However, there is one story that I remember him telling me. This event changed his opinion of her very quickly.

One day on the set of *Cat Ballou*, some of the crew had been eating food off of the wrong catering table. On most working movie sets, the people from craft services set up separate tables, one for the stars, directors, producers and another for the crew. The stars table has all the best food and drinks. Jane walked by as a supervisor was yelling at Daddy for eating at the 'wrong' table. When Jane heard this, she came to my father's rescue. She let it be known to the powers that be, in a very loud voice, that everyone was working hard on the picture. They deserved to be treated better. From that day on, Daddy and the cast all ate the same food, from the same table. Daddy admitted that his respect for her rose a little that day, but just a little.

Daddy also found a day's worth of work on the TV series *The Virginian*. He played the part of a drunk in the jail cell, in an episode called *Letter of the Law*. My friend Simon Oakland was also in this episode.

Mother and Daddy with Michael they absolutely loved him.

(Cynthia Pepper Collection)

Chapter 25

Still Growing Up Under the Yum Yum Tree

I was now 27 years old, and I was a mess. My years of ignoring the business side of my work had caught up to me. I had no idea how much money I had in the bank, if any. Buck and my business manager had taken care of everything financially. I had no idea how to write a check. So I learned.

I had to get a lawyer to handle my divorce. A friend suggested a lawyer to me. They had used him once or twice in the past so I made an appointment. When I arrived at the lawyers, his secretary showed me into his office. After she introduced us she left, closing the door behind her. At some point during our meeting I was overcome with emotion, and started to cry. He took some tissue from the box on his desk and handed it to me. He then ushered me to a large leather couch in the corner. I was so upset with everything that I was going through; I let him lead me there without thinking. I sat on the couch and he sat beside me. It was so nice to have someone that would listen to me and be sympathetic to my plight. As I was wiping the tears from my eyes and trying to explain my story to him, he was suddenly all over me. He was kissing me, grabbing at me and trying to get on top of me. Now I was really confused. This is an officer of the court. He's supposed to help me. Not help himself to me! I pushed the horny bastard off of me, called him a few names and ran out of the office. It would have been my word against his, so I tried to forget about it as quickly as I had left his office. I didn't tell Daddy about it for the same reason I didn't tell him about the elevator incident at the Elaine apartments. He would have killed the guy. The following day, I got a new lawyer. People wonder why there are so many lawyer jokes in the world. "So, how many lawyer jokes are there? Only three, the rest are all true stories."

I still had one tough lesson to learn from Buck in regards to trust. Since our house was empty Buck said, we should sell it and divide the money. We met at his lawyer's office to sign the papers that would give us the ability to sell the house. I was presented with a large number of papers to sign. At this point, a good business person would have taken the papers to their own lawyer to make sure things were in their best interest, but I didn't. I was trusting. I was stupid. I was a sad bundle of nerves and just wanted things to be over, so I signed the papers.

When the house was finally sold, I asked Buck where my half of the money was. I was informed that I had no half as I had signed papers to that effect. I got nothing. It was our combined earnings that bought that house, but I still I got nothing.

During the days that followed, I was finding it hard to get out of bed in the morning. I cried so much in those days I could have filled an empty riverbed with my tears. One morning I dragged myself out of bed, put on a housecoat and met Mother in the kitchen for breakfast.

I was feeling particularly depressed that morning. My marriage was over; I was a single parent with no job, no money, no drive and living with my parents. Mother was about to get ready for work, but she sat down at the table to talk with me. We chatted as I looked deep into my tea cup. Then Mother said: "I got a letter from Patty a few days ago."

Without looking up, I said: "That's nice."

She continued: "It was addressed to your father and me."

"Well, that makes sense." Without looking up, I added: "Is she still living with her friend Carol?"

Patty had been living in New York for a number of years and was doing well as an administrator at the Bellevue Hospital.

Mother said: "Yes she says that she and Carol are doing fine and they love living in New York."

I said: "Good."

Mother then said: "This letter is a bit of a confession. Patty says that she's a lesbian."

Now she had my attention: "What are you talking about?"

Mother said: "Your sister says that she is a lesbian. I think I'm not going to show this to your dad as it just might kill him"

Mother went on: "I know your Dad loves both you and Patty very much, but I'm just afraid how he would react. I love Patty no matter what, but your dad might not take it very well"

I could barely hear what Mother said after that statement. My head was spinning. Patty is a lesbian? My sister is a lesbian? How is that possible? We grew up together, and we even slept together. Why didn't I see this before?

Mother was still talking: "Please don't mention this to your father."

She left the kitchen to continue getting ready for work. I was more depressed than ever. When Mother was telling me about Patty's letter, I thought to myself: "this isn't happening." How could this be? I certainly didn't put two and two together. It had been years since Patty went on a date with a guy. Her roommates had always been women, but I never once thought that she was a lesbian. My thoughts seem so antiquated, but people never spoke of this kind of thing. In 1967, it wasn't very easy for people to discuss or tell others about their alternate lifestyle. Is this why she called me stupid, and said hurtful things like, "you don't know anything!" Was she waiting all these with her secret to see if I could figure it out on my own?

Mother had left for work and I felt like I was knocked over by a huge wave of despair. No husband, no money, no future and now Patty was gay!?

I was lost. I didn't know which way was up! What was the point of going on? I felt so incredibly sad and empty. For a very brief moment, I even thought of ending my life. It just seemed like an alternative to all the pain, but then I thought of Michael. I had to be here for him.

He was my responsibility and I loved him so much. If for no other reason on earth I would be here for him.

Over the next few days, I became more focused on taking care of myself so that I could then, take care of my son. The more I focused on what was right and good in my life, the more open I became to other opportunities. I had more understanding for my sister. I knew that it couldn't have been easy for Patty to write the letter. She really wasn't good at being vulnerable or showing her emotions. I realized that Patty was tortured with her inner feelings, and thought that she was different from the rest of us. Thank God, the changes over the years have made it easier for people to feel free to live their lives openly. Patty didn't have that freedom, only fear. As far as I know, Mother never did show the letter to Daddy. I never mentioned the letter to Patty, or even hinted that I knew. Maybe if I had, we could have had a better relationship.

Even though I was still feeling the stress and strain of a divorce I was able to focus more on what was important, which was taking care of my family. I had to prove to the court, that I could financially provide for Michael and myself. I had an epiphany. If I could be a successful actress once, I could do it again. The perfect project came to me at just the right time.

I was offered the part of Robin Austin in Lawrence Roman's play, *Under the Yum Yum Tree*. The play was a big success on Broadway from 1960 to '61. The movie version was released in 1963 with Jack Lemmon and Carol Lynley. The live stage production that I was to be a part of was going into summer stock. It would play around the country for a couple of months, with an option to extend. I was worried about being away from Michael, but my parents assured me, they would take good care of him. My separation and slow moving divorce, from Buck was anything but amicable. I felt that the play was just what the doctor ordered. Plus, I had to make some money to pay my divorce lawyers.

I was glad to have the opportunity of performing in this production. During our divorce, one of the biggest contentions was concerning the care and custody of our son. There were plenty of threats and worries about my abilities to provide for Michael. My lawyer assured me that working in this play would prove my worth to the court.

The cast of the summer stock version of *Under the Yum Yum Tree* consisted of Edd Byrnes, David Hedison, Peg Shirley and me. I knew Edd from working with him on *77 Sunset Strip* and thought it would be fun to reconnect with him. David had just finished a four year run in his starring role as Captain Lee Crane on ABC's hit television show, *Voyage to the Bottom of the Sea*. Peg Shirley had played the part of Honey in the movie *The Thomas Crown Affair* with Steve McQueen and Faye Dunaway.

We rehearsed the play for two weeks in Los Angeles and then we traveled to the Royal Alexandra Theatre in Toronto, Canada for a week's run. From there, we played most of the large cities on the eastern seaboard of the United States. All the theaters we performed in were large venues. They were mostly 800 to 1500 seat theatres and we filled them all. I had not performed in a summer stock production before, and the fact that we would be traveling so much made my nerves work overtime. I kept thinking that if I pulled this off, meaning if I can do a decent job of acting in this production with all the distractions from back home, I could do anything. At home, my son was in my parent's custody. My lawyer assured me that when the run of this play was over I would return home, and the divorce and custody would be finalized.

On opening night in Toronto, just one hour before going on stage I received a call from my lawyer. He told me that Buck had come to my parent's home and taken Michael away to stay with him. This was a shock to me. The excuse that Buck gave for taking Michael was that my parents were drunks. There had been problems with drinking in my parents past, but they had been cleaning themselves up. There was no way that Mother and Daddy would do anything to harm Michael, and Buck knew that. He was just angry at me.

It would be a huge understatement to just say that I was very upset. I was over 2,500 miles away, in another country and there was nothing I could do until after the show. I had to try to focus on my character, her lines, and her blocking, and be good. My part required me to be on the stage about 80% of the time. With only four of us in the play and no understudies, we had to be ready and focused at all times.

Before the curtain went up, I was still trying to get my tears under control. My cast mates were very sympathetic to my plight, and I couldn't have felt more love and support from them. After the show I went back to my room, made some phone calls back home, and then I cried me a river. I felt helpless to do anything about what was going on. Daddy assured me that everything would be fine and that he would make sure that Michael was safe. By the end of the week, my parents, with the help of my lawyer, eventually got Michael back from Buck.

I had a two month contract to fulfill with the production of Yum Yum. As I had already said, my cast mates were very understanding about what I was going through. Peg was a great person to talk to about my situation, and life in general. David Hedison was such a sweet man. He and his wife, Bridget, were pregnant with their daughter Alexandra. With a child on the way, they were very sympathetic. Then there was Edd.

Initially, Edd was considerate towards my feelings, but then he decided to try something. When doing a sex comedy, like Yum Yum, things get moving pretty fast and furious on stage. The comedy is written down for you to play, but every now and then an actor will strive for more. During our run, Edd decided for, more. There was a scene in the play where my character, Robin - the innocent girl, gets drunk. At one point Edd's character, Dave - Robin's boyfriend, ends up on the floor, on his back, with his head downstage to the audience. My character, in a drunken stupor, ends up on top of him facing the audience. They exchange some funny dialogue, and then move on with the scene. During one particular performance in Toronto, Edd decided that while I was on top of him, it would be funny for him to reach up and grab my breasts. The audience agreed, as it got a big laugh. I was shocked at the time, but what could I do in front of a live audience. I stayed in character and played on through the scene. After the show, I told Edd what I thought of him grabbing me. He just laughed it off as no big deal. I asked him to, please stick to the script, and with what we had rehearsed. The very next night, he did it again.

I remained calm during the scene but as soon as the show was over, I called my agent back in Hollywood. I told him what had happened. My agent then called Edd's agent who later called Edd. The very next show Edd apologized to me and said it wouldn't happen again. He kept true to his word and we've been friendly ever since.

After a month and a half of shows up and down the eastern seaboard, David Hedison left the play. He wanted to get back in front of the camera. He was replaced with Tab Hunter. I was heading towards the end of my contract with the play, and looked forward to seeing my family again. Eventually, Margaret O'Brien took over my role in the play.

I was so happy and relieved to be home with my son Michael. The play was over and I had proven myself to the courts. I could financially take care of both myself and my son. Mother and Daddy had taken exemplary care of Michael. They really bonded while I was away. I knew that if he had to, Daddy would have taken a bullet for his grandson.

From Toronto to St Louis I was proving to the court, and to myself, that as a single parent, I could provide for my son.

(Cynthia Pepper Collection)

Chapter 26

The River Is Down To My Ankles

In 1968, in the middle of our nation's racial problems, NBC got bold. They bought a pilot from 20th Century Fox called *Julia*. This was another Hal Kanter creation. The show was about a young African American woman, Julia Baker, whose husband had been killed in Vietnam. As a single parent, she now had to bring up her son Corey with what she made working as a nurse in a doctor's office. Julia was played by the beautiful and talented Diahann Carroll.

I was very lucky and thrilled to be working with this unique actress. She had played Clara in the movie *Porgy and Bess* with Sidney Poitier, and Dorothy Dandridge. She was also in a favorite movie of mine called *Paris Blues* with Paul Newman, Joanne Woodward, and Sidney Poitier. I was brought in to play Corey's grade school teacher, Ginger Wolfe. Julia's son Corey Baker was played by 6 year old Marc Copage. He was a great little actor to work with.

The first episode I was in was called *Who's a Freud of Ginger Wolfe?* In this episode, Julia is worried about some paintings that Corey has done at school. They were all painted in black. The second episode I did was called *Too Good to Be Too Bad*. In this episode, Julia was the target of some matchmaking schemes.

Julia worked in the office of Dr. Morton Chegley. The doctor was played by veteran actor Lloyd Nolan. He had played a lot of tough gangsters and police detectives in his day but now he was a gruff but friendly, no nonsense doctor.

Both of the episodes I did were directed by Ezra Stone. Mr. Stone had starred as an actor on Broadway, and later a writer for Milton Berle, Danny Thomas, and Fred Allen. However, he will be better remembered as the original voice of Henry Aldridge on the 1930's '40's radio program, *The Aldrich Family*.

I enjoyed working in both of these episodes. I felt like I was part of something important at the time. The *Julia* series was groundbreaking. There were no other shows on the air that were dealing with the current issues of the late sixties. I was very proud to be part of it.

In Julia with the beautiful and talented Diahann Carroll.

(Cynthia Pepper Collection)

While waiting for my divorce to be finalized, I did a guest appearance on the TV show *Lassie*. The episode was called *The Return Home*. I flew to the film location in San Francisco to meet my handsome co-star, Sammy Jackson, and the crew. However, my biggest excitement was meeting the world's most famous collie, Lassie herself. Actually I need to change that to Lassie himself. That's right, Lassie was a boy. He just played the part of a girl in the show, and very well I might add. (Did that make him a dog in drag?) I asked Lassie's handler at the time why they didn't use a female dog. I was told that every dog that ever played *Lassie* was a male. The reason was that male dogs are easier to train than female dogs. (I think all the ladies out there can agree with that.)

The film shoot lasted a few days, and unlike W.C. Fields, I enjoyed working with animals. Lassie was the consummate professional, never late for a scene, and always hitting his mark. It was a lot of fun. I should mention that one day on the set Lassie gave me a kiss on the cheek. Not many people can say that they've been kissed by two international stars, first Elvis and now Lassie. Life just doesn't get any better.

Lassie. Unlike W.C. Fields, I enjoyed working with animals.

(Cynthia Pepper Collection)

Before I left to perform in *Under the Yum Yum Tree*, I went to a party in L.A. that a friend was hosting. I met someone there that I had known when I was in school. He and I really hit it off again. Within a week of my divorce being finalized, we were married. I know what you're saying: "Out of the frying pan and… back into another frying pan Cynthia?" All I can say is that it just felt right at the time. We were married a total of 23 years before we decided to part ways. In that time, I became a stay at home mom. I did a few more TV shows in those years but raising my son Michael had become my joy.

So what happened to my acting career after the 1960's? Did the offers stop coming? The river of work didn't dry up on me, as much as I just stepped out of the river. I was still being offered parts, but I was turning them down.

I did do a couple of shows through those years. I did an episode on *The Flying Nun* called *The Boyfriend*. My character is upset that her fiancé, played by Dwayne Hickman, might be having an affair with Sally Field's character. Once it's revealed that Sally Field's character is a nun, things get a little crazy. Character actors Bob Hastings from *Mchale's Navy*, and Shelly Morrison from *Will & Grace* were also in this episode.

I found Sally Field to be very professional but hard to get close to. Her time was very much in demand, on and off the set. We had a couple of pleasant conversations then we'd do our scenes and that was that.

In 1972, I worked on *The Jimmy Stewart Show*. It was a television comedy in which Jimmy Stewart played a small-town college professor. The plot revolved around his character's teaching and home life. John McGiver was a co-star on the show, and it was great seeing him again. Vincent Price was a guest star in this episode. As you know, he was that scary actor that did all those horror films. Well, I'm here to tell you that he was a pussycat. We had lunch together and talked between scenes. There was nothing scary about him. He was true professional, smart guy, and a real gentleman.

When I first arrived on the set, I recalled the time that Jimmy Stewart yelled at me when we were doing the movie *Take Her She's Mine*. Thank goodness Mr. Stewart didn't remember the incident at all, which made for a few days of pleasant work.

So the scary actor, Vincent Price, was sweet and nice, and the sweet and nice actor, Jimmy Stewart, was scary. It proves two things. Perception combined with a good actor is reality. It also proves that even Jimmy Stewart can have an off day.

My husband, at the time, didn't want me to work at all. I was okay with being a mom and stay-at-home wife during this time of my life, so I complied. However, the acting bug was biting me again. The answer to my predicament was Daddy, and a charity show.

In the mid-seventies, Daddy had been asked by the Masquers Club President, Joe Pasternak, to be part of a night of entertainment, with the proceeds going to a worthy cause. The Masquers Club was initially formed in 1925 by eight Hollywood actors that included Robert Edison, George Read and six others. It was created to promote fellowship among actors and other creative professionals. Their motto was and still is "Laugh To Win". I always thought that was a good attitude to have in life. As time went on the Masquers would boast more famous members, such as John Gilbert, Gene Autry, Bob Hope, Louis B Mayer, W.C. Fields, Tony Curtis, Lou Costello, Cary Grant, Jerry Lewis, and Kirk Douglas, just to name a few. I don't know when Daddy officially became a member, but he was a member for a long time. He would eventually work his way up the ladder of the Masquers to be part of the Masquers Board.

Daddy and I worked up a two person act to be performed at the Masquers. We did our comedic song and dance act, which helped raise money for a local charity. The charity got the money, and I got to perform. I loved being on stage with Daddy. He was now in his 70's and moving a lot slower than he used to, but when the lights came on they lit a spark in him that was so wonderful to see again. He was masterful, funny and he loved the whole night just as much as I did.

Daddy had performed numerous times within the hallowed halls of this revered club, but for this particular night he wanted me to be a part of his show. I was so proud to do it. We were a part of a great variety show that night. We told some jokes, danced, and sang for the crowd. (To be honest Daddy sang and I just tried to keep up.) I knew there were a lot of rich and famous people in the audience, but I was just focused on doing a good job. I didn't want to be worried about who we were performing for.

After the show, Daddy introduced me to a number of his friends and fellow performers. Eventually, he brought me to meet his friend, and the shoe millionaire, Harry Karl. Mr. Karl reminded me of a tall older Cary Grant, but with a strange creepy side. He had been married to actress Marie "The Body" McDonald, but that had not ended well. After saying hello, Mr. Karl introduced us to his wife, Debbie Reynolds.

I said: "Hello Miss Reynolds." I couldn't believe that I was meeting my idol.

She shook my hand and said: "Oh Cynthia, call me Debbie. I enjoyed your performance with your Dad. He's still got it. You were both great."

I didn't know if she meant it or was just being polite, but I said: "Thank you. That means a lot to me." As we sat down at their table, I continued: "Musicals are my favorite movie genre. I loved you in *Unsinkable Molly Brown, Tammy and the Bachelor* and, of course, my all-time favorite movie *Singing in the Rain*."

She laughed and said: "Wow you really are a fan."

We sat and talked for quite a long time. Debbie and I talked about our similar characters. She was Tammy, and years later, I was Margie. Those characters even had similar pigtails. I asked her why she didn't reprise her role as Tammy in the two sequels that followed. She said that she had been asked, but was pregnant at the time and; "The studio waits for no man, or pregnant woman." So they gave the part to Sandra Dee.

During our conversation, Debbie mentioned that she was President of a charity organization and asked if I would I be interested in joining?

"Would I?"

Before she and Mr. Karl left for the evening, she gave me her number. She said that she would put in a good word for me and be my sponsor with the Thalians. Daddy could see that I was very excited, and he was so happy for me. First, I sang with Daddy, and we really enjoyed our time up on the stage together. Then, to top off the evening, I got to meet and talk with someone I had always admired, and was going to be working with... Life doesn't get much better than that.

With Debbie as my sponsor, I joined the Thalians in 1974. The Thalians were first formed in 1955 by a group of talented young stars. They got together to change the perception that young 'Hollywood" stars just partied, then married and divorced. They wanted to show that young actors were more responsible than their public image implied. The initial group included Nicky Blair, Bill Brown Jr., Milton Cohen, Gary Crosby, Kim Dibbs, Bill & Nori Gold, Jack Haley Jr., Mac Krim, Hugh O' Brian, Bob Petersen and Margaret Whiting. The first meeting was held at Jayne Mansfield's Pink Palace in Beverly Hills. The Thalians decided to devote their time and energy to children with mental health problems. Over the years, large amounts of money were raised for this great cause.

Every year, the Thalians would raise money by hosting the Thalians Ball. We would begin to sell tickets to the annual event long before the actual date of the ball. They were sold at the studios, malls, and door to door if need be. We really pushed those tickets.

At home, working on a script.

(Cynthia Pepper Collection)

The ladies of the Thalians would also be asked to dance in the actual show. It was a lot of work, but I loved it. Our choreographer was Alex Romero. I loved working with Alex. He danced and was assistant choreographer, in my favorite film, *An American in Paris*. He choreographed, or assisted in the choreography for a lot of great dance routines for some of the classic films including *Annie Get Your Gun, Kiss Me Kate, Seven Brides for Seven Brothers, Gigi* and *Jailhouse Rock* with Elvis. As a matter of fact, Alex is the one that choreographed the famous dance scene for the song *Jailhouse Rock.*

He had already rehearsed the male chorus of dancers, so they were ready. Later, when he was teaching the dance to Elvis, he realized that Elvis wasn't a dancer. He couldn't do what Alex was trying to teach him. Alex had the insight to let go of the routine and asked Elvis to show him what he could do. Elvis showed him his moves. Alex followed along, copying his moves. Then he made some notes, ran to the male chorus, and said: "Forget everything I showed you, we're starting new." They learned the new dance and the rest is history. Alex was smart enough to work with someone's strengths and not worry about their weaknesses. I think that's exactly what he did with us. When we first got together, he said: "Ok ladies, show me what you've got." He used our strengths. I only danced in two of the shows, but really enjoyed the experience.

The Thalians Ball was usually held at the Beverly Hilton Hotel and attracted many big stars on the night of the show. They would generally honor someone with what was called the "Mr. Wonderful" award. Through the years, they had to add the "Mrs. Wonderful" award when honoring a woman. Each year the honoree was a bigger star than the last.

In 1974, the star to be honored was Lucille Ball. That show included Steve Allen, Eve Arden, Desi Arnaz Jr. Lucie Arnaz, Carol Burnett, Sammy Davis Jr., Doris Day, Gloria DeHaven, Shecky Greene, Ruta Lee, Jayne Meadows, Liza Minnelli, Andy Williams and Raquel Welch. We rehearsed for weeks to get the dance numbers memorized. You know you're in a big show when the opening bit of the night is Billy Barty riding an elephant onto the stage. (Do you realize how much skill is involved in dancing around whatever the elephant leaves on the stage? Some of these leavings were bigger than Billy himself. Ah, Show Business.)

I remember being backstage during this particular show, with my dance troupe. The whole time we were fixated on how fantastic Doris

Day looked. She was in incredible shape. We all thought that Raquel Welch would be the knockout beauty of the night, (and she's no slouch), but Doris Day had the lock on that race.

In 1976, the Thalians paid tribute to not one, not two but three movie stars. Bing Crosby, Dorothy Lamour and Bob Hope. It was an homage to the many Road Pictures they had done together. We only had a few minutes before the curtain went up, but I spoke with Mr. Crosby backstage and mentioned Daddy. He was more than happy to talk about "the old boy" as he would call him. He talked fast and with passion about Daddy, but then he apologized as he had to run to make the curtain. I know that he appreciated Daddy's musical abilities, and his friendship.

This show was a big event. Everyone who was anyone was there. They even had John Wayne involved with presenting the awards for the night. Peggy Lee sang for the gala attendees, and we danced our little buns off for the crowd. Our rehearsal time lasted about 3 weeks... we really put in many hours of dance. We had a tap dancing number a jazz number and another number that I can't even recall now. (At least there were no elephant droppings to jump over in this show.)

One of the ladies I danced with was Barbara Luna, (you may remember her as the sexy Marlena Moreau in TV's *Star Trek* episode called *Mirror Mirror.*) I also danced with Anne Convy, [Bert Convy's wife, at the time) and a lady by the name of Diana Hyland. Diana won an Emmy for her role in the television movie *The Boy in the Plastic Bubble,* which also starred John Travolta. At the time of our dance rehearsals and show, Diana was dating John Travolta. I found Diana to be very pretty and at the time, quite fragile looking. She had a sweetness and sort of an ethereal quality about her. She talked a lot about John during the short time I knew her. Her conversation was always of a loving nature when she spoke of him. Even with an age difference of 18 years, it seemed like an amazing relationship.

At the time I knew her, Diana had a very young son, Zachary, whom she loved dearly. You just knew by the way she spoke of him that he meant everything to her.

A year later, I was shocked and saddened to hear, that Diana had become ill. Within a short time, she succumbed to cancer. What a loss. She was a very talented and special person.

The last TV work I did towards the end of the 70's was a made-for-TV movie for CBS called Crisis in Mid-air. I played the part of a stewardess named Marsha. (Remember these were the 70's, so the term 'flight attendant' wasn't being used yet.) It starred George Peppard and Karen Grassle. The supporting cast included Desi Arnaz Jr. and Fabian. It constituted a couple of days of work for me and beyond that, I have very little recollection of the project.

The Elvis Connection #9 - 1970's

Vincent Price was in *The Trouble with Girls*. This movie had a great lineup or co-stars including Marlyn Mason, Sheree North, Dabney Coleman, and John Carradine.

In 1974, Comedian and actor, Shecky Greene was in the same Thalians Ball show that I was in. In 1956, Shecky was part of the show at the New Frontier Hotel in Las Vegas with a young performer billed as the 'Atomic Powered Singer,' Elvis Presley. This was the very first time that Elvis performed in Vegas.

The same Thalians Ball had Steve Allen performing. Steve Allen had put Elvis on his TV show, *The Steve Allen Show* weeks before Ed Sullivan did and for that alone Steve deserves a mention.

When not riding elephants at the Thalians Ball, Bill Barty, found himself in two of Elvis' films. *Roustabout* and *Harum Scarum*.

Chapter 27

Ivan, Goodbye Again

There is a poignant addition to my 1963 New York City visit. Before I left Hollywood I had heard through a mutual friend, Gary, that my high school sweetheart Ivan was married and living there now. We had not been in direct contact with each other since he left to study in Europe while I was still in high school. Other than a few sweet and friendly letters we sent to one another, we had very little contact.

I was still married at the time, but I thought it would be ok to get in touch with Ivan, to see how his life was going and to catchup after all these years. I have to admit that I was curious as to what our feelings towards each other would be. I had no expectations, but I was curious.

We met for lunch at the Empire State building. This building was the focal point of one of my favorite romantic movies, *An Affair to Remember* with Cary Grant and Deborah Kerr. They were to meet at the Empire State building, but on the way to their meeting, unbeknownst to Cary's character, she was hit by a car and ended up in a wheelchair for the rest of her life. After that, it was the disability that kept them apart. It was silly of me to even have that movie in my head at all, but there it was.

I was quite nervous when I first saw Ivan, after all the years we were apart. It was strange, but this whole scene took me back to school, and the year I first met him. In my heart, I was a teenager again. Surprisingly I still had the same feelings for him as I did all those years ago.

After lunch, we started walking and of course, talking. We discussed everything from old friends to old music and how he was still managing his diabetes. We seemed to walk forever. New York was now his town and he seemed to really enjoy showing me around. We talked and laughed and talked some more. There was never a lack of conversation between us. We discussed our lives now, jobs, and life in general. When we talked about our marriages, we discussed the good and the not so good things about them but we never disrespected our spouses.

As the day was turning into night and before darkness set in we decided to visit his dad. Mr. Haas now lived in Greenwich Village. His apartment was a four story walk up and had a very bohemian feel to it. He was warm and friendly when he greeted me. We ate dinner later at Luchow's on 14th Street in The Village. At that point in time, Luchow's was America's most famous German Restaurant. For years, they dominated the New York celebrity dining scene. They even had a genuine Viennese Quartet playing in the corner. Sadly, this great old restaurant was destroyed by fire in 1982.

After dinner, we took Mr. Haas back to his sparse apartment and made sure he was good for the night. A couple of years later he moved back to Vienna where, in 1968, he died from complications of asthma.

Now the hour was getting late, and Ivan and I both knew that our wonderful time together was coming to a close. He wanted to make sure that I got back to my hotel safe and sound so he hailed a cab and rode with me to my hotel. We talked outside for a few minutes more, and it was there that he confessed that he still loved me and would always love me. I started to cry. I was happy to hear that but at the same time, I felt quite sad, knowing that we couldn't go back in time and that we could never be anything but friends. We hugged one another for the longest time in the bitter sweet New York air. Neither one of us wanted to let go. He gave me the sweetest kiss and then we said our goodbyes. I could feel a small part of my heart ache as it did before, when we parted all those years ago. This was the way it had to be.

A few years later, I heard from the same mutual friend that Ivan and his wife had moved to Hollywood. Our friend asked if it would be all right to give Ivan my phone number...I said sure. I had remarried by this point and knew that my current husband wouldn't be upset if I kept in contact with an old friend.

When I met up with Ivan again I was shocked at his appearance. Since I had last seen him, his diabetes had taken its toll. He was almost completely blind he was dependent on others for transportation and many other aspects of his daily life. Of course this didn't matter to me but once again I thought of the movie *Affair to Remember*.

After our initial meeting, we went out many times for lunch. I would pick him up at his friend's house and off we would go. A couple of times we went to Hollywood's oldest restaurant, Musso Frank Grill on Hollywood Blvd. I think it was Ivan's favorite. He would take my arm and I would guide him the best I could. These were great, fun times for us. When we weren't getting together for lunch, we would often just talk on the phone. The last time I spoke with him will forever haunt me.

Ivan called to talk to me and I complained about having a headache... I guess I kind of rattled on a bit about my discomfort. I wasn't in the mood to talk just then. He told me he would be in dialysis that coming week and would call me when the week was over. I said ok and quickly hung up the phone so that I could take care of my head pain. On Sept. 8th 1978, I was reading the Sunday newspaper and happened to see an article about two patients who died while receiving treatment for dialysis. As I read on, the paper said that the two patients were in the same room receiving treatment when something went horribly wrong and both of them had died. I can't remember exactly what went wrong, but I just remember being stunned by the article. It was just a routine dialysis treatment which caused these two people to die. I read one of the names in the article, Ivan Haas. No. Could that be my Ivan Haas... middle name Michael? Could it be just a terrible coincidence? I was afraid, but I had to know. I called our mutual friend and it was confirmed that it was Ivan and somehow they couldn't get a hold of me to let me know sooner...Ivan was 38 years old when he passed away.

I've often wondered what path our lives would have taken if he had stayed here instead of being shipped off to Europe for school all those years ago? What if our relationship had more time to blossom? What if we had married? What if... but it's no use trying to figure that out now. No more "what if's." It's better to live in the "what is."

I still think of him once in a while and I'm of the mind and faith that I will see him again one day.

The Hollywood Show

In the early 90's, I was in the midst of a separation from my second husband. My son Michael was in his twenties and living his own life. I had to find out where I belonged in life. I wasn't working or doing anything in the world of entertainment. My acting career seemed like ten lifetimes ago. I missed a lot of my old Hollywood friends that I had come to know and work with through the 60's and 70's. I was searching for something to do.

One day I was having lunch with my friend Diane and her friend Joanne. As the luncheon was ending Joanne asked me if I would like to go to the Hollywood Show. I asked: "What is that, a play?" She explained that it was an event at a local venue where celebrities sit at tables, sign autographs, and mingle with their fans. I asked why celebrities would do that. Joanne said that they made money doing these shows. For a lot of actors and musicians that were no longer in the limelight, this was a way to help them make some income. I knew first hand that being a celebrity didn't always come with a pension plan.

I asked: "Who'll be there?"

She didn't know for sure, but said, "I'll bet there will be someone there that you'll know."

It sounded like fun and I needed some fun in my life at that time. Diane was busy and couldn't go. I told Joanne that it would just be the two of us and that I'd meet her there.

We met outside of the hotel ballroom so that we could go in together. We entered this massive ballroom. The high ceiling gave it a very echo like sound throughout. For the first couple of minutes, it felt very cold and intimidating but that would quickly change. I glanced around the room and saw rows and rows of tables. There must have been about 70 tables side by side. Sitting behind these tables were celebrities from all different eras. The cast from television shows like *Leave it to Beaver,* and *Father Knows Best.* To my left there was Cindy Williams to my right there was Henry Winkler and throughout the room there were so many other beloved stars of days gone by. I started to get excited with the prospect of seeing some old friends.

My good friends Beverly Washburn and Randy Carlson. Beverly was in many classic films like Shane and Old Yeller.

(Cynthia Pepper Collection)

As I looked around the room, I started to recognize even more familiar faces. The first friend I identified was Beverly Washburn. It had been years since we had last seen each other. I ran over to her and gave her the biggest hug. She was so surprised and happy to see me. She grabbed my hand and said: "Come with me. We can walk around together. There are a lot of people here that would like to see you." By this time, Joanne had gone on her own to meet and talk with celebrities that she wanted to meet. I can't blame her. It was like one-stop shopping of all the actors and musicians that you grew up. There were so many familiar faces from the world of television, radio and the movies all sitting in one room.

Beverly and I walked and talked as we caught up on the past missing years. She walked me up to a particular table and there was another familiar face from 30 years ago, Stanley Livingston. The last time I had seen Stan he was just a young boy on the set of *My Three Sons*. It was such a joy for me to see him again. We hugged, laughed and chatted about those days. I was almost crying for joy because I had reconnected with so many of my old friends in only one day.

As Beverly and I walked on, we met up with a friend of hers named Tim Neeley. She introduced us and he said: "Cynthia, where have you been? I've been looking all over for you." For a moment, I wondered what he meant by that. I didn't think that I'd been hiding from anyone or that I was that hard to find, but then again it had been a long time since I had worked in the business. He then asked: "Would you be interested in coming to the next show? You could bring some pictures and spend a few hours talking to the fans. What do you say?" This was the reconnection that I was looking for. Would people still know me? Would anyone care? I had to find out.

I said: "Tim, I would love to attend the next show. Where do I sign up?" Beverly explained that Tim was the promoter that brought in the celebrities for the shows.

A few months later I was a guest at the Hollywood Show. I had my own table and displayed what few pictures I had to offer. When I first set up I was worried that people would not know me or my past work, but that was certainly not the case. Fans started dropping by my table and I quickly got into the swing of things. They bought my pictures, asked for my autograph and had a lot of questions. They wanted to know how I got started, what was it like to have my own television show, what was it like to work on *My Three Sons*, what was Hollywood like in the 60's?

Then there were the questions about Elvis. Hundreds of questions about Elvis and I answered each and every one of them. I really enjoyed talking to everyone who came by my table.

Towards the end of the day, a sweet lady approached me and noticed the pictures I had of Elvis and me. She introduced herself as Bobbie Cunningham and said that she was the president a California based Elvis Presley fan club. She then smiled and asked: "Would you be interested in being a guest at an Elvis weekend, in Palm Springs?"

I was perplexed. I didn't even know that there were such things as Elvis weekends. She continued: "Of course we would supply your transportation, accommodations and any other expenses that you may incur. I think you would have a great time, and we would love to have you there." Without knowing what I was getting into, I told her that I would love to be a part of the Elvis weekend.

The Palm Springs event was a great experience. They had some other people there that had known Elvis on the dais. They called us VIP's and treated us like royalty. I certainly didn't think of myself as a VIP. I was just as much an Elvis fan as everyone else that attended. We shared our Elvis stories and signed some autographs. There was even a couple of Elvis impersonators that performed. At this time the term "Elvis Impersonator" was still an acceptable title. I was later told that the term Elvis Tribute Artist or ETA was now the fashion in the Elvis world. ETA to me has always stood for Estimated Time of Arrival, but I can change.

The Palm Springs weekend was the beginning of my second involvement in the Elvis world. Of course, the first involvement came in 1963 with Elvis himself. Ever since that day at the Hollywood Show I've thanked God for meeting Bobbie and having her introduce me to a world that I didn't even know existed.

Elvis fans are some of the best, intense, yet fun loving fans in all of show business. Since that first introduction, I've been invited to numerous Elvis festivals around the world including Canada, Australia, England, Ireland, Germany and Denmark just to name a few. Thank you again Elvis.

In 2005, my son was turning 40 years old. "Wow, where did all that time go?" His very good friends decided to throw him a surprise birthday party at a pub in Studio City called The Fox and the Hounds. It was a wonderful informal gathering of about twenty-five people. I was invited to be there, but so was my ex-husband, Buck. I was a little apprehensive to go since Buck was going to be there. I still had some old wounds and scars from our bitter divorce and custody battle so many years ago. I wasn't sure how he would react with me being there. Buck had remarried, and his life seemed to be in a good place for him, but still I was hesitant. Then I realized that this was my son's

40th and there was no amount of imagined pain that I wouldn't go through for Michael.

Here I am with my best friend Vicki McIntyre-Watters. This was taken at our Hollywood High School 40th Reunion. She passed away in 2010. I miss her every day.

(Cynthia Pepper Collection)

After I arrived and gave Michael his present and a great big hug and kiss. I saw Buck across the way with his wife Connie. After a while, Buck came over to my table. He bought me a drink and then said: "Hey Kiddo, you want to dance?"

I said: "Sure." His smile let me know that everything was fine. As we danced we talked about how proud we both were of Michael. We both agreed that Michael was the one thing that we did right in our marriage. I guess the adage of "time heals all wounds" is a true one. It was so good to know that after a lot of heartache we were able to reconcile our relationship. Buck and I remained friendly after that.

Reunited with my friend, Tim Considine

(Cynthia Pepper Collection)

Relaxing by the pool with my very good friend Stan Livingston. That's odd, I don't remember "Chip" having a beard.

(Cynthia Pepper Collection)

With Amanda. Spanky McFarland's sister.

The very funny Jerry Stiller.

Carol Burnett is a comedy acting Legend.

(Cynthia Pepper Collection)

Having a great time with Van Johnston and Pamela Tiffin at a 20th Century Fox luncheon in New York for Richard and Darryl Zanuck.

(Cynthia Pepper Collection)

Chapter 28

Saying Goodbye Is Never Easy

In the late 1960s, Daddy was performing in Las Vegas, with Phil Harris, at one of the casinos. In the past, he had done a lot of shows in Vegas with a number of his old cronies. After one late night show, Daddy was walking back to his room when a sharp pain went ripping through his chest. The staff got him to the hospital in time to stabilize him and his newly found heart trouble. The doctors determined that the only course of action was to equip him with a pacemaker. The operation went very well. After a little convalescing in the hospital Daddy was home and good as new, well almost. When he got home, he was different. He slowed down a lot. His drinking had reduced way down and, as a result, there were a lot fewer confrontations with him and Mother. She seemed to take this change to heart.

Daddy was very close to Michael. Daddy once said to Mother: "I guess I wasn't such a good father to the girls. I'm going to try to make it up by being the best Pop-pops I can be to Michael." Pop-pops is what Michael affectionately called him.

I must say, Daddy did succeed. He spent as much time as he could with Michael. Daddy would often pick him up from school and take him to lunch, or to a comic book store. Daddy, being who he was, would sometimes even take Michael to the race track to meet his pals Willie Shoemaker, and Johnny Longden, among others. I know what you're thinking: "Who takes a kid to a horse race?" That was my father. The track was his second home. Sometimes, Daddy's crony from his Vaudeville days, Charlie Foy, would meet them there and that would result in a whole lot of fun for everyone. Daddy loved Michael and just wanted to pal around with him. Mother was the doting grandma that made sure Michael was safe at all times, but Pop-pops was his playmate. There was a lot of love to go around in the Pepper house for Michael.

In 1979, Michael had learned to play cribbage. He promised his Pop-pops that he would teach him the game so they could play together. Unfortunately, Michael never got to keep that promise. That was the year Daddy got really sick. There were a number of ailments that had him hospitalized but ultimately it was his heart that gave out.

Paul "Mousie" Garner and Daddy. Mousie was with Ted Healy's Stooges in Vaudeville and later with Spike Jones. He and Daddy were the best of friends.

(Cynthia Pepper Collection)

On April 1, 1979, (April Fool's Day) Daddy passed away. We were all devastated. You know your parents won't live forever, but you don't want to think of the end until you're forced too. Michael was very upset, but he was also very brave at Daddy's funeral... Michael wanted to show his love for his Pop-pops so he wrote a note and asked if he could put it in the casket with him. The note read: "Pop-pops, I'm sorry I didn't get to teach you how to play cribbage, but I promise you, someday I will." He placed his note into his Pop-pop's hands just before they closed the casket lid.

At the Forest Lawn gravesite there was family, friends, coworkers, singers, actors, vaudevillians and other Hollywood people that knew and loved Daddy. He would have loved the fact that his plot was overlooking the Warner Bros. studio where he had done a lot of his work. After a few words were spoken we all held hands and stood around his grave silently reflecting upon his life. Then, without warning someone began to sing *Tura Lura Lura (That's An Irish Lullaby)*. It was one of Daddy's favorite songs. He would sing it all the time. To this day I don't know who started that wonderful joyous chorus but we all joined in. Daddy would have loved hearing his friends and family singing over him. I believe somehow he heard us and was singing along. Maybe he'd stop singing just long enough to remind Mother that she was still a better dancer than a singer. To be honest, there were no bad voices that day.

Patty

Sometime during the early 70's, Patty moved back to California and started working in administration at the Department of Water and Power for the city of Los Angeles. I knew very little of her job but from all accounts she was a very good administrator. She had very good organizational skills which made me think that Patty would have made a great actors' agent. She knew show business and was a very savvy minded person. She just seemed to have an aversion to the entertainment business in general.

Patty was a functioning alcoholic. She wouldn't drink much through the week, but she could really put it away on the weekends. When she was drinking she would get mean, nasty, and very hurtful. That was when we would really butt heads. So many vile insults were being hurled towards me that I could barely duck let alone fire much of anything back. I was always trying to figure out why she would say these things. People drink to forget, or escape, from reality but what was she running from? Was she ashamed of being gay? Was she jealous of my success in the world of entertainment? Did she not get enough hugs as a kid?

Patty, Mother and Me.

(Cynthia Pepper Collection)

In 2000, Patty was having a myriad of health problems and decided to retire from her job. She had always been a slave to her asthma, but there seemed to be a number of other medical issues that were catching up to her. She was in a lot of pain. I'm sure that a number of these problems were brought on by her alcoholism. She eventually became bedridden, and had to have constant care at home. She could afford the nurses and healthcare professionals she needed to care for her, but her less than cheery disposition caused many of her caregivers to quit after a short time on the job. She had gone through more than fifty caregivers in a two year span. Her illness was making her insufferable to all. Our on-again off-again relationship was definitely off again. We tried to keep in touch by phone, but they weren't always the best calls. I visited Patty only a couple of times while she was bedridden. During the visits I was yelled at, talked down to and at times, ignored. I decided to just stay away. She called once and asked why I wasn't visiting her. I told her that I didn't want to visit her just so she could verbally abuse me again. She then proceeded to verbally abuse me over the phone. I took it for a while but eventually hung up on her.

I always wanted to have a warm and loving sisterly relationship. I liked to think that way down in her heart, Patty felt the same way too. We just couldn't find it.

In 2005, Patty was hospitalized. At the time I was living in Las Vegas so I flew to Los Angeles to see her. The hospital staff was attending to her needs when I arrived, so I waited outside her room. The nurse asked me if I wanted the Minister to say a prayer for her, and would I also like to be there? I said: "Thank you, I would very much like to be included." It was now obvious that she didn't have long to live. I went inside her hospital room. It was a simple white room with a couple of machines helping to sustain her life. This was to be the last meeting between sisters. Patty was in a coma due to the morphine she was given for her pain.

As I waited for the minister I looked around the room and saw so many cards, flowers and gifts addressed to my sister. They all had well wishes from other people in Patty's life. I was happily surprised at this outpouring of sympathy for my sister. They were from her friends and coworkers, people that I didn't even know existed in her life. They were filled with so much love and compassion. Within a few minutes, the minister arrived and proceeded with his prayer. It lasted no more than 2 or 3 minutes. I was hoping that somehow Patty knew that I was there and could hear the words that the minister had spoken.

After we had said our "Amen's", I kissed Patty's forehead, stroked her hair and said: "I Love you." The minister and I left the room together. I thanked him for his time and for helping me pray. As the minister turned to walk away I could feel my throat tighten and tears welling up in my eyes. I knew that I would never see my sister again and felt such a loss in my heart. The comfort I took with me that day was in knowing that Patty was now free of pain. I also made peace in my heart with my sister that day. Patty passed away a week later.

Her roommate, Carol, did confide in me once: "Patty never got over your father having an affair on your mother." I wasn't aware of any particular affair that Daddy may have had, but I was pretty sure that he hadn't been completely true to her through the years. I'm pretty sure that Mother hadn't been a complete saint either. Maybe that's why we were sent to live with relatives in Fresno when we were kids. Maybe that's what they were working out, and Patty had more knowledge of the actual situation than I did. This might be the reason that she'd call me stupid and then would add: "...you don't know anything", many times over the years. These questions came to me much later in life so I never got a chance to ask Patty or even Mother and Daddy for that matter. I was respecting their privacy back then, but I wish now that I had been a bit more nosey.

Mother

It was a sad, heartbreaking mystery to watch my mother's slow descent into the black hole of Alzheimer's.

She was in her mid-eighties when she was first diagnosed. Before that, there had been many signs that the disease was slowly taking over, but we didn't recognize it. We thought it was just Mother becoming a little eccentric in her old age. It started when she began to get very upset with herself because she couldn't remember certain names or dates. After that, things got worse. Mother was still living at De Longpre Ave, even after Daddy had passed away. She was comfortable there but unsupervised.

I dropped by for a visit one day to find my mother cutting a one foot square hole in the living room carpet. When I asked her what she was doing, she said that the cat had thrown up on the rug and she had to get the stain out. When I asked why she didn't just wash it out of the carpet, she said that this was better. Sometime after that I got a call from the property manager of the De Longpre apartments saying that there was a problem with my mother. I drove to Mothers and when I arrived she was accusing the De Longpre caretaker of sexually abusing her. I looked into her claims, but I was convinced that there was no truth to her accusations. Months later Mother had a stroke. When she was in the hospital recuperating, she caused a few problems for the staff during her walks. She would walk up to people, open her hospital gown and expose herself to anyone and everyone. The hospital explained how inappropriate this was so I thought that the best thing that we could do for Mother was to have her come live with us. She couldn't live alone anymore.

Patty was still alive as Mother was going through her tough times, but Patty was having her own problems. She wasn't getting around like she used to. It was up to me to look after Mother. It's difficult for any child to have to be a parent to the parent especially when that parent had been such a rock in their life. She used to have all the answers but now she didn't even know what the questions were.

Things were going well at first but in time she became unstable again. There was an incident where she threw a glass of water over my head. I had just walked into her room to check up on her when out of frustration she heaved the water glass in my direction. It missed my head and smashed off the wall. It wasn't her fault. She couldn't control herself and was becoming dangerous.

After Daddy had passed away Mother decided to get back into show business. She got work in some commercials. An actress needs a good head shot, this was hers.

(Cynthia Pepper Collection)

One summer day, I had been out of the house running a few errands for most of the day. When I had returned home Mother had a big trunk of Daddy's old mementos strewn about the table and floor. Until now, this trunk hadn't been opened in years. The trunk contained old photos, letters, posters and other such items from Daddy's long career in show business. It was his whole life in the trunk. Mother had a pair of scissors in her hand and was cutting everything up. She wasn't doing it in anger; she just decided that she didn't need these things anymore and they needed to be disposed of. There were old Vaudeville posters, pictures of Daddy with the elite people of the 1920's. There were letters from Jack Benny, Bob Hope, Bing Crosby, Judy Garland, General Douglas MacArthur, General George Patton among others. The letters were all cut, clipped and hacked beyond repair. I was in shock. I asked incredulously: "What are you doing?"

She calmly answered: "I just thought I'd straighten out these pictures.

She just coolly looked at me as if I was the one in the room doing the odd things. This incident combined with so many others made me fear for her safety and made me realize that there might be something more going on here than we knew. It was time to have her diagnosed by a professional.

After a lot of testing, the doctor determined that Mother had Alzheimer's disease. He explained that she'd be better off in a facility that was equipped to handle those stricken with Alzheimer's. It is such a terrible disease. The brain just keeps shrinking as the illness progresses. It's one thing to misplace the car keys and eventually find them. It's another to misplace the car keys, find them and then forget what they are for.

I visited Mother one day at the facility where she was living. I came into her room with some flowers for her. She looked at me and said: "Hello."

I said: "Hello Mother. I brought you some flowers to brighten your room."

She looked at me curiously and said thank you. As I was looking for a good place to display her flowers, she asked: "Who are you?"

I turned and said: "It's me Mother, Cynthia, your daughter." She said: "Oh, that's nice."

I knew then that she'd soon be forgetting everything. A whole lifetime of memories would be gone for her. I felt so bad for my mother. I also felt so lost and alone. I was now taking care of a parent that didn't even know me.

There is no upside to Alzheimer's. The only good thing was that Mother was spared the grief of attending Patty's funeral. Mother was so riddled with the disease she wasn't cognizant of the fact that Patty had died. Parents shouldn't outlive their children.

Eventually, the disease overpowered Mother until she could no longer fend for herself. She fell into the darkest cave imaginable. In her last years, she was completely unable to speak or recognize anyone. Over time, she fell into a comatose state and had to be fed through a tube.

I was living away from Los Angeles as my mother was going through her worse times so it was difficult to see her as much as I wanted to. When I did visit her, I would hold her hand and tell her how much I loved her. I hoped that she could hear me and feel my love. Mother died March 31st 2006. It was just one day short of 27 years since Daddy had passed away. I always knew that her mind had died long before her body gave out. She was 92 years old. Oh, how I miss her.

Steve

I've not said a lot about my second marriage. Our time together had its ups and downs. By the early 1990's, we separated, and eventually divorced.

During my separation, I wasn't looking to jump back into anything too quickly. I was still living in Los Angeles at the time. My friends Vicki and her husband Ronnie asked me if I'd like to get away for the weekend in Las Vegas. I agreed, as I needed to get away, and clear my head. We had a great time in Vegas.

At the end of the weekend I had some time to kill before we were to head back home, so I decided to play a couple of hands of Blackjack. I wasn't a big gambler and hardly ever played the table games. I found a table where the stakes were perfect for my budget, a dollar a hand. I bought ten dollars' worth of chips and placed a bet. The dealer busted, and I won. I was up a dollar. Yahoo! The other people at the table said that I had brought them luck. I didn't feel all that lucky, but who am I to jinx a good thing. The handsome gentleman seated beside me was ordering a drink. I was drawn towards his English accent. He said hello to me, and for the next couple of hours we proceeded to talk, smile, and laugh. Oh yes, we played some blackjack too. I didn't think much beyond the fact that, we were just two people enjoying a fun afternoon together. Eventually, I had to leave. He suggested we exchange phone numbers. I was a bit apprehensive at first, but he had the most beautiful and trusting eyes. When I left the casino I was up thirty dollars and the beginning of a new and promising relationship, with Steve.

Initially, he didn't know that I was an actress or any of my past work. I also knew that he wasn't interested in me for my money, because I didn't have any. He loved me for me and that felt wonderful.

When Steve and I decided to be together, my family got instantly bigger. He had two children from a previous marriage, Christine and Sam. I thought my childrearing days were over, but I was wrong. I didn't begrudge the situation because I was in love with Steve. My son, Michael, was a child in the 1960's and 70's which was an interesting and difficult time to bring up a child. With my new family, the 1980's and 90's brought a whole new set of family challenges, but we made it work. Today we are as close as ever.

I knew Steve would have to adjust to what strange happenings my life and my friends would bring to him. One night, Steve, and our good friends, Dick and Melissa Grob got together for dinner at the Orleans Hotel and Casino, just off the Vegas Strip. We were aware that Debbie Reynolds was performing her wonderful, one woman show at the Orleans Showroom and I thought, what a perfect time to see if I could talk to her after the show. It had been over 20 years since we had last spoken, and she may not even remember me. While Steve and Dick stayed at the bar to have a few drinks, Melissa and I waited outside the theatre exit.

I wrote Debbie a note that included my phone number. I was hoping that she would take it and read it whenever she got the chance. Just then the doors opened and Debbie came out. I went over to her and said: "Debbie, my name is Cynthia Pepper. We worked together on the Thalians show a few years ago. I just want to give you this note and say that I hope you are having a good time here in Vegas"

When I handed Debbie the note, she was very sweet and said: "Of course I remember you."

Truthfully, I really didn't know if she had remembered me or was just being nice. We chatted a few more minutes, said our goodbyes and walked away.

As Melissa and I headed back to our husbands, I said: "I'll just have to wait and see if she calls. Who knows, maybe she will."

Melissa was hopeful that she would, and so was I.

One week later I was in the shower at home when the phone rang. Steve answered it. He shared his phone conversation with me, after the fact. To know Steve is to love Steve but he can be very direct at times. He picked up the phone and said: "Hello."

The female voice on the other end said: "Hello, may I speak with Cynthia?"

Steve asked: "Who's calling?"

The voice answered: "Debbie Reynolds."

Steve: "Yea right."

Debbie: "I'm being serious. I'm Debbie Reynolds and I'd like to talk with Cynthia, please."

Steve: "You're kidding."

Debbie: "No I'm not."

Steve said: "She's in the shower right now can I have her call you back?"

She agreed. Steve wrote down her number on a small piece of paper and hung up.

When I got out of the shower Steve gave me a paper saying: "Debbie called."

I said: "Debbie who?"

He smiled and said: "Reynolds. Debbie Reynolds"

At first I thought he was pulling my leg. Can you blame me? It's not every day that Debbie Reynolds calls your house.

I grabbed the phone and dialed the number on the piece of paper. After hearing her say hello, I knew it was Debbie. I'd know that voice anywhere. I was very surprised and, needless to say, happy, that she had called.

Steve was watching something loud on the TV so I took the phone into the bathroom to have a little privacy. Since there was only one good place to sit in our bathroom, I put the lid down and sat on the toilet as we chatted.

We must have talked for about 30 minutes. It was one of the most bizarre and funny conversations that I've ever had with anyone.

My wonderful and amazing husband Steve.

(Cynthia Pepper Collection)

We started off talking about our respective ex-husbands. We talked about all the grief and frustration that came from those unions. Then Debbie told me a funny story about driving down Sunset Blvd with her daughter Carrie.

They were cruising along Sunset Blvd, talking, and generally having a nice time together. Their conversation turned to Debbie's frustration with the problems she had with her ex-husbands. Carrie suggested to her mother that she roll down her window and shout to the world... "He's an Asshole!" Carrie told her to do it five times. Debbie thought about it for a minute, rolled down the window and yelled: "He's an Asshole!" five times. When I asked her how that made her feel, she said that that little exercise made her feel better and somehow cathartic. I told her that I was glad that it worked for her.

Eventually, our talk turned to my frustration with ex-husbands. Debbie said: "You know it would be good for you to vent the same way."

I said: "Yes, well I'll have to give that a try someday, when I'm driving in an area where people don't live."

Debbie then said: "No you should do it right now, with me. You'll feel so much better."

After much cajoling on her part, I finally agreed. So there I was sitting on my toilet, (still with the lid down) with Debbie Reynolds yelling right along with me on the other end of the line... "He's an Asshole! He's an Asshole! He's an Asshole! He's an Asshole! He's an Asshole!"

After our last declaration of vented frustration, we both laughed. After we finally pulled ourselves together, she remarked how funny it was that here was sweet Tammy and sweet Margie, displaying such potty-mouths. The public would have paid big money to see that.

Later, I assured Steve that we were yelling about past husbands and not him. That exercise proved to be a great stress relief for me. Thanks Debbie.

"Life is a banquet, and most poor suckers are starving to death!"

- Rosalind Russell (Auntie Mame)

Living Life Now

Well, that's my life story, so far. Thanks for allowing me to share it with you.

So what now? I'll continue to travel and make personal appearances wherever the jobs take me. I plan on working even more with animal charities and do my part to prevent cruelty and suffering to animals.

After 23 years of not performing, I'm enjoying being back in the river of work. It's not the lucrative Hollywood river that the 1960's offered me, but it's warm, exciting and at times, much better place to be.

I'm thrilled when I'm approached by a stranger at an event and they say things like: "I loved you in…" or "I grew up with you." Until I was able to go out and meet the fans, I didn't really appreciate how many people, 'grew up with me.'

Most people assume that if an actor has done a few TV shows and a couple of Hollywood film roles, that they are rich. Not so. With a play on words from one of Elvis' songs, this book was almost titled, 'Fame Without Fortune'. You see, Fortune doesn't always follow fame. It's a hard lesson to learn. My Daddy learned it and so did I.

My fortunes these days are my friends and family. I'm appreciative of all the joy and happiness they bring me.

I'm grateful for my son Michael and so delighted that he is married to an exceptional woman named Eve. He's a terrific stepfather to Cormac and Caleb. A shared life is the life to Live.

I'm blessed to have Steve. He's my Bear. He supports me in everything I do. Our secret is to know how and when to make each other Laugh.

I'm humbled at the amount of people that remember, and appreciate the work that I've done in the past. Their joy truly fills my heart with Love.

There you have it folks… The secret to life - Live, Laugh, Love.

Elvis Fans, Young & Old

To all the fans at the autograph shows, and the many enthusiasts at all the Elvis festivals that I attend around the world I'd like to say thank you and that I appreciate you. You've made me very happy and busy person.

To show you how impressive the legend of Elvis is, and continues to be, I was recently a guest of honor at the Parkes Elvis Festival in Australia. Their theme was *Kissin' Cousins.* The entire town got into the theme and participated. There were people attending from all over Australia and New Zealand. Each one of them was allowed to express their love and respect for Elvis, in their own way. To me that's what all of the Elvis shows and festivals are all about. Elvis fans around the world can celebrate and express their love in a positive fashion, and I love being part of it all.

It never ceases to amaze me just how far reaching Elvis Presley, his movies and his music has affected people over the years. I have no doubt that it will continue for many years to come. I feel that I'm an ambassador to the celebrity of Elvis, and I hope that I always have the opportunity to honor his memory well.

Acknowledgements

I need to acknowledge some special people that have helped, directly or indirectly in creating this book.

I'd also like to recognize those that have been or who are currently part of my life, career, and family. With a loving heart, I appreciate you all more than you will ever know. (If I missed your name by accident, please don't fret. I'll put you in my next book.)

Patsy Anderson
Ed Bonja
Diane Borden
Vivian Bourbonnais
Joyce Browne-Breslin,
Diane Phillips Buechler
Randy Carlson
Steve Christopher
Ace Crye
Jean Curnyn
Chris Davidson
Tony Davies
Kathy & Craig DeNike
Kay Carpenter Dorner
Sue & Ron Ebner
Donna & Donny Edwards
Eve & Michael Edwards, & Caleb,
& Cormac
EPE
Mark Forlow
Arlene Feld
Ellie & Mike Geller
Bud Glass
Rick Goeren
Melisa Hank
Kim Hall
Jane & Pat Hanly
Suzy & Victor J Hanson
Anne Helm
Steve Horn
Russ Howe
Tommy Ivo
Lorraine & John Job
Sam & Christine Jupp
Steve Jupp
Hal Kanter
John Kavanaugh & the "Ireland
Elvis Fan Club"
Lorraine & Ken Kiblews
George Klein
Henrik Knudson, & Gitte
Darwin Lamm
Kay & Paul Lipps
Sue Lorenz & "Viva Las Vegas
Elvis Fan Club"
Sue Manuzek
Mickey Beauchamp-Martin,
Vicky & Steve Mason
Barbara Tolch McCormack
Gary Moncur

Tim Neeley
Chuck O'Brian
Rosemarie Garrity O'Brien & "Collingwood Elvis Festival"
Ava Overstreet
Angie & Morgan Parks
Robin & Steve Parry
Judy Richard & "All Shook Up Elvis Fan Club"
Christopher Riordan
Dick Rippey
Matt Roush
Jean & Christine Sader
Cathy & Frank Saladino
Rick Saphire
Sarah & Rob Scott
Chris & John Smart
Dianne Woods & Brad Smith
Kathy Spehar
Mary-Jo & Robert Standring
Linda & Charles Stone
Phillip Sturman
Westley Tackett
Louise & Sam Thompson
Jen Thurman
Daniel Van Tassel
Robin & Jimmy Velvet
Linda & Dino Verticchio
Vicki, Ron, Dean, Kelly & Alex Watters
Ryan Wood
Jim Yokum
Kimberly & Varouge Mesrobian, & Connor

Special Thanks to:

Marian Cocke

Yvonne Craig

Karen & D.J. Fontana

Dick & Melissa Grob

Stan Livingston

Beverly Washburn

I'd like to extend a special thank you to my dear friend and co-writer, Victor J Hanson, without whom this book may never have been written. Also, thanks to his wonderful wife, Suzy for all her love and support during this endeavor.

ABOUT THE AUTHORS

Cynthia Pepper is a Hollywood movie and TV actress from the Gold-Golden Age of Hollywood. She's been working professionally since the late 1950's. She co-starred with Elvis Presley in MGM's "Kissin' Cousins". She became a star with her own TV series, "Margie" on ABC. Cynthia was born in Hollywood, California and currently resides in Las Vegas, Nevada.

(Photo courtesy of Susan Hanson)

Visit Cynthia at: www.Cynthia-Pepper.com

Victor J Hanson is a comedian, musician, actor, writer, and entertainer. When not touring his one-man comedy show, "Splitting Hairs", he can be found applying his skills as a guitarist performing with numerous "A" list Elvis Tribute Acts from all around the world.

(Photo courtesy of Robert Standring)

Visit Victor at: www.VictorJ.com"

Kissin' Cousins

(Courtesy of Alamy Limited)

I'd love to hear from you.

You can send me a message by visiting my website:

www.Cynthia-Pepper.com

(Cynthia Pepper Collection)